# The Basics Book
## Seven Keys to Good Writing
### Third Edition

Also by Larry Edgerton

*The Editing Book: Crafting Graceful Prose*
*Approaches to Critical Thinking and Writing: Close-Reading the Arts*

# The Basics Book

## Seven Keys to Good Writing

### Third Edition

Larry Edgerton
*University of Wisconsin-Madison*

Previously titled *What We Owe the Reader: A Resource Workbook for Writers*

# Kendall Hunt
publishing company

www.kendallhunt.com
*Send all inquires to*:
4050 Westmark Drive
Dubuque, IA 52004-1840

Copyright © 1994, 1996, 2009 by Kendall/Hunt Publishing Company

ISBN 978-0-7575-6258-7

All rights reserved. No part of this publication may be reproduced, stored in a retrieval system, or transmitted, in any form or by any means, electronic, mechanical, photocopying, recording, or otherwise, without the prior written permission of the copyright owner.

Printed in the United States of America
10  9  8  7  6  5  4  3  2  1

# CONTENTS

*Preface xiii*
*Acknowledgments xvii*
*Introduction: Finding and Focusing Ideas xix*

## Key 1: The Basics of Organization  1
What's the Big Picture?  1
Am I Asked to Show Something or Prove Something?  2
How Do I Organize the Content?  2
What Goes into the Setup?  4
What Goes into the Development?  7
How Many Pages Am I Supposed to Write?  11
Why Should I Use Models?  13
Where Do I Start?  14
How Should I Outline?  15
Who's My Audience?  18
What Goes into the Wrap-up? *or* How Do I (When Should I) Write a Conclusion?  21
What Title Should I Use?  25

## Key 2: The Basics of Paragraphs and Transitions  27
What Is a Paragraph?  27
How Long Should a Paragraph Be?  31
How Do I Fix Bad Paragraphs?  32
How Do I Go from Here to There?  35
    1. Transition Words and Phrases  35
    2. Repeated Key Words  38
    3. Common Denominators  38

**Key 3: The Basics of Sentences  41**
    Is That a Fragment or a Sentence?  41
    Simple Sentences or Less Simple Sentences?  44
        How Many Simple Sentences?  45
    How Do I Create Sentence Variety?  45
        1. Combine Simple Sentences  46
            a. Use a comma + a conjunction  46
            b. Use a semicolon  46
            c. Use a semicolon + a transition  46
            d. Turn a simple sentence into a fragment  46
        2. Vary Sentence Beginnings  46
            a. Add a transition  46
            b. Add an adverb  46
            c. Add an adverb clause  46
            d. Add a prepositional phrase  46
            e. Add a direct object  47
            f. Add an adjective  47
            g. Add a present participle  47
            h. Add a past participle  47
            i. Add an infinitive  47
            j. Add an absolute  47
            k. Add an appositive  47
        3. Vary Sentence Length  47
        4. Vary Sentence Diction  49
    Active vs. Passive?  52
    What Goes Wrong with Our Sentences?  56
        1. Separating Sentence Parts  57
            a. Subject-Verb split  57
            b. Modifiers that describe the wrong word  57
        2. Dangling Modifiers  57
        3. Pronoun Shifts  58
        4. Vague Pronoun Reference  59
        5. Lack of Parallel Structure  60
        6. Necessary Word Left Out  62
        7. Mismatched Verb Forms  63

       a. Tenses  63
       b. Inconsistent active and passive  65
   8. Wordiness  65
       a. Bad jargon preferred to plain words  65
       b. The passive  65
       c. Redundancies  65
       d. Sentences with *there is/are/were* and *it is*  65
       e. Strings of prepositional phrases  66
       f. Needless repetition  66
       g. Hollow or pompous phrases  66
   9. Sexist Language  67

## Key 4: The Basics of Word Use  69

What Is Institutional Language?  70
What Are the Characteristics of Bad Jargon?  73
   1. Turning Verbs into Nouns  73
   2. Cramming Nouns Together  74
   3. Stacking Prepositional Phrases  75
   4. Using Weak Verbs  77
   5. Choosing the Passive over the Active  77
   6. Choosing Complex Diction over Plain  78
   7. Grouping Words and Phrases in Twos and Threes  79
   8. Using Words that Echo Other Words  81
       a. Syllables that echo each other  82
       b. Alliteration and assonance  82
What Is the Vocabulary of Bad Jargon?  83
   A Vocabulary of Bad Jargon  83
What Words Should I Watch Out For?  86
   1. A Short List of Individual Words  86
   2. A Long List of Word Confusions  87
   3. A Long List of Wordy Phrases  99
What Words Should I Use?  111
   1. Strong Verbs  111
   2. The All-Purpose Fancy Word List  112

### Key 5: The Basics of Grammar  117

    The Eight Parts of Speech  118
    Pronoun Problems  119
        Problem  1: Subject Pronouns  120
        Problem  2: Subject Pronouns in Comparisons  121
        Problem  3: Subject Pronouns after Verbs of Being  122
        Problem  4: Object Pronouns after Verbs  123
        Problem  5: Object Pronouns after Prepositions  124
        Problem  6: Who or Whom?  124
        Problem  7: That, Which, or Who?  127
    Agreement Problems  128
        Problem  8: Pronoun Agreement  128
        Problem  9: Subject-Verb Agreement  130
    Verb Problems  133
        Problem 10: Irregular Verbs  133
        Problem 11: Lie or Lay?  136
        Problem 12: The Subjunctive  139
    Adverb and Adjective Problems  140
        Problem 13: The Adverb and -ly  140
        Problem 14: Adjectives and Linking Verbs  141
        Problem 15: Good or Well? (Continued)  142
        Problem 16: Real or Really? (Sure or Surely?)  142
        Problem 17: Adjective Comparison  143
        Problem 18: Where Do I Put the Adverb?  143
        Problem 19: The Possessive and the Gerund  144

### Key 6: The Basics of Punctuation  145

    What's the Least Punctuation I Need to Know—
      and Still Survive? 145
    What Are the Eight Punctuation Patterns?  150
    How Can Just Eight Patterns Punctuate Almost All the
      Sentences in the World?  156
    What Other Punctuation Do I Have to Worry About?  158
        1. A Few More Patterns that DO Need a Comma  160
           a. Commas with a series  160

b. Commas with interrupters  160
   c. Commas with dates  161
   d. Commas with adjectives  161
   e. Commas with deleted words  162
   f. Commas with quotations  163
2. A Few Patterns that DON'T Need a Comma  163
   a. To separate a subject from its verb  163
   b. To separate a verb from its object  164
   c. Before AND + a fragment  165
   d. After ALTHOUGH, EVEN THOUGH, SINCE, WHILE, IF, AS, BECAUSE, BEFORE, and AFTER  165
   e. After the FANBOYS: FOR, AND, NOR, BUT, OR, YET, SO  165
   f. After HENCE, NEXT, NOW, THEN, and THUS  166
   g. Before a title  166
3. The Semicolon with a Series  167
4. The Dash  167
   a. After an introductory fragment  167
   b. In the middle of a sentence  168
   c. At the end of a sentence  169
5. The Colon  170
   a. After a verb of being  171
   b. After a preposition  171
6. The Apostrophe  172
   a. To show possession  172
   b. To show something left out  173
7. Quotation Marks with Periods, Commas, Your Own Title, and Emphasis  174

Is That All?  175
Forty-Nine Basic Punctuation Patterns  175
   The Apostrophe  175
   Quotation Marks  176
   The Comma  177
   The Colon  178
   The Semicolon  178

      Capitalization 179
      The Question Mark 180
      The Exclamation Mark 181
      The Period 181
      The Hyphen 182
      Parentheses and Brackets 184

**Key 7: The Basics of Revision 187**
      How Should I Revise? 187
      Nineteen Sentence-Editing Suggestions 189
      What Usually Goes Wrong? 191
      Forty-Four Editing Reminders 191
          Content and Paragraphs 191
          Sentences 192
          Words 192
          Punctuation 193
          Grammar 197
          Tenses 198
      How To Revise a Problem Manuscript: A Case Study 198
      How Should I Proofread? 203
      Nineteen Proofreading Strategies 204

**Editing Exercises 207**

**Key 1 209**
      Exercise 1—Finding the Big Picture 209
      Exercise 1—Sample Revision 210

**Key 2 211**
      Exercise 2—Revising Paragraphs 211

**Key 3 213**
      Exercise 3—Misplaced and Dangling Modifiers 213
      Exercise 4—Effective Sentences 215
      Exercise 5—Wordy Sentences 217

**Key 4 219**
      Exercise 6—Redundancy 219

**Key 5**  221
    Exercise 7—Editing Test  221

**Key 6**  225
    Exercise 8—Run-on Sentences  225
    Exercise 9—Essential and Nonessential Fragments  227
    Exercise 10—Colons  229
    Exercise 11—Apostrophes  231
    Exercise 12—Dictation  233
    Exercise 12—Dictation Answers  237

**Key 7**  241
    Exercise 13—The Forty-Four Reminders Quiz  241
    Exercise 14—Final Revision  249

**Twenty-Three Writing Projects**  251
    Project 1: Writing a Profile: The Writer  253
    Project 2: Compiling a Journal of Ideas  253
    Project 3: Looking Inside Yourself for Ideas  253
    Project 4: Looking Outside Yourself for Ideas  254
    Project 5: Looking Outside Yourself for Ideas: Eavesdropping  254
    Project 6: Brainstorming in a Group  254
    Project 7: Identifying Thirteen Logical Fallacies  254
    Project 8: Summarizing One Source (Not Stating Opinion)  257
    Project 9: Summarizing One Source (Stating Opinion)  258
    Project 10: Summarizing Sources (Not Stating Opinion)  258
    Project 11: Summarizing Sources (Stating Opinion)  258
    Project 12: Summarizing Sources: The OED—"Air," "Earth," "Fire," and "Water"  258
    Project 13: Writing a Research Paper: Popular Culture  259
    Project 14: Writing a Position Paper: The Environment  264
    Project 15: Writing a Second Position Paper: Social Issues  265
    Project 16: Writing a Personal Essay  266
    Project 17: Writing a Second Personal Essay  270
    Project 18: Writing an Argumentative Essay: Alice vs. Humpty  270
    Project 19: Writing a How-To Essay  271

Project 20: Writing a Book Review  271
Project 21: Writing a Movie Review  272
Project 22: Writing Literary Analysis Using Comparison and Contrast  273
Project 23: Writing about the Ideal Job (with a Résumé and Cover Letter)  275

**Glossary  277**

**Suggested Readings  281**

**Index  283**

# PREFACE

Most readers come pretty trustingly to a page of print. We assume that the writer knows his or her business—that the writer:

- Will make a point
- Will state it plainly and quickly
- Will develop the point
- Will organize the subpoints and examples
- Will write clear sentences
- Will choose words carefully
- Will use standard grammar
- Will use standard punctuation
- Will proofread

This list doesn't ask very much. We demand more for our money from a car dealer or landlord. Most readers simply hope that the writer will make a clear point. And make it through a clean window—so that we don't have to find the message behind distracting bug splats and rain streaks. Can you glimpse the message in the next paragraph? Or do the distractions in structure and language stop you?

> In my estimation our political leaders don't seem too notice what we all want, there head is in the clouds, as its to plain to see. How are you suppose to vote with enthusiasm when the choice is between a Republican and a democrat eventhough, in theory their different from each other. I don't like like politics and won't vote in the future if some politician says something like "Trust me;" thats an insult to: our intelligence. Well something is really wrong. The problem with politics is that its' goal, aren't allways alot like the common

mans or women. What I want to know is: why isn't Newsweek and Time and other magazines publishing articles, such as: What Wrong with Americas politics? Theres many things that make me angry. Also I do'nt think TV use to be as bad as it is. Each tv station now has their own political bias. Watching t.v. daily T.V. dosen't tell one much about political truth, as an of, 60 Minutes, called "How politics on TV Effects You", a good title pointed out.

The author of the paragraph, a bright communication arts major, said his point was that **The problem with politics is that its' goal, aren't allways alot like the common mans or women.** But the problem of a dirty window kept his classmates and professor from paying attention. They were too busy wiping glass.

At least this writer had a point. Sometimes writers forget—or never know—why they are writing. They forget they have a reader.

The reader-writer relationship works like any other social contract: I'll do something for you if you'll do something for me. I'll read your writing—**but you must give me something in return.** I'll buy your novel if you promise to tell a good story; I'll read your essay if you promise to prove your point—in clear language.

In writing for a reader, writers face common problems. In fact, any experienced teacher or editor can predict these problems. For example, introductory paragraphs often forget to introduce the material—to provide a **Big Picture**\* (see the **Glossary**, page 277) or road map to show where the writer has headed.

Or concluding paragraphs fail to conclude. And if there's a choice between **affect** and **effect**, odds predict that the writer will choose the wrong one.

Why?

Part of the answer says that it's hard to figure out the point of our writing—and then lay out ideas in a well-formed structure.

Another part of the answer is that our eyes and ears become tainted by common use—but incorrect use, according to the grammar books. Most of us write, "It's **me**" instead of, correctly, "It's **I**" because almost everybody chooses "**me.**" When the whole world gets it wrong, you're bound to write it wrong. Scarcely a soul today knows the difference between **lie** and **lay**, and if you trust your ear (don't you often choose a word because **it sounds righ**t?), you'll probably pick the form you shouldn't: **lay** when you mean **lie**.

Another part of the answer says that we let logic lead us along when we're sentence-editing. And logic can lead to trouble. Writing conventions don't always behave logically, like the final period in the following sentence. Isn't it reasonable to put the period at the end of

>I told my friend, "See you at the gym tonight".

because you're thinking that, once you've finished the main statement, the quotation marks come after the last word? Then, logically, to seal it with a period?

Such reasoning may be logical, but it's wrong, at least according to American practice. Our conventions direct that you place the quotation marks **outside** the period and comma—for no good reason other than somebody says you have to. Here, logic will lead you astray.

Still another reason why we face the same writing problems comes from our schooling: English classes can fill up a writer's head with a lot of silly stuff. Remember these so-called "rules"?

1. Don't start a sentence with **and** (or **but** or **because**).
2. Don't end a sentence with a **preposition**\* (those little words like **with**, **to**, **from**, and **up**).
3. Don't use **I**.
4. Don't use contractions (e.g., don't use **can't** for **cannot**).

These "rules" belong to the mythology of "good writing." We're taught if we want to write well, not to break them. But fine writers routinely start sentences with **and**, end sentences with prepositions, use **I**, and delight in contractions.

Writers who know better have developed a healthy distrust of rules. They understand that there's much bad advice floating around out in the world. Until recent years, some writing classes offered little but rules—especially misguided ones like "Don't start a sentence with **and**."

It's true that we can speak and write any way we want. That's democracy in action. But some essays still convince better than other essays. Some sentences still sound more graceful. And some grammar constructions still read right and some still read wrong.

Who's to say what's right and wrong? All of us—since we make up the language.

But the hitch is that unless we agree to what's right and wrong—another contract we fashion between reader and writer—we won't be able to communicate. We'll each speak a language of our own. It may be a marvelous language, full of wit and poetry, but nevertheless remain unintelligible to our audience.

So—because we want our readers to understand—we agree to write **"It doesn't matter any"** instead of **"It don't matter none."** Our language necessarily has to demand some conformity. Otherwise, we'll have chaos. We establish conventions to ensure accurate communication, writer to reader.

The reader's job is to read well; the writer's job is to write well. It's thus the job of the **writer**—not the reader—to state a clear point in clear language. For writers, this job defines what we owe the reader.

And to know what we owe the reader, we have to learn seven keys to good writing—the *basics* of good writing.

---

Key 1: Knowing the Basics of Organization
Key 2: Knowing the Basics of Paragraphs and Transitions
Key 3: Knowing the Basics of Sentences
Key 4: Knowing the Basics of Word Use
Key 5: Knowing the Basics of Grammar
Key 6: Knowing the Basics of Punctuation
Key 7: Knowing the Basics of Revision

# ACKNOWLEDGMENTS

Thanks to Carol, Sarah, and Aaron; thanks to my friends; (especially to Max Rankenburg for his careful proofreading eye); thanks to my students; and thanks to the students who have become my friends.

# Introduction

## Finding and Focusing Ideas

Many writers struggle getting started on a project, no matter the length—whether a one-page letter or an eight-hundred-page book. Filling up white space can be intimidating. And meanwhile the clock keeps ticking . . . you've got a deadline that warns not to procrastinate too long.

But you can't get started. You find yourself blocked.

So how do you get started? Unblocked?

Try easing into a project. That is, if you don't have any ideas in mind, it can be dangerous to plunk down cold in front of a notebook or computer. Staring at empty space, no ideas handy, can lead to writer's block.

"Easing into a project" means that, before starting a draft, you should "brainstorm" (or "freewrite" or "prewrite")—which means that you should doodle, write notes to yourself, make lists, outline: in short, do stretching exercises before you start running the mile.

Some writers are lucky. Fully developed ideas pop into their heads, and they have no trouble getting started; they simply turn the faucet, the words appear, and they write all the way to the end of the draft. Their ideas tell them which direction to head, so they don't outline, let alone brainstorm.

Other writers may start with just a glimmer of an idea. They don't yet know all the developed details, but they do have enough of an idea to start, and they'll refine and focus that idea in the first draft. As they write, they discover exactly what it is they're saying. (See Key 1, pages 14-18, on **Where Do I Start?** and outlining.)

But many writers have no idea **how** to start, let alone **where**, and if they wait too long—make too much of the project—they find themselves facing writer's block. And once writer's block sets in, it's a dry rot that damages how you see yourself and how you move through the world.

Because we link writing to intelligence, creativity, and self-worth, writer's block can cause unbelievable doubt and guilt. You may think that you'll never be able to write—let alone be a writer.

So as a tool to crack writer's block, brainstorming can be a pretty good tactic for the writer—life-saving, in fact. Use brainstorming to hone ideas, whether you're blocked or not. All writers can use it, even writers spilling over with ideas.

Brainstorming falls into two stages:

> Stage One: Finding Ideas
>
> Stage Two: Developing and Focusing Ideas

The following seven strategies will help you get started when you're searching for ideas; then help you develop and focus the ideas that you find. (If you already have an idea, skip Stage One and go right to Stage Two.)

# Stage One: Finding Ideas

## Strategy 1: Look inside yourself for ideas

We often do our best writing when we're passionate about some topic—a political issue like the destruction of national forests or the government's refusal to put more money into AIDS research; or death or divorce (especially if we've experienced either firsthand); or a hobby (the interest you spend too much time and money on). A topic that can excite you, whether with love or hatred, often declares itself the right one to write about. And since you've thought a lot about it, you're probably an expert.

What is it that makes your heart beat fast? What article do you turn to first in the newspaper? What topic do you talk too much about? What topic do you know more about than any of your friends?

That topic will give you all kinds of ideas for writing. Listen to your secret soul; it knows what you want to write about.

A related way to find ideas is to cast yourself back to your childhood. What do you remember most often? Most vividly? Childhood memories can call up terrific ideas. When we're children, our senses operate at their peak: We never touch or taste or see or smell or hear with such open enthusiasm. Sitting before your notebook or computer, describe a childhood memory that involves one of the senses. Why do you remember this moment? Now meditate on how this memory affects your life today. And before you know it, you have an idea to write about.

### Strategy 2: Look outside yourself for ideas

But if you have to write about a topic in which you have no interest whatsoever—and no ideas at all—you'll have to prime the pump by finding ideas outside yourself. One easy way is by paging through *Newsweek* and *Time*. What's in this week's news? Terrorism? Censorship of movies or music lyrics? Drugs? A fad? Borrow the topic of the day for your writing project. If you don't want to write about current events, look through past issues of *Newsweek* or *Time*. What were the topics of 1946? 1961? 1978? 1992? 2009?

Another easy way is to listen to what people are talking about. Eavesdrop on your friends and coworkers. What's the topic of this morning's coffee break? Overheard conversations can furnish terrific ideas that you might never have found on your own. Keep lists of ideas that you've overheard.

Other easy ways to find ideas are to ask friends and family for suggestions, consult teachers or librarians (they can show you places to look for ideas), go to the movies (Hollywood stays on top of hot topics), or—if nothing else triggers the juices—open the dictionary and put your finger down on a word: That word can generate associations with other words, and before you know it, you'll have an idea to work with.

Brainstorm in places where you feel comfortable. Buy a stack of paper and lay out your favorite pens. If coffee spurs you, pour the coffee. Some of us like to brainstorm in absolute silence; others of us like noise—from our favorite music to the white noise of a busy restaurant. Agatha Christie used to lie in the bathtub, munching apples, dreaming, plotting her murder mysteries. Sometimes great ideas come while we do work that requires little thought, like painting a wall or washing the dishes. Solitary exercise like running or a good walk can promote finding ideas.

When you brainstorm, stop just at the point when the idea is breaking through the egg, right when you can pin several solid notions to the page. Write them down. Then go for a walk, even if it's only across the street to buy a cup of coffee. Stopping for a few minutes can work magic on the imagination, and moving around—though not enough to become sidetracked—can reveal connections and push you off in a new direction.

Be sure to write down your ideas in an idea journal. Leonardo da Vinci filled up journals with his ideas and drawings; Beethoven recorded likely tunes in his notebooks; many professional writers keep a journal for general ideas and a journal for specific projects. Wonderfully, you'll discover that ideas lead to ideas. In time, finding ideas will become second nature; in fact, after training yourself to come up with ideas, you'll come up with too many. Professionals nearly always have more ideas than they can use.

## Stage Two: Developing and Focusing Ideas

### Strategy 3: Find out what you're thinking

Once you have an idea, write it across the top of a blank page or screen. Now set a kitchen timer for thirty minutes and start writing about your idea. **Write as fast as you can.** Don't stop until the alarm sounds.

During your thirty timed minutes, write whatever comes to mind about the idea. What do you like about it? Hate about it? Why is it important to you? To other people?

Try to force yourself to write the entire length of the thirty minutes. Lose yourself to the writing . . .

When the alarm sounds, stop and count up the words you've written. You've probably written at least 100 words every five minutes or 600 or more words over the thirty minutes. Typed, that comes out to two double-spaced pages!

Writing for timed stretches is a great way to break out of writer's block, whether you're just starting or in the middle of a draft. Use this technique whenever you get stuck.

## Strategy 4: Develop your idea by free association, comparison, and contrast

Read out loud what you've written. It may not be Shakespeare, but it's a start—and more than you had thirty minutes ago.

Next circle all the ideas that surfaced as you wrote. You started with one idea: Now you have several. List them on another piece of paper, leaving space after each idea. Then:

1. For each idea, **free associate** (recording your response). For example, if your idea is **tattooing**, jot down all that comes to mind about **tattooing**:

   *Designs, ink, pain, body mutilation, pierced ears and body parts, needles, AIDS, popularity, age groups, socioeconomic profiles of people with tattoos, tattoo artists, relation to graffiti artists, history of tattoos, celebrities with tattoos, tattoos and peer pressure, tattoos and fashion, professional vs. homemade.*

2. **Compare your idea with other ideas.**

   *Tattooing = decorating the body = like body piercing. Tattooing = permanently modifying the body. Part of general Zeitgeist that says body alterations okay; style statement. Traditionally associated with outsiders/outlaws like Hell's Angels = fashion statement with an attitude.*

3. **Contrast your idea with other ideas.**

   *Tattooing is permanent, unlike body piercing, hair and clothing styles. It's traditionally associated with a class/money attitude, unlike hair/clothing styles.*

At this point, unless you're writing a book, you've probably found more ideas than you want, so keep only those you intend to develop. The shorter the project, the fewer ideas you'll need.

Study the list of ideas. How well do you know the material? Well enough to organize it and write a first draft? Or do you need to tackle research?

### Strategy 5: If necessary, research your idea

If you find that you don't know enough about your idea to develop it further, head for the library, call up experts, and check out the Internet. Once you've researched it, repeat Strategy 3, adding the fruits of the research.

### Strategy 6: State the project's MAIN IDEA (Big Picture) in a sentence or two (no more than thirty words total)

Don't cheat here. It's the most important strategy.

- Rewrite until your idea is clear.
- Then tell your idea to a friend. If the friend doesn't understand, rewrite.

### Strategy 7: Draft a letter to yourself describing the project you want to write

Your letter should describe the project's overall shape and intention: What **kind** of project is it? Letter? Résumé? Literary analysis? Movie review? What's the **goal** of the project? Why is it worth writing about? Who's the **audience**? How much does the audience know about the topic? A lot? Little? What **material** will back up your main idea? How much and what kind of **research** do you need? When your audience finishes reading the project, what **main idea** do you want them to remember?

Write the letter in one big jolly burst: Don't get up till it's finished. If the project is short, limit the letter to a paragraph; if it's long, limit it to a page.

When you finish the letter, you're ready to consider a more detailed view of the project—the Big Picture; Setup, Development, and Wrap-up; length; models to imitate; outlining; audience; and title. In other words, you're ready for Key 1: *The Basics of Organization*.

# Key 1

# The Basics of Organization

- What's the Big Picture?
- Am I Asked to Show Something or Prove Something?
- How Do I Organize the Content?
- What Goes into the Setup?
- What Goes into the Development?
- How Many Pages Am I Supposed to Write?
- Why Should I Use Models?
- Where Do I Start?
- How Should I Outline?
- Who's My Audience?
- What Goes into the Wrap-up or How Do I (When Should I) Write a Conclusion?
- What Title Should I Use?

## WHAT'S THE BIG PICTURE?

You'll never write anything that's worth a damn if you can't state the Big Picture—a summary of what you're writing—in a sentence or two.

And this summary should be stated in your introduction.

You don't necessarily have to state it **before** you begin writing—that is, you don't have to know the Big Picture before the first draft. But when you've completed the draft, before submitting the work for review or publication, you should be able to state the Big Picture.

> **Big Picture:** Advertising techniques influence voting.
>
> **Big Picture:** Hollywood's portrayals of people of color create popular stereotypes.

> **Big Picture:** Employees should follow certain steps to report a job-related accident.
>
> **Big Picture:** The bald eagle has made a dramatic comeback from near extinction.

## AM I ASKED TO SHOW SOMETHING OR PROVE SOMETHING?

The Big Picture can be used to show or prove a point. And, generally, our writing falls into two categories:

- **Writing that SHOWS something**
- **Writing that PROVES something**

Writing that shows something can take many forms, from a business letter that **shows** the benefits of buying insurance to an online site that **shows** the popularity of California as a vacation site.

Writing that proves something can also take many forms, from a business letter that **proves** that you owe money for a service to an essay that **proves** that Spielberg's camera work heightens audience suspense.

All four examples of the Big Picture have a main point to make—but those that **show** something do not state an argument, while those that **prove** something do state an argument (and some books call this argument a **thesis**).

Regardless of which kind of writing that you produce—writing that shows something or writing that proves something—organize the content the same way.

## HOW DO I ORGANIZE THE CONTENT?

The Big Picture sums up the content of the entire project—and the content will usually break into three parts:

1. **The Setup\* (or introduction)**
2. **The Development\* (or body)**
3. **The Wrap-up\* (or conclusion)**

Scriptwriters often use these terms to describe the three acts of a Hollywood movie: the **Setup**, which lasts approximately the first half hour and introduces the main problem facing the main character; the **Development**, the middle hour of the movie, which complicates the plot and creates more problems for the main character; and the **Wrap-up**, the last twenty or thirty minutes, which wraps up the plot by solving the main problem.

Movie and TV scriptwriters realize the importance of breaking a story into three acts—the Setup, Development, and Wrap-up. So do musicians. Most music, whether it's a folk song or the first movement of a Beethoven symphony or a tune by George Gershwin or the Beatles, breaks into three parts.

Why?

Worlds we make up—movies, TV sitcoms, music, business letters, English essays—seem to demand three-part construction. Remember your confusion walking into a movie a half hour after it's started? You sit down with a box of popcorn and wonder what's going on. You've missed the Setup. You've missed the Big Picture.

We crave fullness in movies and music and books and letters and English 101 essays. We like beginnings, middles, and ends—maybe because our lives fall into the three acts of childhood, adulthood, and old age.

If an act is missing—like the first twenty minutes of the movie, the first movement of Beethoven's Seventh, or the first fifty pages of a novel—we feel ripped off. Just as we feel cheated if the movie stops before the last reel or somebody has yanked out the final page of the murder mystery we're reading. Or when we hear about the death of a man or woman cut down in the prime of life: What happened to their Act III?

And if you write an essay or business letter that lacks a Setup or Development or Wrap-up, your reader will feel ripped off.

Too often in what we read, the Setup is missing or handled badly (there's no statement of the Big Picture and the Main Sub-points), and we feel ripped off, disjointed, discombobulated: **Where's this writer going? Why?**

A common nightmare is the experience of plowing through a software manual. **There's never any Big Picture!** The computer junkies who write those manuals assume that we know as much as they do—and they plunge in without providing any orientation. They don't tell us all the stuff we need to know: like the Big Picture of the software we're trying to learn. Instead, they dive in, throwing out intolerable clusters of abbreviations and **jargon**.* Many software manuals lack a first act, so you have to piece together the Big Picture as you turn pages.

**Beware of leaving out the Big Picture**—which you surely will if you can't express it in a sentence or two. You can't expect your reader to sift through your opening paragraphs and assume the Big Picture. You need to do the job yourself.

You don't have to know the Big Picture when you sit down to write. But by the time you've completed a draft and prepare for the revision, you'd better know the Big Picture. Remember that few drafts work unless you state the Big Picture somewhere in the Setup.

## WHAT GOES INTO THE SETUP?

A **Setup** has two parts:

1. **The Big Picture**—what you show (something generally known) or what you prove (something generally not known); this is your **thesis**.
2. **The Main Sub-points**—the material that supports what you show or prove.

Each sub-point will support the Big Picture. Imagine a lawyer trying to persuade a jury that her client has *not* committed a murder (her Big Picture thesis). She cites three facts to prove the client's innocence:

1. **He has an alibi.**
2. **The police have found no witnesses.**
3. **A guy named Louie Spottwood has confessed.**

But these facts—the sub-points supporting her thesis—need proof, just like her Big Picture. Over the course of the trial, to get her client off, she'll have to prove each one.

Do you see, then, the essential difference between the two types of Big Picture? The first simply shows what is generally known; you don't have to prove a thing. The second type has to prove what is generally not known.

If you're **showing**, you don't have to come up with original matter: You're researching and gathering other writers' material. **Proving**, on the other hand, means you come up with original material, something nobody has written about.

Thus: In a class, if you're asked merely to show, then you don't have to find an original slant on a topic. You're obliged to do no more than to compile research and show the reader what you've learned.

But if you're asked to prove a point, then your instructor expects an original slant on a topic. You must prove the idea that you've come up with.

Does this setup show or prove?

> **Leonard Bernstein's musical *West Side Story* has enjoyed growing popularity since its 1957 Broadway**

premiere. In 1961, Hollywood produced a movie that won many Academy Awards and saw huge box office success. Following the original cast album, a number of recordings, from full orchestral suites to Muzak arrangements, were released, introducing the listening public to Bernstein's music. And local theater groups around the world, from high school and neighborhood drama clubs to professional companies, have presented *West Side Story* to enthusiastic audiences.

---

**Big Picture:**
1. Since 1957, *West Side Story* has enjoyed growing popularity.

**Main Sub-points:***
2. The 1961 movie expanded the musical's audience.
3. Many recordings have expanded the musical's audience.
4. Theater productions have expanded the musical's audience.

---

Summed up, this Setup contains four pieces of information.

Each sub-point supports the Big Picture, namely that, since its premiere, *West Side Story* has continued to gain popularity. The Big Picture is a general statement that requires further support. The sub-points offer that support.

Does the *West Side Story* Big Picture show something or prove something? The line may not be clear. Since readers interested in Bernstein and his music probably know of the growing popularity of *West Side Story*, the Big Picture shows its readers common knowledge—not proves an unknown fact. But what about people who know nothing of Bernstein: For them, do you show or prove?

A good rule of thumb is this: If, after research, you discover that people in the field know about your topic, then you're showing. But if you discover that you have new information—a topic that specifically hasn't been written about before—then you're proving.

Does it matter if you're showing or proving?

Not in terms of **structure**—since showing and proving both require a Big Picture and Main Sub-points.

Let's imagine several situations. Is the writer showing or proving?

> **Situation One:** The editor of a popular publication like *Time* or *The New Yorker* gives a writer the following assignment: "Tell the reader about the latest advances in AIDS research."
>
> **Situation Two:** A scientist publishes the results of her lab research in a scientific journal. She's pursuing an AIDS cure that no other scientist has so thoroughly investigated.
>
> **Situation Three:** You sign up for a night class in "The Films of Steven Spielberg." Your first assignment is to write an essay that discusses the critical reception of *Jaws*.
>
> **Situation Four:** In the same night class, your professor asks you to examine some elements of *Jaws*—writing, direction, camera work, special effects, or music—and comment on how effectively Spielberg handles that element.

In Situation One, the writer is **showing**, not proving. He gathers information about the various advances through reading and interviews. The writer is not announcing a new cure. Rather, he is laying out what's generally known (by experts in the field) for a mass readership.

In Situation Two, the writer is **proving**, not showing. She has new information to tell the world: the Big Picture of breakthrough AIDS research. Her journal article will try to convince the reader of this breakthrough (and her Main Sub-points will offer proofs to support the Big Picture).

In Situation Three, you're asked to **show**, not prove. Your professor wants a compilation of critical opinion, not your own opinion. Thus, your Big Picture will be something like the following:

> **For the most part, a favorable reception greeted Spielberg's *Jaws* when it debuted in 1975.**

Your Main Sub-points will then include several examples from the 1975 reviews to support the Big Picture claim that critics responded favorably. Library research will tell you what scholars generally know; your task is merely to gather and present common knowledge.

1. Critic X said that . . .
2. Critic Y said that . . .
3. Critic Z said that . . .

In Situation Four, you're asked to **prove**, not show. Your professor wants **your own interpretation**, not an interpretation that you have taken from a source. Since it's your interpretation, you have to prove the argument: why

Spielberg effectively handles the writing or acting or special effects. Your Setup Big Picture might look like this:

> In *Jaws*, Spielberg's camera work effectively heightens the dramatic suspense.

The Development then develops the Main Sub-points to prove that Spielberg's camera work heightens the dramatic suspense in *Jaws*.

## What Goes into the Development?

The **Development**, or the middle section, may be the easiest of the three parts to write. In the following breakdown, note that each of these sub-points states a mini-Big Picture, each requiring its own proof, so that your overall structure might follow this structure:

---

**SETUP Big Picture. In *Jaws*, Spielberg's camera work effectively heightens the dramatic suspense.**

    Main Sub-point 1: In the shark attacks, Spielberg uses horror-film editing techniques to shock us.

    Main Sub-point 2: Spielberg shoots scenes to include us in the action.

    Main Sub-point 3: Spielberg's odd camera angles catch us off guard, thus creating audience anxiety.

**DEVELOPMENT Main Sub-point 1. In the shark attacks, Spielberg uses horror-film editing techniques to shock us.**

    First Level Sub-point 1 (for proof, an example of horror-film editing in *Jaws*)

    First Level Sub-point 2 (a second example)

    First Level Sub-point 3 (a third example)

**DEVELOPMENT Main Sub-point 2. Spielberg shoots scenes to include us in the action.**

    First Level Sub-point 1 (for proof, an example of a scene shot to include us in the action)

    First Level Sub-point 2 (a second example)

    First Level Sub-point 3 (a third example)

**DEVELOPMENT Main Sub-point 3. Spielberg's odd camera angles catch us off guard, thus creating audience anxiety.**

    First Level Sub-point 1 (for proof, an example of an odd camera angle that creates anxiety)

    First Level Sub-point 2 (a second example)

    First Level Sub-point 3 (a third example)

Although you can certainly develop with three sub-points, you can use more—as few or as many as you want. There's nothing sacred about sticking to three. In fact, the longer the essay, the more sub-points needed. In the Setup, once you've stated the Big Picture, list as many sub-points as you want to discuss.

Two good ways to expand the Development are:

1. **To add Main Sub-points to the Setup (instead of three, use ten or twenty or a hundred—or as many as you want).**
2. **To add sub-point levels under your Main Sub-points (instead of three, use ten or twenty or a hundred—or as many as you want).**

**Main Sub-point 1**
First Level Sub-point 1
    Second Level Sub-point 1
    Second Level Sub-point 2
    Second Level Sub-point 3
First Level Sub-point 2
    Second Level Sub-point 1
    Second Level Sub-point 2
First Level Sub-point 3
    Second Level Sub-point 1
    Second Level Sub-point 2
First Level Sub-point 4
    etc.
First Level Sub-point 5
    etc.
First Level Sub-point 6
    etc.
**Main Sub-point 2**
    etc.
**Main Sub-point 3**
    etc.
**Main Sub-point 4**
    etc.

Or with even more detail:

**Main Sub-point 1**
- First Level Sub-point 1
    - Second Level Sub-point 1
    - Second Level Sub-point 2
    - Second Level Sub-point 3
- First Level Sub-point 2
    - Second Level Sub-point 1
        - Third Level Sub-point 1
        - Third Level Sub-point 2
        - Third Level Sub-point 3
        - Third Level Sub-point 4
        - Third Level Sub-point 5
    - Second Level Sub-point 2
        - Third Level Sub-point 1
        - Third Level Sub-point 2
- First Level Sub-point 3
    - Second Level Sub-point 1
        - Third Level Sub-point 1
        - Third Level Sub-point 2
            - Fourth Level Sub-point 1
            - Fourth Level Sub-point 2
                - Fifth Level Sub-point 1
                - Fifth Level Sub-point 2
                - Fifth Level Sub-point 3
            - Fourth Level Sub-point 3
        - Third Level Sub-point 3
        - Third Level Sub-point 4
    - Second Level Sub-point 2
- First Level Sub-point 4
    - etc.
- First Level Sub-point 5
    - etc.
- First Level Sub-point 6
    - etc.

**Main Sub-point 2**
- etc.

**Main Sub-point 3**
- etc.

**Main Sub-point 4**
- etc.

All sub-points will not have sub-points. But breaking into sub-sub-sub-points is a good way to expand the Development. What began as a one-page essay can quickly become ten pages, one hundred pages, or even a book. The secret is moving to first, second, third, fourth, fifth—or more—sub-point levels. The farther you move into sub-point levels, the farther you excavate, the more material will fill up the Development.

A book typically begins with an introduction that provides the Big Picture (the chief purpose of the book) and then lists the chapters (or Main Sub-points). Each chapter then breaks into sub-points that break into sub-points that break into sub-points. . . . (Flip back to the Contents of this book: Note the sub-points, especially the sub-point levels under Key 3 and Key 6.)

But a one-page essay usually doesn't break into sub-points beyond the Main Sub-points:

> **Setup:**
> 
>     Big Picture
>     Main Sub-point 1
>     Main Sub-point 2
>     Main Sub-point 3
> 
>     **Total Paragraphs in Setup: one**
> 
> **Development:**
> 
>     Main Sub-point 1—developed (one paragraph)
>     Main Sub-point 2—developed (one paragraph)
>     Main Sub-point 3—developed (one paragraph)
> 
>     **Total Paragraphs in Development: three**
> 
> **Wrap-up:**
> 
>     Wrap-up points
> 
>     **Total Paragraphs in Wrap-up: one**
> 
> _____
> 
>     **Total Paragraphs in essay: five**

You may recognize this bare-bones five-paragraph format. It's routinely taught in high schools as "The Five-Paragraph Theme." There's nothing wrong with writing themes that have five paragraphs, but what you write can certainly have more—why not 11,297 paragraphs?

There's nothing sacred about five paragraphs.

Nor is there anything sacred about limiting your Main Sub-points to **three**: You can use **two** or **four** or **ten** or **11,297** sub-points—and as many (or as few) sub-points for each levels as you wish.

## How Many Pages Am I Supposed to Write?

This is an extraordinarily important question, and no one should take it lightly. Too often teachers and employers shrug and say, "Write as many as you need to."

Great. Now what? **So how many is that?**

The politically correct answer—write as many as you need to write—understands that the amount of material you have to develop should dictate the number of pages: The needs of the content should drive the number of pages produced. Ideally, with this view, you shouldn't even think about the page count. You just jump in and do the job. If you're adequately developing the material, the theory goes, you'll produce the right number of pages.

Some writing instructors even appear offended if a student innocently asks, "How many pages am I supposed to write?" The question seems to betray a student who's more interested in the mechanics of the assignment than in thinking, a student more worried about practical, earthly matters like page counts than the content—in which, presumably, the student will discover great truths that have little to do with counting things (like money and pages). Hence the sigh and shrug and "Write as many as you need to."

But, in fact, you have to know **precisely** how many pages you need to write. The real world demands this. A writer submitting an eighteen-page "novel" will never see it published as a novel. A "research paper" that's a page and a half won't be much of a research paper. A business letter that's 529 pages probably won't get read. Professional writers always research page counts for their projects. A novelist knows that a novel must reach a certain length; essayists know that journals publishing essays won't consider work too short or too long. Hollywood scriptwriters know that a movie script fewer than 90 pages or more than 120 pages probably won't be filmed—since a page equals about a minute of screen time, feature-film scripts shorter than 90 minutes or longer than 120 minutes suffer in finding a producer.

Page counts matter because of the conventions we all live with: We expect a novel to be at least 100 pages but no more than 1000 pages. We expect movies to be at least an hour and a half but probably no more than two and a half hours. We expect business letters to be no longer than three or four pages.

For whatever project you're working on, try to find a model. If it's a class research paper, look at other research papers for the same class. How many pages do you count? If you're writing an article for a specific publication, how long are its usual articles? If you're writing a suspense novel, visit the book store and pull the suspense novels off the shelf and note the average length. If your boss wants a certain kind of memo or report, dig through the files until you find one like she wants—then make yours just as long.

This page-counting technique is not so artificial as it may seem. In fact, what we write tends to have a certain length because, over the years, we've grown to expect those lengths. The notion developed that a novel should have a ballpark page count because readers came to expect a certain number of pages—just as we expect that, when we go to the movies, the movie will last more than fourteen minutes.

Here's a good rule of thumb: **The three parts of your writing project will usually fall into the following proportions:**

- Setup = 1/4 total length
- Development = 5/8 total length
- Wrap-up = 1/8 total length*

*You may not need a Wrap-up; see, "How Do I (When Should I) Write a Conclusion?" (page 21)

That is to say, if you write a one-page letter, you'll probably write three paragraphs (or about eight sentences). The first paragraph will take about two sentences (or 1/4 the total length); the second paragraph will need three to five sentences (or 5/8 the total length); the third paragraph will need just a sentence or two (or 1/8 the total length).

So, an eight-page essay will, more or less, break down like this:

- Setup = 2 pages
- Development = 5 pages
- Wrap-up = 1 page

Total pages = 8

For an eight-page paper, you may not need two full pages for the Setup, which means you can add length to the Development. The longer the project, the more the 1/4 total length rule works for the Setup; shorter projects require a shorter Setup.

Proportions may vary from project to project; in some cases, you may not need a Wrap-up. Nevertheless, these furnish ballpark estimates, and they apply with surprising frequency from the one-page letter to the two-hour movie to the first movement of the Beethoven symphony to the one-hour TV drama to the ten-page summary memo to the two-hundred-page Ph.D. dissertation to the four-hundred page suspense novel.

Count the pages of a good model. Then figure the same number for your own project.

And while you're at it, take notes on the model:

**What goes into the Setup?**

**The Development?**

**The Wrap-up?**

## Why Should I Use Models?

The best way to learn to write will always be to look at good models. The best way to study a model will always be to take it apart like a watch.

Jot down notes like—

1. Big Picture?
2. Main Sub-points?
3. How many paragraphs?
4. How many paragraphs for the Setup?
5. How many paragraphs for the Development?
6. How many paragraphs for the Wrap-up?
7. Total number of pages?

Remember—

1. You don't have to limit yourself to three Main Sub-points.
2. The Big Picture doesn't have to come in the first sentence—but it should come somewhere in the Setup.
3. Apply the 1/4-5/8-1/8 rule of thumb to plan for length.

## WHERE DO I START?

If you can plan what to say before you start writing, you're lucky. But if you can't, then don't sweat the writing process. Lots of us don't know what we're going to write until we've written it.

For those who can outline before starting, you may want to abandon that time-honored outline foisted upon us in grade school:

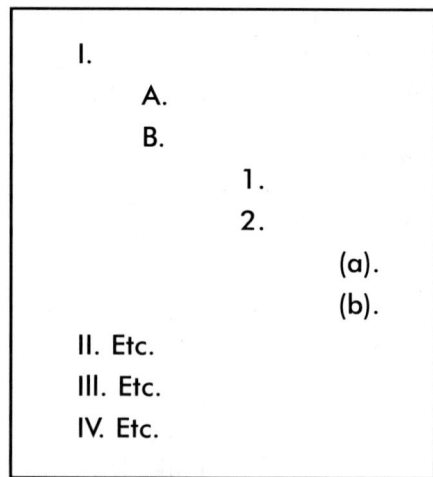

You know this kind of outline. It's an orderly piece of symmetry—each letter A matching a letter B; each Arabic number matching another Arabic number; the parentheses matching other sets of parentheses.

No doubt, such an outline creates a tidy, handsome work of art on the page. Consider all those matching pairs! Fifth-grade teachers love traditional outlines. Their orderliness testifies to a neat world whose neat children know how to follow directions and wipe their feet and noses.

But such an outline is a dangerous, manipulative tool that sabotages our writing.

You want to know why.

Such outlines sabotage our writing because, in the name of symmetry, they force us into dreaming up a second point to match a first point—**when a second point may not exist!**

We're told that if you have
- I.
  - A.

you also have to have a **B.** to go with it:
- I.
  - A.
  - B.

Likewise, every 1 has to have a **2**; every (a) has to have a (**b**).

And that's nonsense. You don't always have two statements to make about a topic. Roman numeral/letters-of-the-alphabet outlines force you into dreaming up points that do no more than fill up a slot on a chart. As a result, the outline sucks in material you'd never otherwise use and bloats the original good ideas.

Avoid these grade-school outlines.

## How Should I Outline?

Recall that writers split into two groups—those who do know what they're going to say before they start writing, and those who don't know what they're going to say before they start writing.

Those in Group One outline ahead of the writing. Those in Group Two believe they should outline, but they find outlining difficult and antithetical to their spontaneity, so they avoid outlines altogether.

If you belong to Group One and have no difficulty outlining, please consider the following advice:

1. Don't use traditional outlines (Roman numerals and letters of the alphabet).
2. Outline twice (before you start but also **after** you finish the project).

### Don't Use Traditional Outlines

Traditional outlines force you into filling slots you'd never consider if symmetry didn't demand matching up all those pairs of parentheses and numbers.

A better outline to use is an informal grouping of similar material. Let's say that you come up with a topic—My Two Favorite Kinds of Fruit.

You have the topic, but what can you say about it, about your two favorite kinds of fruit (which are grapes and apples)? To say something about it, you need to limit the subject. You decide to talk about your favorite *varieties* of grapes and apples.

And you brainstorm, listing the varieties that you like:

> *Concord grape*
> **crab apple**
> *red grape*
> **APPLE**
> *green grape*
> **McIntosh apple**
> **delicious apple**
> **GRAPE**

Each fruit represents an idea. Looking over the list, you may realize that some categories (**GRAPE** and **APPLE**) are Big Picture ideas, while others are sub-points—three varieties of grapes and three varieties of apples.

So under Big Picture/main idea of **GRAPE**, you group the sub-points, and under the Big Picture/main idea of **APPLE**, you group the sub-points:

> *GRAPE*
> > *Concord grape*
> > *red grape*
> > *green grape*
>
> **APPLE**
> > **crab apple**
> > **McIntosh apple**
> > **delicious apple**

We've ended up with two main groups (**GRAPE** and **APPLE**) and two sub-point groups (varieties of grapes and apples).

Likewise, we can arrange other ideas in similar groupings: Big Picture with the sub-points grouped under.

---

**TYPES OF TV SHOWS** (Big Picture idea)
  *classic sitcoms*
  *talk shows*
  *news*

**TYPES OF RADIO SHOWS** (Big Picture idea)
  *pop music*
  *sports*
  *news*

Or:

The Big Picture idea of the Types of TV Shows splits into three categories: classic sitcoms, talk shows, and news. And the Big Picture Idea of the Types of Radio Shows splits into three categories: pop music, sports, and news

So far, TV classic sitcoms and radio pop music do not have sub-point categories. As you study the list, you may decide that you want to plug in further sub-point categories such as:

> TV classic sitcoms
>     half-hour
>     hour
>
> Radio pop music
>     Golden Oldies
>     Top 40

And then, under sub-point categories, even further sub-point categories:

> **TV classic sitcoms (Main Sub-point)**
>   **half-hour** (First Level Sub-point 1)
>     **family** (Second Level Sub-point 1)
>       professional (Third Level Sub-point 1): *The Cosby Show*
>       working class (Third Level Sub-point 2): *Roseanne*
>     **working single adults** (Second Level Sub-point 2)
>       TV newsrooms (Third Level Sub-point 3): *Murphy Brown*
>       cops (Third Level Sub-point 4): *Barney Miller*
>       bars (Third Level Sub-point 5): *Cheers*
>       courts (Third Level Sub-point 5): *Night Court*
>   **hour** (First Level Sub-point 2)
>     etc.

An informal outline that groups by category doesn't require the rigidity of the traditional outline—and, in the process, doesn't force you to invent categories to satisfy the needs of symmetry. In other words, you won't be writing BS to plug gaps.

You'll be writing no more than needed; the logic of the outline will be the logic of the content—not the logic of an outline that demands a (2) for every (1). If you fill up a slot with a topic, you will do so because the content **requires** it, not because an outline has issued the order.

Group One—those writers who outline before they begin—should also try outlining after they've completed a draft. Here's a quick way of outlining:

- **Number each paragraph.**
- **In a sentence, state the paragraph's main idea, the mini-Big Picture. (If you've done your job, you'll have a topic sentence in place. If you can't find the topic sentence, insert the one you've stated that summarizes the paragraph.)**
- **Group your list of Big Picture topic sentences.**

**Have you grouped all grapes with grapes, all apples with apples?** If not, fix the problem. Outlining after the draft will thus force the writer to stick to the Big Picture.

**Now:** Group Two, your turn.

If you can't outline before you begin a draft, so be it. Not being able to outline before writing doesn't make you a bad person. It just means that you have to outline **when you finish.** Then you check to see if your spontaneous creation makes sense, if it hangs together logically. An outline following the draft supplies this chance to check your work and fix the problem.

**Finally:** If you outline before you write the draft, make sure you know the Big Picture. That Big Picture should act as your beacon as you write. Jot it on a three-by-five card and tape it to the wall. Every sentence and paragraph must hook up to the Big Picture.

If you can't outline before writing the draft, start writing anyway.

And write until the draft begins to make sense. Then, once you're finished, state the Big Picture. By now you should know it. Revise until you reach the point at which you can insert the Big Picture into the Setup. Tape the Big Picture to the wall and revise, making sure that every sentence and paragraph hook up to it.

## Who's My Audience?

Teachers cause real mischief when they fail to mention that a writer should think about writing for an audience. As students, we're told to write five pages on the Civil War—or John Steinbeck or photosynthesis. Most of that we steal from *Wikipedia*.

Audience? What audience? It's our teacher, right?

**No.** Your ideal group of readers acts as your audience. How would you approach writing an article on baseball? If you worked for *The World Book*, you might come up with the following entry on "Baseball":

**Definition**
**Rules**
    Playing field
    Equipment
    Defensive positions
        Infield
        Outfield
        Battery
            Pitcher
            Catcher
    Offensive positions
        Batting
        Put-outs
        Hits
        Rotation
**Scoring**
**Strategy and skills**
**History**
**Outstanding players**
**Baseball glossary**

As the author of an encyclopedia article, you assume that the audience needs to know **everything**—but in brief form. So you tell everything, though briefly, from defining the term "baseball" to listing outstanding players.

But how often will you have an audience that wants—or needs—to know everything? Not often.

Unfortunately, a lot of writers learn to write by cribbing encyclopedia articles, and what they write for the rest of their lives resembles a bad *World Book* entry.

In truth, whether you're writing to show or writing to prove, you must select more narrowly than the authors of *The World Book*. Readers usually don't want to know everything about a subject—that's why we have encyclopedias. Rather, they want to know selected facts.

And that's where the concept of an audience comes in: Most readers want to know either general information about a narrow topic (for example, the latest advance in AIDS research) or specific information about a narrow topic (for example, the latest advance in AIDS research). If you're writing about general information, you probably will need to provide history or background and key terms and key players to bring the general reader up to speed.

A general article on the latest advances in AIDS research might

1. **Define AIDS**
2. **Provide a history of the disease**
3. **Review the background of recent research advances**

before it comes to explores the Big Picture, which is

### A brief discussion of current AIDS research.

You define the term "AIDS," provide a history, and review the background because not all readers of a general, popular magazine (like *Time, The New Yorker, Newsweek, Vanity Fair,* and so on) automatically know what "AIDS" stands for or how the disease originated or what cures researchers have explored in the lab.

But physicians reading about the latest advances in *The New England Journal of Medicine*, a publication for medical doctors, presumably know what "AIDS" stands for, how the disease originated, and what the current research consists of. They **have** to know this sort of information; that's their business. What doctor would you trust who didn't?

If you're writing for *The New Yorker* or *Time*, you'll tell your audience more general background than if you're writing for *The New England Journal of Medicine*.

Considering your audience means just one thing: How much are they likely to know? Very little? Or a lot?

If you're writing a *Sports Illustrated* article about special pitches, you don't have to define curves, knuckle balls, screw balls, forks, and sliders. You certainly don't have to define "baseball" and explain what a pitcher does for a living. Those are givens for the *Sports Illustrated* audience. But if you're writing for a Swedish magazine whose audience knows nothing about baseball, then your work is cut out: definitions, history, and background.

1. **Imagine your ideal audience.**
2. **How much will they likely know about the subject?**

Then begin—either providing definitions, history, and background—or moving straight to the point with no more background than the specific situation demands.

Remember that audience = knowledge (whether the audience knows a little or a lot about the topic).

Remember that a general audience needs to know a lot more general knowledge than a specific audience.

Before sitting down to write, meditate on how much your audience needs to know. A lot or a little? If your audience needs to know a lot, then the Setup and Development will take a considerably different form.

Here's an important point also to remember: If you're **showing**, you're probably writing for a **general** audience. If you're **proving**, you're probably writing for a **specific** audience.

Thus, furnish more background for a piece that shows. Why? It's obvious. Any audience that needs to be shown probably doesn't know very much about the topic. So you'll have to fill them in.

But a piece that proves can often assume its audience knows a fair amount about the topic. They're beyond beginners, so you can move right to the point to prove.

## WHAT GOES INTO THE WRAP-UP OR HOW DO I (WHEN SHOULD I) WRITE A CONCLUSION?

When we're students, we don't learn much about outlining and writing for an audience. What we hear about conclusions isn't very helpful, either. Too often, our heads are filled with disastrous "rules" about how to write the conclusion—or Wrap-up.

Probably the worst piece of structural advice is that

**Every piece we write needs a conclusion.**

Not true. The shorter the piece, the less likely it will need a conclusion. Some pieces never need concluding. A one-page memo, for example, has only one purpose: to talk about one topic. You begin a memo with a Big Picture, which you then explore in the Development.

The memo needs no conclusion because there is no reason to summarize what you've just written. Only a lazy reader will forget the points stated two or three lines above.

Think about the person to whom you are sending the memo: another employee who has no need of a summing up. And consider a memo's function: a short, informal discussion, reminder, or listing of specific material. By the same token, don't attach a conclusion to an in-class exam (when it's expected you'll cross out words and generally write informally) or a birthday letter to your mother (imagine how stuffy and comic this would be).

**A reminder:** No matter how short or informal the writing, use the Big Picture and Development. And remember that the longer the work and the more formal the situation, the more likely you'll have to write a Wrap-up or the audience will feel ripped off.

But the shorter and/or less formal the writing, the less likely you'll need a Wrap-up. And the audience won't feel ripped off.

That awkward "and/or" construction covers for short, formal pieces of writing that do require a conclusion. A business letter, for instance, requires a Wrap-up. You add only a sentence or two ("I hope to hear from you. If you have questions, please call me."), but you may need the gesture to avoid bluntness.

So in general: **If you've done your job as a writer, most short works need no conclusion.** That is, if you've clearly spelled out your Big Picture and Main Sub-points, you don't need to repeat your Big Picture and Main Sub-points in a conclusion. "Short" means up to five pages.

If the writer has done the job, why conclude at all? Three reasons:

- To be polite (to wrap up gracefully, like the final sentences of a business letter).
- To remind the reader of the main points.
- To hook up the Big Picture to another Big Picture.

Let's take each in depth:

1. **To be polite**. Business letters constitute an odd breed of writing. Their formality demands a leave-taking like shaking hands when you leave church. With a short business letter, you write a Wrap-up to avoid bluntness, not to sum up what you've just said.
2. **To remind the reader of the main points.** This becomes necessary only when you're afraid that the reader might forget those main points. If you're a lawyer whose final speech to the jury has lasted over a long sixty minutes, then of course you'll repeat the Big Picture and three Main Sub-points:

**My client is innocent of murder.**
1. **He has an alibi.**
2. **The police have found no eyewitnesses.**
3. **A guy named Louie Spottwood has confessed.**

You repeat the Big Picture and three Main Sub-points because you're dealing with life and death. You want to drive home these points—after a detailed discussion of each (why you've spent sixty minutes in front of the jury)—as your final, lingering words. You repeat them as reminders—**in case the jury has forgotten**.

But if there's no danger of the audience forgetting, then don't repeat. A one-page memo that states the Big Picture and three Main Sub-points and then restates them all at the bottom of the page would be redundant, at best:

---

TO: The Jury
FROM: The Defending Attorney
SUBJECT: My Client's Innocence
DATE: December 2, 2010

My client is innocent of the murder charge.
  1. He has an alibi.
  2. The police have no eyewitnesses.
  3. A guy named Louie Spottwood has confessed.
In conclusion, my client is innocent of the murder charge because he has an alibi, the police have found no eyewitnesses, and a guy named Louie Spottwood has confessed.

---

However, if you're writing a work that goes over five or so pages, then conclude by restating the content of the Setup. Try, however, to **change the wording** to spare the reader another round of familiar material. And try to do more than simply regurgitate familiar material restated in new words.

3. **To hook up the Big Picture to another Big Picture.** You want to hook up what you are writing to another issue (a bigger or related issue). This issue is another Big Picture.

That is to say, when you're wrapping up the conclusion, after you've restated the Big Picture and Main Sub-points, tie your main idea to another main idea—one that's related.

**THE BASICS OF ORGANIZATION**

For example, if you're proving how Hemingway suggests homoerotic friendship in his short story "The Three-Day Blow," then in your Wrap-up suggest that:

> **An exploration of homoerotic friendship figures not only in "The Three-Day Blow," as this essay has tried to prove, but in other stories from** *In Our Time*, **as well as in Hemingway's early novels,** *The Sun Also Rises* **and** *A Farewell to Arms.* **Indeed, the nature and forms of male friendship were to preoccupy Hemingway throughout his creative and personal life.**

Note how the Big Picture—that Hemingway explores homoerotic friendship in "The Three-Day Blow"—gets hooked up to related Big Pictures (the uses of this topic in other Hemingway stories and novels) and to the bigger Big Picture (as seen in both his life and art, Hemingway's longtime interest in the nature and forms of male friendship).

In many essays, the final sentences of the essay do not **close off the topic for good,** but rather **open it up to** other directions to explore, other related Big Pictures for other essays to examine. (If you're writing a book, this technique lets you travel from one chapter to the next.)

The final chapter of a book investigating German nationalism may end by summing up the conditions that led into World Wars I and II and then draw parallels by **relating those to today's politics.**

In fact, most good histories use their final pages to connect their topic to other, related current concerns (how does American policy in Vietnam explain present U.S. policy in third-world countries? how does African-American migration in the Depression contribute to present inner-city politics?).

To wrap up these remarks on the Wrap-up:

1. You probably won't need a Wrap-up with short, informal writing.
2. Thus: the longer and more formal writing, use a Wrap-up.
3. You're more likely to need a Wrap-up for writing that proves rather than shows (because you're trying to drive home new information).
4. The last time in the Wrap-up that you mention the Big Picture, hook it up to another, related Big Picture (one that could become the topic of your next essay, chapter, or book).

## WHAT TITLE SHOULD I USE?

The Big Picture will tell you. If you're writing about AIDS, don't title your work "AIDS." That's too broad and vague. Look at the Big Picture. If you're writing about a breakthrough cure for AIDS, then the title should address that cure:

**Drug X: A New Cure for AIDS**

For example, if you're writing about *West Side Story*, go to your Big Picture and pull out the key words:

**Leonard Bernstein's musical *West Side Story* has enjoyed growing popularity since its 1957 Broadway premiere.**

**Key words** = *West Side Story*, growing, popularity

Now arrange those key words in a title that reflects the Big Picture:

**The Growing Popularity of *West Side Story***

Calling your essay "*West Side Story*" won't specifically address the Big Picture.

And follow these conventions with your title:

1. Hook up the title to the Big Picture.
2. Don't borrow the title of the work you're discussing for your own title (i.e., don't call your essay *Hamlet* or *West Side Story*; Shakespeare and Bernstein have already used them).
3. Don't quote, italicize, or underline your title (but—depending on what's appropriate—quote, italicize, or underline a title within the title: The Growing Popularity of *West Side Story*. (See p. 176 for an explanation of what titles you quote, italicize, or underline.)
4. If you wish, you can capitalize your title: THE GROWING POPULARITY OF *WEST SIDE STORY*.

# Key 2

# The Basics of Paragraphs and Transitions

- What Is a Paragraph?
- How Long Should a Paragraph Be?
- How Do I Fix Bad Paragraphs?
- How Do I Go from Here to There?

## WHAT IS A PARAGRAPH?

Ponder the following:

1. All paragraphs don't have a Big Picture (sometimes called the topic sentence).
2. The topic sentence doesn't have to come at the beginning of the paragraph.
3. All paragraphs don't have sub-points.
4. A paragraph can be as short or as long as you want.

In other words, a paragraph can be just about whatever you want it to be. So what is a paragraph?

**It's a collection of words about one topic.**

That's not a bad definition—except that it also defines a novel, insurance policy, sonnet, and billboard ad. Nevertheless, you'll be hard pressed to find a better definition because paragraphs are fluid shapes that vary in content and length according to what's needed. Paragraphs thus can be as short (like a **fragment**\* or a sentence) or as long as you want. (Faulkner wrote paragraphs that go on for fifty pages, but you should probably keep yours shorter.)

**In its classic form, a paragraph is a mini-essay, with a mini-Big Picture and mini-Main Sub-points.** Whether you call the main sentence a Big Picture or topic sentence, this sentence functions like the Big Picture that controls the overall shape of your project. In other words, in its classic form, each paragraph has a controlling sentence and sub-point sentences to support the controlling sentence (just like in this paragraph: with the **boldfaced** Big Picture/topic sentence).

Here's a paragraph that you saw in Key 1. It's a traditional paragraph with a topic sentence and three support sentences (**boldface** identifies the topic sentence; numbers mark the support sentences):

> **Leonard Bernstein's musical *West Side Story* has enjoyed growing popularity since its 1957 Broadway premiere.** (1) In 1961, Hollywood produced a movie that won many Academy Awards and saw huge box office success. (2) Following the original cast album, a number of recordings, from full orchestral suites to Muzak arrangements, were released, introducing the listening public to Bernstein's music. (3) And local theater groups around the world, from high school and neighborhood drama clubs to professional companies, have presented *West Side Story* to enthusiastic audiences.

Note that you begin with a statement that previews the paragraph. The reader learns that *West Side Story* has been growing more popular since the 1957 Broadway premiere. Now it's time to provide examples to back up that statement:

**Topic Sentence**
    Example 1
    Example 2
    Example 3

This structure looks no different from the Big Picture structure that we examined in Key 1:

**Big Picture**
    Main Sub-point 1
    Main Sub-point 2
    Main Sub-point 3

Remember that with the Big Picture structure, you're never limited to just three Main Sub-points. If you're writing a book, you'll want as many Main

Sub-points as you have chapters. And within each chapter, you'll have sub-points to support your Main Sub-points.

Likewise, a paragraph doesn't have to limit itself to three examples. You can write as few or as many as you wish.

> **Procrastination is a deadly disease.** (1) For years, I've suffered from attacks of it. (2) Despite my best intentions, despite my daydreams of glory, despite three-a.m. fears that my life is going nowhere, I still put off tackling what my heart tells me to do. (3) I weed the garden, paint the bathroom, figure next month's bills, take the dog for a second walk, read a bad novel—in short, come up with time-killers that steal days and nights from what I should be doing. (4) Just as cancer can steal years from our lives, so can procrastination.

Not all paragraphs work by topic sentence/example. Some paragraphs unpack a story that moves from the Big Picture through a series of sentences that develop the Big Picture:

The structure here still follows a Big Picture overview that controls the paragraph ("Procrastination is a deadly disease").

Yet sentence 1 isn't really an **example** of how procrastination behaves as a deadly disease. Rather, it functions as background. Sentence 2 elaborates the topic by telling how the speaker puts off what his heart knows he should be doing. Sentence 3 offers forms of procrastination. Sentence 4 sums up the paragraph by circling back to the words "deadly disease" to show how procrastination, like cancer, can shorten our time to do what we want most to do.

The only real "example" sentence is 4. It's the one sentence that demonstrates how procrastination acts as a deadly disease (as the Big Picture/topic sentence claims). Sentences 1, 2, and 3 hover around the topic, expand on it, push it in various directions. These three sentences play variations on the theme of the Big Picture/topic sentence.

Some paragraphs present a Big Picture/topic sentence followed by examples. Others, as we've just seen, work by playing variations on the theme: one related sentence that leads to another related sentence that leads to another . . .

Here's a second illustration of the theme and variations paragraph:

> **I like action movies because they kick you in the gut.** Action movies require little thinking. You don't have to think in the midst of a car chase or when a guy slips off a skyscraper ledge or a mutant hacks up a pack of Cub Scouts. Action movies are about feeling—not the thinking you do when you read. On the other hand, when you read, you can put down the book and reflect on the passage—even a passage with a car chase. But action movies don't give you time to reflect. You're on a roller coaster ride that lasts till the movie ends. Action movies are roller coaster rides, with the same ups and downs and wild thrills that slam your stomach before you can think about how scared you are.

This paragraph presents a basic theme (i.e., that action movies hit you viscerally rather than intellectually) that develops after the first sentence. The logic that ties the paragraph together is the logic of **theme**: The sentences provide various ways of restating that theme and developing it.

Paragraphs in general seem to follow one of two routes:

1. **Traditional structures**—like topic sentence/examples
2. **Looser structures**—like theme and variations

Whichever structure you use, remember the basic rule about all paragraphs:

> - **Use one topic per paragraph.**

But sticking slavishly to the rule can lead you into a booby trap—enormous paragraphs that swallow up three or four pages. You'll argue, "But my paragraph **is** about one topic!"

And indeed it may be. So use common sense. If you see that the topic you're exploring will demand several pages—that you'll end up writing one whale-sized paragraph—take pity on the reader and **paragraph-break at subpoints**. You want to end up with two or three paragraphs a page.

Remember, too, that every paragraph may not have a topic sentence. You may find yourself setting up a topic sentence that will serve as the topic sentence for several, related paragraphs:

> PARAGRAPH ONE: You establish the Big Picture for a topic that needs substantial exploration.
> PARAGRAPH TWO: You continue exploring the topic but break here to make life easier for the reader.
> PARAGRAPH THREE: You continue to explore.
> PARAGRAPH FOUR: And here you wrap up the topic. You're still referring to the Big Picture in Paragraph One.

The weight and meaning of the Big Picture/topic sentence are carried from one paragraph to the next. But, again, take pity on your reader. If you travel too far from the topic sentence, reintroduce it so the reader doesn't forget the Big Picture. Topic sentences serve as road signs to keep the reader focused on the highway.

Here's another good rule of thumb:

**Use paragraphs like those you see in your model.**

## How Long Should a Paragraph Be?

A paragraph should be as long as the model calls for: Paragraphs develop their material according to the rules of the genre. Paragraphs in a research paper will no doubt take longer to unfold than paragraphs in advertising copy.

If you're writing a business letter, write paragraphs that look like business-letter paragraphs. That means (for a one-page letter) that you begin and end with short paragraphs (one or two sentences for each) but that the middle paragraph—your Development section—deserves three to five sentences **because here you're elaborating the main idea**.

A good model will show you how to use paragraphs. It will show you when to use long paragraphs, when to use short paragraphs, when to write paragraphs with a Big Picture, and when to write classic paragraphs that not only begin with a Big Picture but also include supporting sub-point sentences.

A good model can be an article in a magazine that you admire. Or a good letter by somebody in your office. Or a sample essay that your professor hands out. Or a book by your favorite writer.

We devise paragraphs according to the genre that our model belongs to. The word **genre** means the **kind** of writing that the model represents. Novels form a genre (they're a work of the imagination, between 100 pages and 1000 pages). Novels separate into sub-genres: romance, western, mainstream, mystery, and so on. Within sub-genres, there are further genre separations. Mystery novels break into hard-boiled (tough-guy private eyes), the cozy (amateurs who stumble on a crime), the procedural (cops at work as they unravel who done it), and so on. And within those sub-sub-genres, the genre breaks down even farther.

Each genre—from the business letter to the police procedural—tends to call for certain kinds of paragraphing. Pick up a novel by popular writers like Stephen King and Dean Koontz, and you'll discover that their paragraphs fall on the short side. In fact, they love one-sentence paragraphs.

How come?

The horror-novel genre, to which King and Koontz both contribute many lively examples, uses short paragraphs to pull the reader along. One-sentence paragraphs lead you down the page like tugs on a leash. You can't get away. You have to keep reading. Your eyes burn—feverish with the suspense.

Moreover, we're all children of the TV age, presumably with thirty-second attention spans after years of gazing at thirty-second commercials and music videos. Popular fiction also uses short paragraphs because they're easier to follow; modern readers seem to get lost inside long paragraphs—paragraphs that last for more than a half page. So to respond to modern reading psychologies, popular writers keep their paragraphs short.

Another myth taught in grade school is that we should never write one-sentence paragraphs.

Nonsense!

It depends on the genre.

End of discussion.

## How Do I Fix Bad Paragraphs?

Let's define as "bad" a paragraph that doesn't do the task expected. That is, if the genre you're working in demands one kind of a paragraph and you write another, then that's a "bad paragraph." A loosely structured paragraph may work fine in a letter to a friend but look entirely out of place in formal business correspondence. By the same token, a personal essay (like a blog entry) may appear stiff if it's constructed of nothing but topic sentence/example sentences, whereas research essays are long strings of topic sentences supported by sentences with examples. "Good" and "bad," then, exist largely in the eye of the genre.

If you're expected to write a loosely structured paragraph, you'll probably have no trouble since these approximate how we talk: a bunch of sentences circling around a topic, spinning out variations on some theme. The one problem you'll encounter is going too far: letting the paragraph become too loose. As you edit, remind yourself that you may be taking a scenic journey but that you don't have to stop at every interesting location. You can't forget the journey's destination.

But if you're expected to write a traditional paragraph along the lines of topic sentence and examples, three major problems can derail you:

- **You underdevelop**
- **You overdevelop**
- **You forget the Big Picture**

Here's an **underdeveloped** paragraph:

> *West Side Story* is liked by lots of people. It's always been popular, from the movies to radio, TV, and CDs. Also, it's presented a great deal on stage.

Fix such a paragraph by asking Who, What, When, Where, Why, and How questions:

1. Who wrote *West Side Story*? (Leonard Bernstein)
2. What is *West Side Story*? (Broadway musical)
3. When was it written? (1957)
4. Where was it premiered? (Broadway)
5. Why should I write about it? (To explore its growing popularity)
6. How has it shown its growing popularity? (Through the movie, CDs, and stage performances)

Providing the context of the Big Picture (the who, what, when, where, why, and how—with plenty of examples) will fully develop the paragraph.

Here's the **overdeveloped** version:

Leonard Bernstein's musical *West Side Story* has enjoyed growing popularity since its 1957 Broadway premiere, **the same year that Frank Loesser, another composer of genius, brought out his operatic delight** *The Most Happy Fella* **and Iowa's own genius, Meredith Willson, let loose** *The Music Man* **on the Broadway stage. What an amazing year. (As a note of interest, one should add that both Loesser and Willson, unlike Bernstein, who worked with lyricist Stephen Sondheim on this particular show, wrote the words for their brilliant tunes—if "tunes" is the right word!)** As regards *West Side Story*, in 1961, Hollywood produced a film that won many Academy Awards and saw huge box office success—**all of it, of course, highly deserved, especially in light of the competing films from that spectacularly forgettable year.** Following the original cast album (**you'll recall it, I'm sure**), a number of recordings, from full orchestral suites to Muzak arrangements (**and these I'm sure you won't— if you're lucky**), were released, introducing the listening public to Bernstein's music. And local theater groups around the world, from high school and neighborhood drama clubs to professional companies, have presented *West Side Story* to enthusiastic audiences. **These companies may vary in quality, but there's no doubt that they approach their task with zeal and ardor for the master's masterpiece—and thank God! one must surely shout, for us listeners all.**

The boldface highlights the overdeveloped additions—which, though essentially "relevant," still cause too many road stops along the way. The real issue here is **the growing popularity of *West Side Story* since its 1957 premiere.** No more or less. The writer gushes out material that may interest him but that overwhelms the paragraph's lone mission: to provide examples for the Big Picture (the growing popularity of *West Side Story*).

The third problem is **to forget the Big Picture**:

Leonard Bernstein's musical *West Side Story* has enjoyed growing popularity since its 1957 Broadway premiere. That year saw several landmark musicals presented on the Broadway stage. Despite the blandness of the 1950s, Broadway theater managed to produce some of its finest work. Television, too, was in its golden age, with cutting-edge hour dramas and comedy like *The Honeymooners* and *I Love Lucy*, not to mention the late-night brilliance of talk-show hosts Steve Allen and his successor, Jack Paar. In fact, one can argue that the decade of the fifties gave us our best TV programming.

Astonishingly, the paragraph has traveled from Bernstein to a final sentence about fifties TV programming. How did this happen? It's easy when you write by association—when one idea reminds you of another idea and then another. . . . The chain of associations wanders from *West Side Story* to Broadway musicals of 1957 to the 1950s to television in the 1950s to the quality of TV programming in the 1950s.

How do you fix the problem?
Go back to the Big Picture. **Each sentence must refer to it**.

And remember, whether you're writing a traditionally structured paragraph (topic sentences and examples) or a loosely structured paragraph (theme and variations), to keep your eye on the Big Picture.

## How Do I Go from Here to There?

Editors call the device for going from here to there a **transition**. We often hear comments like "It doesn't flow" or "You need a transition"—both of which can mean that you're jumping from one topic to the next. So how do you fix the problem?

Professional writers and editors practice at least three techniques for going from here to there:

1. **Transition\* words and phrases**
2. **Repeated key words**
3. **Common denominators**

### 1. Transition Words and Phrases

The first technique to go from here to there is to use ordinary transitions (see page 37). You plug in **however** or **on the other hand** or a **conjunction\*** (like **and** or **but**) between two sentences:

> Action movies are about feeling—not the thinking you do when you read. **On the other hand**, when you read, you can put down the book and reflect on the passage—even a passage with a car chase. **But** action movies don't give you time to reflect.

Or between two paragraphs:

> I like action movies because they kick you in the gut. Action movies require little thinking. You don't have to think in the midst of a car chase or when a guy slips off a skyscraper ledge or a mutant hacks up a pack of Cub Scouts. Action movies are about feeling—not the thinking you do when you read. On the other hand, when you read, you can put down the book and reflect on the passage—even a passage with a car chase. But action movies don't give you time to reflect. You're on a roller coaster ride that lasts till the movie ends. Action movies are roller coaster rides, with the same ups and downs and wild thrills that slam your stomach before you can think about how scared you are.
>
> **However**, because action movies don't make you think, they don't last too long in the memory. In the end, one action movie is pretty much like another—just like one roller coaster ride pretty much resembles another. All you can do to improve the ride is to add extra hills and curves. And in the end, all the rides—whether in the movie theater or at the fair—become one big blur.

Depending on function, ordinary transition words and phrases fall into a dozen categories:

## Categories of Transition Words and Phrases

| TO SHOW ADDITION | TO SHOW ASSENT | TO SHOW CONTRAST |
| --- | --- | --- |
| TO SHOW DETAILS | TO SHOW EMPHASIS | TO SHOW END |
| TO SHOW EXAMPLES | TO SHOW PLACE | TO SHOW PURPOSE |
| TO SHOW RESULTS | TO SHOW SIMILARITY | TO SHOW TIME |

We can flesh out these dozen categories into the following:

# A List of Transition Words and Phrases

| TO SHOW ADDITION | TO SHOW ASSENT | TO SHOW CONTRAST |
|---|---|---|
| again<br>also<br>besides<br>equally important<br>finally<br>first, second, etc.<br>further<br>furthermore<br>just as important<br>moreover<br>too | after all<br>at any rate<br>at least<br>clearly<br>nevertheless<br>of course<br>still<br>yet | by contrast<br>however<br>in contrast<br>in spite of this<br>instead<br>nevertheless<br>notwithstanding<br>on the contrary<br>on the one/other hand<br>still<br>whereas |
| **TO SHOW DETAILS**<br>especially<br>in particular<br>namely<br>specifically<br>to enumerate | **TO SHOW EMPHASIS**<br>above all<br>certainly<br>in fact<br>in short<br>in truth<br>indeed<br>most important<br>obviously<br>of course<br>really<br>surely | **TO SHOW END**<br>at last<br>finally<br>in conclusion<br>in short<br>in summary<br>on the whole<br>overall<br>to sum up<br>to summarize |
| **TO SHOW EXAMPLES**<br>for example<br>for instance<br>further<br>furthermore<br>in addition<br>in the first place<br>to illustrate | **TO SHOW PLACE**<br>beyond<br>nearby<br>opposite<br>there<br>to the left<br>to the right | **TO SHOW PURPOSE**<br>for this/that purpose<br>to do this/that<br>to this/that end<br>with this/that in mind<br>with this/that in view |
| **TO SHOW RESULTS**<br>accordingly<br>as a result<br>for that reason<br>for this reason<br>otherwise<br>therefore<br>thus | **TO SHOW SIMILARITY**<br>by the same token<br>equally important<br>in the same manner<br>in the same way<br>like<br>likewise<br>similarly<br>too | **TO SHOW TIME**<br>after a while<br>afterward(s)<br>at present<br>at the same time<br>directly<br>earlier<br>in the meantime<br>later<br>meanwhile<br>next<br>presently<br>simultaneously<br>soon<br>then |

## 2. Repeated Key Words

The second technique to go from here to there is to repeat key words. Typically, you pull a key word or key words out of the last sentence of one paragraph and repeat it, or them, in the first sentence of the next paragraph.

**LAST sentence of one paragraph to the FIRST sentence of the next paragraph:**

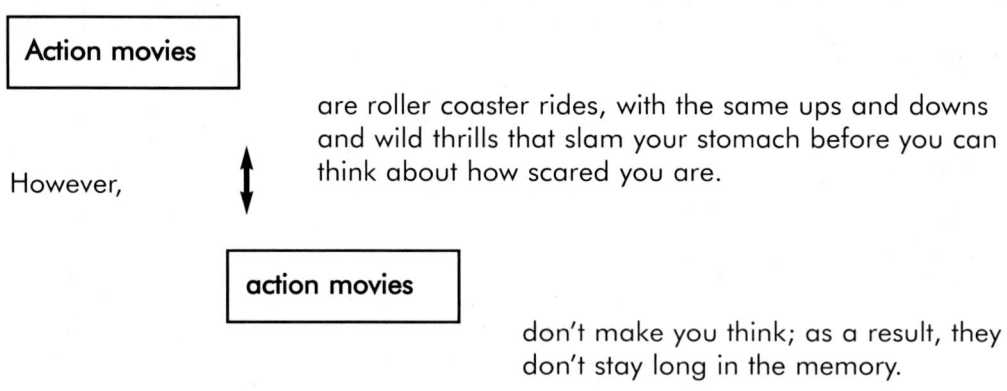

The boxed key words link up the first paragraph to the next. Imagine a series of paragraphs. Now put links between them using key words. Suddenly each paragraph hooks up to the paragraph that follows. You can't go wrong with this technique. (And note that the transition **however** functions as still one more link between the paragraphs.)

## 3. Common Denominators

The third technique to go from here to there is the most fun of the three. Take any two topics and find some common denominator (just as 2 is a common denominator of 4 and 8).

    motorcycles
    **Bill Clinton**

How can you possibly go from a paragraph about motorcycles to a paragraph about Bill Clinton?
Easy . . . Find the common denominator.

**Start with the last sentence or two of a paragraph:**

> All across the world, young people have taken to the roads on their motorcycles—the romantic symbol of the loner and the outlaw.

**Then find a common denominator:**

> **Like the loner on the motorcycle, the jazz musician in sunglasses exemplifies what it means to be cool.**

**Between that paragraph and the next paragraph:**

> When Bill Clinton appeared on a talk show wearing sunglasses and playing his saxophone, he knew how to tap into America's national obsession with being cool. Clinton knew that his youth could only help him in an election against the older Bush if he portrayed himself as an outsider, a cool young politician trying to buck the system.

---

**Motorcycles and Bill Clinton are divided by a common denominator:** *cool*.

**Use the common denominator as a pivot between any two topics:**

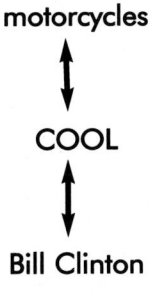

---

Thus:

> All across the world, young people have taken to the roads on their motorcycles—the romantic symbol of the loner and the outlaw. **Like the loner on the motorcycle, the jazz musician in sunglasses exemplifies what it means to be cool.** When Bill Clinton appeared

THE BASICS OF PARAGRAPHS AND TRANSITIONS

on a talk show wearing sunglasses and playing his saxophone, he knew how to tap into America's national obsession with being cool. Clinton knew that his youth could only help him in an election against the older Bush if he portrayed himself as an outsider, a cool young politician trying to buck the system.

Similarly, you can go from just about any topic to just about any other topic by figuring out the logical link. And that link, like ordinary transitions and repeated key words, hooks your paragraphs together in a long, solid chain that will flow like the Mississippi, start to finish.

# Key 3

# The Basics of Sentences

- Is That a Fragment or a Sentence?
- Simple Sentences* or Less Simple Sentences?
- How Do I Create Sentence Variety?
- Active vs. Passive?
- What Goes Wrong with Our Sentences?

## IS THAT A FRAGMENT OR A SENTENCE?

Every good writer should know the difference between a fragment and a sentence. If you don't, your writing will take a dive in at least two regrettable directions:

- **You'll write fragments when you should write sentences (and that's a bonehead mistake open to ridicule).**
- **You'll commit all kinds of punctuation errors (more about this under Key 6).**

A fragment is a group of words needing more information to complete it—either BEFORE or AFTER the fragment—to turn a partial idea into a whole idea ➔ into a sentence.

For example, if we write,

When it rains ➔
Although the game ended late ➔
If I were you ➔
← because he wanted to do the right thing
← since she was available then
← which was full of gas fumes

we've written fragments. Each one needs information to complete it:

> When it rains, I GET WET.
>
> Although the game ended late, WE STOPPED FOR SUPPER.
>
> If I were you, I WOULDN'T HESITATE TO CALL WILLY MURDOCH.
>
> RONNIE PAID THE TICKET because he wanted to do the right thing.
>
> I MADE THE APPOINTMENT WITH MY LAWYER since she was available then.
>
> MRS. SNETHEN VACATED HER CABIN, which was full of gas fumes.

Traditional writing frowns on using fragments. It prefers sentences. Indeed, for some teachers and editors, fragments signal bad writing—and you'll get your knuckles cracked.

But, in truth, good writers **do** use fragments and always have.
But sparingly.
And carefully.

Notice those two fragments. ("But sparingly" and "And carefully.") They drive home the main point: that you're allowed to write fragments but that their use must be sparing and careful.

For that's how writers typically use fragments. In a professional's hands, fragments normally appear at the end of a sentence or paragraph to nail down a point.

*Whack.*

Or appear in a paragraph of their own.

Like this.

If you want to introduce fragments into your writing, remember the following:

- **Before writing the fragment, consider your audience**. (Fragments are okay in advertising copy but not so good in a formal research report.)
- **Thus: The more formal the writing, the less appropriate the fragment**.
- **Teachers usually don't like them.**
- **Many readers ridicule a clumsy use of fragments.**

What constitutes "a clumsy use of fragments"? Generally, it's situations like these:

| MAIN STATEMENT | FRAGMENT |

**Ronnie paid the ticket. BECAUSE HE WANTED TO DO THE RIGHT THING.**

**I made an appointment with my lawyer. SINCE SHE WAS AVAILABLE AT THAT TIME.**

**Mrs. Snethen vacated her cabin. WHICH WAS FULL OF GAS FUMES.**

All three fragments are clumsy because a period has split them from their main statements.

As a rule,

**Don't separate a fragment from the main statement with a period.**

Otherwise, your writing will look like an amateur's.

Professionals know how to avoid fragments. It's easy: Just connect the fragment to the main statement:

**Ronnie paid the ticket <u>because he wanted to do the right thing</u>.**
**I made an appointment with my lawyer <u>since she was available at that time</u>.**
**Mrs. Snethen vacated her cabin, <u>which was full of gas fumes</u>.**

(You're probably wondering when it's proper to put a comma in front of the fragment, as in the sentence about Mrs. Snethen. See patterns 2 and 3, p. 151.)

Remember that the intelligent, careful, occasional use of a fragment is a good thing. You just can't try it too often or in the wrong genre.

As a second rule,

**Use fragments only when you're trying to drive home a point.**

Like this.
And as a third rule,

**Don't use fragments too often.**

They quickly wear out their welcome.
Like this.

If the reader begins to notice your fragments, you're using them too often. Probably one or two a page will be the right number.

## SIMPLE SENTENCES OR LESS SIMPLE SENTENCES?

The normal sentence order in English is:

**SUBJECT + VERB***
**I            slept.**

The subject tells who or what takes charge of the sentence; the verb tells what gets done:

**I slept.**

The simplest simple sentences have no more than a subject and verb:

**I slept.**
**I walked.**
**Myron juggled.**
**Will swam.**
**Belinda sang.**

Sometimes you may want to add stuff after the verb:

I slept **through the night**. (The addition is a **prepositional phrase**.)

Or:

I hit **the ball**. (Now it's a **direct object**.*)

Or:

I drove **carefully**. (And now it's an **adverb**.*)

Or:

Billy sent **Martha a birthday card**.

(This one has two additions: an **indirect object*** [Martha] and a **direct object** [birthday card]).

And so on. You can add all sorts of stuff after the verb.
Just as you can add all sorts of stuff before the subject:

**The tall, old** man hit the ball. (Three **adjectives*** come before the subject, "man.")

For our purposes, a **simple sentence** states, in the simplest way possible, what you want to say. It is **a subject followed by a verb**, sometimes with stuff in front of the subject, sometimes with stuff after the verb. And sometimes both:

**The tall, old** man hit the ball **through the window**.

Simple sentences—even the simplest—are terrific, and good writing can't survive without them. Never let yourself believe that writing simple sentences will somehow say that you have a simple mind. To the contrary. Fine writers have always used simple sentences—and always will.

## How Many Simple Sentences?

Nevertheless, a steady diet of simple subject-verb sentences can become a miserable monotony to the ear:

> <u>I went</u> to the store. <u>I bought</u> some bread. Then <u>I drove</u> home. My <u>wife and I cooked</u> dinner. Next <u>we washed</u> the dishes. <u>I dried</u>. <u>I like</u> to dry. The <u>cat meowed</u>. So <u>I stopped</u> to feed the cat. <u>She stopped</u> meowing. <u>I am</u> glad <u>I fed</u> the cat. The <u>cat was</u> also glad. My <u>wife was</u> also glad. <u>Such is</u> life.

Boring, right? Can you imagine two hundred pages of these singsong simple sentences? For some of us, it would be like a long, long evening of unrelenting polka music or an interminable concert by a high school marching band pumping out one Sousa march after another:

**One**-two-three-four
**One**-two-three-four
**One**-two-three-four
**One**-two-three-four . . .

Our ears and eyes crave variety. Music, sentences—and life!—without variety will drive us crazy.

So to spare your reader, you must introduce a change of pace into your writing.

**One**-two-three-four
One-two-**three**, one-two, one-two—**three** . . .

# HOW DO I CREATE SENTENCE VARIETY?

Try these techniques:

> 1. Combine simple sentences
> 2. Vary sentence beginnings
> 3. Vary sentence length
> 4. Vary sentence diction*

**THE BASICS OF SENTENCES**

1. **Combine Simple Sentences**
    a. Use a **comma** + a **conjunction** to combine two simple sentences:
        I have a new bike**, and** I ride it a lot.
        Jerry visited Poland last year**, and** Misty visited Germany.
    b. Use a **semicolon** to combine two simple (related) sentences:
        I have a new bike**;** I ride it a lot.
    c. Use a **semicolon** + a **transition** to combine two (related) simple sentences:
        I have a new bike**; therefore**, I ride it a lot.
    d. Turn a **simple sentence** into a **fragment**:
        I have a new bike. = **simple sentence**
        → Because I have a new bike = **fragment**
        Misty visited Germany. = **simple sentence**
        → while Misty visited Germany = **fragment**
       Then add the **fragment** to another **SIMPLE SENTENCE**:
        → Because I have a new bike, I RIDE IT A LOT.
        JERRY VISITED POLAND LAST YEAR,
        → while Misty visited Germany.

2. **Vary Sentence Beginnings**

Simple sentences start with a subject and follow that subject with a verb:
   **Jim studied.**

Try these twelve techniques to move beyond monotonous subject-verb openings:
   a. Add a **transition*** (see the **Glossary**, page 280):
       HOWEVER, Jim has to study tonight.
   b. Add an **adverb:***
       UNFORTUNATELY, Jim hasn't kept up with his studies.
   c. Add an **adverb clause:***
       BECAUSE HE HADN'T STUDIED, Jim worried that he'd flunk the exam.
   d. Add a **prepositional phrase:***
       IN A REAL PANIC, Jim realized that he had to study.

e.  Add a **direct object**:* (**Note**: No comma needed when the direct object comes first.)
    HIS DAILY ASSIGNMENTS Jim had ignored for weeks.

f.  Add an **adjective**:*
    SCARED OF THE EXAM, Jim began to study hard.

g.  Add a **present participle**:*
    WORRYING (WORRY + ING) ABOUT THE EXAM, Jim stayed up all night to study.

h.  Add a **past participle**:*
    DEPRIVED OF STUDY TIME BY WORK, Jim cut back his hours at McDonald's.

i.  Add an **infinitive**:*
    TO KEEP UP HIS GRADE AVERAGE, Jim maintained his study schedule.

j.  Add an **absolute**:*
    THE EXAM APPROACHING, Jim decided to buckle down.
    TRUE, Jim had to study.

k.  Add an **appositive**:*
    A SCREW-OFF BEFORE THE EXAM, Jim now had to study.
    (Jim, A SCREW-OFF BEFORE THE EXAM, now had to study.)

## 3. Vary Sentence Length

It may surprise you to discover that your sentences will probably each have about the same number of words; that is, they will if you're not paying attention to word count. Sherlock Holmes could have identified the author of this anonymous memo simply by counting words and comparing the count to known perpetrators of similar memos:

> ### PAROLE BOARD ACTION
>
> (1) A report from your social worker indicates that a parole plan has not yet been developed. (2) Your desire to transfer to the Fond du Lac area has been noted but not facilitated at this point. (3) Your case is still assigned to Jefferson County and we have no verification of a residence in the Fond du Lac area. (4) There seems to be some question in regard to the Theresa living situation that should be explored further prior to your next interview. (5) A pre-parole investigation is required prior to your next parole hearing in order to determine the efficacy of a plan in Fond du Lac County.
>
> Attention Social Service: (6) We would appreciate your assistance in providing us with a firm parole plan via the inmate pre-parole status procedure forms. (7) The need for acceptance in Fond du Lac County and a release by the assigned agent in Jefferson County is essential prior to Inmate's release.

This memo is remarkably dull—for reasons ranging from a missing Big Picture (what does the writer want to say?) to the plodding, singsong sentences to the strings of prepositional phrases to the bad jargon and passives.

And another factor contributing to the dullness is that each sentence has about the same number of words:

Sentence (1) = 16
Sentence (2) = 19
Sentence (3) = 22
Sentence (4) = 23
Sentence (5) = 25
Sentence (6) = 20
Sentence (7) = 25

**Sentence average = 21**

Given an average sentence length of twenty-one words, imagine two hundred pages of sentences all twenty-one words long, all marching along, one flat sentence after the other . . . More miserable monotony to the eye and ear. **One**-two-three-four. **One**-two-three-four.

Apparently, if we're not thinking about it, we write sentences that "fingerprint" us, as telling as our blood type and DNA code. Unfiltered, unedited, sentences will spill out in uniform batches, depending on the number that typically fingerprints you.

Sound crazy? Pull out a page of your own prose and count the words, sentence by sentence. So what? What's the point?

Repetition is an ancient device to induce drowsiness. That's why bad writing—the monotony of the language—can put us to sleep. Crooning a lullaby in a softly creaking rocking chair, we coax a child into sleep. Over the pleasant clacking throb of train wheels bumping train tracks, we'll slide off into a nap. And during that long, long night of polkas or the band concert that never wants to end, don't you nod off, hypnotized into slumber by the steady, repetitive, monotonous beat?

**One**-two-three-four . . . **One**-two-three-four . . .

## 4. Vary Sentence Diction

"Diction" means the words you choose when you write or speak. Key 4 will look at words in all sorts of situations, but, briefly, remember that a paragraph composed of mostly one-syllable words can deaden the ear (and induce sleep), just as a paragraph of mostly more-than-one-syllable words can have the same effect (and confuse the reader).

**One-Syllable Words** (in **boldface**)

**I went to the store. I bought some bread. Then I drove home. My wife and I cooked** dinner. **Next we washed the** dishes. **I dried. I like to dry. The cat** meowed. **So I stopped to feed the cat. She stopped** meowing. **I am glad I fed the cat. The cat was** also **glad. My wife was** also **glad. Such is life.**

**More-Than-One-Syllable Words** (in **boldface**)

The **agenda legitimized** the plan's **efficacy** in **order** to **present** the **procedure effectively, underscore** the **overall intention**, and **suggest** more **positive** means of **interpretation**, both in terms of the **protocol** for **pest-resistant applications** and **structural** and **fiscal considerations** to **augment** the **department's image**, as well as the **protocol** for **seeking, expanding**, and **developing** a **rationale** for **increased spending** and **public awareness**.

Obviously, a paragraph of one-syllable simple sentences has its shortcomings, and a paragraph whose words have more than one syllable, presented in one whopper sentence, has even worse problems. What's the answer?

Good writers swing like a pendulum between the simple and the complex, though they generally favor the simple.

- Use both simple words and sentences AND complex words and sentences.
- BUT use simple words and sentences more often than complex words and sentences.

This swing between the two poles (while favoring the simple) can mean that both your sentences and your diction will show constant variety. In the hands of a wonderful writer, the result can thrill the ear.

Listen to this passage from Henry David Thoreau's *Walden* (published in 1854):

> 1. For my part, I could **easily** do **without** the **post-office**. 2. I think that there are **very** few **important communications** made through it. 3. To speak **critically**, I **never received** more than one or two **letters** in my life—I wrote this some years **ago**—that were worth the **postage**. 4. The **penny-post** is, **commonly**, an **institution** through which you **seriously offer** a man that **penny** for his thoughts which is so **often safely offered** in jest. 5. And I am sure that I **never** read any **memorable** news in a **newspaper**. 6. If we read of one man robbed, or **murdered**, or killed by **accident**, or one house burned, or one **vessel** wrecked, or one **steamboat** blown up, or one cow run over by the **Western Railroad**, or one mad dog killed, or one lot of **grasshoppers** in the **winter**,—we **never** need read of **another**. 7. One is **enough**.

Thoreau stays on the simple side but makes trips into the complex. The highlighted words have more than one syllable; of the total 145 words in the passage, 35 have more than one syllable. That figures at only 24% of the total word count—leaving a splendid 76% that have just one.

Sentence length varies considerably:

Sentence 1 = 10        Sentence 5 = 14
Sentence 2 = 12        Sentence 6 = 54
Sentence 3 = 26        Sentence 7 = 3
Sentence 4 = 26

After the gathering crescendo of Sentence 6, that final sentence of three words acts like a final chord coming down to cap a melody. The passage shows a beautiful use of sentence variety: from starting with two sentences of approximate length, moving then to two sentences **twice** as long and **equally** as long. Then moving to a shorter sentence of fourteen words before jumping into that long, accumulating sentence of fifty-four words! And then into three solid words expressed in a simple sentence: *One is enough.*

*One is enough*: Two words of one syllable followed by a lengthening two-syllable finale. This is sentence variety to aspire to.

Likewise, although some sentences start with the plain subject-verb, others vary the pattern:

| | |
|---|---|
| Sentence 1: For my part = Prepositional phrase<br>Sentence 2: I think = Subject-Verb<br>Sentence 3: To speak critically = Infinitive phrase<br>Sentence 4: The Penny-post is = Subject-Verb | Sentence 5: <u>And I am sure</u> = Transition (Note how Sentence 5 challenges the "never start a sentence with 'and'" myth.)<br>Sentence 6: <u>If we read of</u> . . . = Adverb clause<br>Sentence 7: <u>One is</u> = Subject-Verb |

And, likewise, Thoreau uses sentence-combining to avoid one plain simple sentence after another. Sentences 3 and 6 start with fragments that Thoreau could have written as simple sentences:

To speak critically = **I will speak critically.**
If we read of one man robbed = **We can read of one man robbed.**

Sentence 6—with its fifty-four words—combines nine short simple sentences that turn into one expanded fragment:

**If we read of one man robbed, or murdered, or killed . . .**

before coming to the final statement or Big Picture:

**we never need read of another.**

Thoreau combines the following sentences into Sentence 6:

**We can read of one man robbed.**
**We can read of one man murdered.**
**We can read of one house burned.**
**We can read of one vessel wrecked.**
**We can read of one steamboat blown up.**

THE BASICS OF SENTENCES

> We can read of one cow run over by the Western Railroad.
> We can read of one mad dog killed.
> We can read of one lot of grasshoppers in the winter.
> We never need read of another.

Combined, these become:

> **If we read of one man robbed, or murdered, or one killed by accident, or one house burned, or one vessel wrecked, or one steamboat blown up, or one cow run over by the Western Railroad, or one mad dog killed, or one lot of grasshoppers in the winter,—we never need read of another.**

And what satisfaction we're thus granted by this long and suspenseful sentence.

So, to review, has Thoreau:

1. **Combined simple sentences?**
   Yes.
2. **Varied sentence beginnings?**
   Yes.
3. **Varied sentence length?**
   Yes.
4. **Varied sentence diction?**
   Yes.

We can learn a moral by reading this passage: *Use Thoreau for a sentence-paragraph model.*

## ACTIVE VS. PASSIVE?

It's your choice whether you write:

**I hit the ball.** (Grammarians call this construction the **active.**\*)

Or:

**The ball was hit by me.** (Grammarians call this construction the **passive.**\*)

Grammatically, neither is right nor wrong. However, you may want to choose the active. It's shorter, and up front you know who did what in the sentence (you learn with the first word **who** hit the ball; the passive makes you wait till the end to discover it was **me**).

You can shorten the passive by writing **The ball was hit**. But now it's worse: Who's responsible for hitting the ball? Who knows?

The passive, then, either lengthens the sentence and delays telling who's responsible—or, with shortening, omits the subject.

Hence good stylists don't like it very much. They're fond of warning us to **avoid the passive, avoid the passive**.

But active vs. passive is an issue of style, not rule-breaking. Choosing **The ball was hit** rather than **I hit the ball** breaks no rule; it only weakens your writing by **adding words** and introducing an inefficient word arrangement that **fuzzes up clarity and meaning**.

Now let's return to that parole board memo:

---

### PAROLE BOARD ACTION

(1) A report from your social worker indicates that a parole plan has not yet been developed. (2) Your desire to transfer to the Fond du Lac area has been noted but not facilitated at this point. (3) Your case is still assigned to Jefferson County and we have no verification of a residence in the Fond du Lac area. (4) There seems to be some question in regard to the Theresa living situation that should be explored further prior to your next interview. (5) A pre-parole investigation is required prior to your next parole hearing in order to determine the efficacy of a plan in Fond du Lac County.

Attention Social Service: (6) We would appreciate your assistance in providing us with a firm parole plan via the inmate pre-parole status procedure forms. (7) The need for acceptance in Fond du Lac County and a release by the assigned agent in Jefferson County is essential prior to Inmate's release.

---

Why does this prose sound so impersonal? vague? institutional?

For a start, of the seven sentences, four fall into the **passive** (1, 2, 4, and 5). You don't know who's responsible for what. The inmate reading this doesn't know if **he** is supposed to develop a parole plan—or if that's the job of the social worker. Or somebody else. **Who's** "noted but not facilitated" the "desire to transfer to the Fond du Lac area"? **Who's** supposed to look into the "Theresa living situation that should be explored further"? And "a pre-parole investigation is required" by **whom**?

**Who's** in charge of what? You can't tell.

Passive (impersonal, vague, institutional) writing ducks responsibility for its actions.

**THE BASICS OF SENTENCES**

**The ball was hit.** By whom? Who takes responsibility?
**Mistakes were made**. By whom? Who made them?

Consider these sentences in the active:

**I hit the ball**.
**I made the mistakes**.

Or instead of:

A report from your social worker indicates that a parole plan **has not yet been developed**.

Consider:

A report indicates that your **social worker has not yet developed** a parole plan.

Instead of:

Your desire to transfer to the Fond du Lac area **has been noted but not facilitated at this point**.

Consider:

At this point, **we have noted but not facilitated** your desire to transfer to the Fond du Lac area.

And instead of:

There seems to be some question in regard to the Theresa living situation that **should be explored** further prior to your next interview.

Consider:

There seems to be some question in regard to the Theresa living situation that your **social worker should explore** further prior to your next interview.

And, finally, instead of:

A pre-parole investigation **is required** prior to your next parole hearing . . .

Consider:

**We require** a pre-parole investigation prior to your next parole hearing . . .

Replacing the passive with specific subjects (**social worker, we**) and turning these vague, irresponsible sentences into the active won't just make the sense clearer. More important, it's a matter of ethics: You as writer are ethically obliged to help the reader of the memo. Like many prisoners, he may have a limited education—and perhaps have no more than grade-school reading level.

Above all, the memo should strive to **communicate**. What else? That's the main purpose of any memo. Or of any piece that we write.

So why do so many writers leave out the subject and convert a sentence into the passive?

One answer is that it's easy to slide into the passive. If you're a bureaucrat, you can churn out page after page of it:

> A decision **was made** to enact the Forbes memorandum. All additions to that memorandum **will be gathered** at regular intervals of time, **updated**, and **disseminated** electronically. Staff **will be expected** to review said additions. Any response **will be responded** to.

> Who's **deciding**?
> Who's **gathering**?
> Who's **updating**?
> Who's **disseminating**?
> Who's **expecting**?
> Who's **responding**?

Ethics aside, additional word count aside, the major problem with the passive is that it's inefficient. After reading these sentences, you'll have to phone or email the sender to find out who's supposed to do what. And that's a sloppy, time-consuming pain for the reader.

But you should understand that bureaucrats (and the rest of us) sometimes **want** to use the passive. Sometimes it doesn't matter if you say:

> The church addition **was built** around 1890.

Or:

> Her hip **was replaced** at University Hospital.

Or:

> Garbage **will be picked** up around dawn.

Or:

> Two children's fares **will be counted** as one adult's.

Who cares who built the addition or who replaced the hip or who will pick up the garbage or who will count the fares? Nobody. In this case, the passive works fine. Here, we use the passive as a convenience.

**If nobody cares who did what, use the passive.**

And, sometimes, being a sneaky, sleazy bureaucrat, you may deliberately want to avoid saying who did what.

**If you have a good reason for hiding an identity, use the passive.**

But you don't want to use the passive just because it's handy or because everybody in your office of bureaucrats writes in the passive. Remember that it creates vague prose, ducks responsibility—and adds all those extra words.

Thus: **The passive generally should be avoided.**
Oops.
Rather: **Generally avoid the passive.**

## What Goes Wrong with Our Sentences?

Besides clumsy fragments, the passive, and a lack of variety? Lots of things. But the list isn't so long that you can't learn it quickly. Review these common problems:

1. Separating Sentence Parts
    a. Subject-Verb split
    b. Modifiers* that describe the wrong word
2. Dangling Modifiers
3. Pronoun* Shifts
4. Vague Pronoun Reference
5. Lack of Parallel Structure
6. Necessary Word Left Out
7. Mismatched Verb Forms
    a. Tenses
    b. Inconsistent active and passive
8. Wordiness
    a. Bad jargon preferred to plain words
    b. The passive
    c. Redundancies
    d. Sentences starting with **there is/are/were** and **it is**
    e. Strings of prepositional phrases
    f. Needless repetition
    g. Hollow or pompous phrases
9. Sexist Language

1. **Separating Sentence Parts**
   a. **Subject-Verb split**

   Sentences have a natural logic:

         S V

   **After leaving the house, I drove to work.**

   So why write:

   S    split   V

   **I, after leaving the house, drove to work.**

   This awkward construction makes life hard for the reader. You shouldn't have to wait till Hell freezes over to discover the verb.

   As a rule, **Keep the subject and verb next to each other.**

   b. **Modifiers that describe the wrong word**

   The natural logic of a sentence requires that words that belong together should stay together (like the subject and verb). In other words, if you write

   **Ralph stuck a cap on his head that he'd just bought at the Farmer's Market,**

   you're doing something wrong.

   What's the logic?

   1. Ralph hasn't just bought his head at the Farmer's Market.
   2. He presumably bought his cap at the Farmer's Market.
   3. "Head" should follow "stuck."
   4. "Cap" should follow "head."
   5. "That he'd just bought" should follow "cap."
   6. And "at the Farmer's Market" should follow "bought."

   **Ralph stuck (a) on his head (b) a cap (c) that he'd just bought (d) at the Farmer's Market.**

   As a rule, **A word (or phrase) should stay next to the word it describes.**

2. **Dangling Modifiers**

   Read the following out loud:

   **Driving recklessly, the bus went out of control.**

Drinking orange juice daily, the cold went away.
Eating lunch in the cafeteria, the computer broke down.

Hear the problem? Each sentence lacks a connection between the **modifier** (the words **before** the comma) and the main statement (the words **after** the comma). That lack of connection causes a problem in logic:

1. How can a **bus** drive recklessly? (A bus **driver** has to drive.)
2. How can a **cold** drink orange juice daily? (A **man** has to drink orange juice daily.)
3. How can a **computer** eat lunch in the cafeteria? (A **woman** has to eat lunch in the cafeteria.)

And the problem in logic—the lack of connection between the modifier and the subject (**bus, cold,** and **computer**)—causes the modifier to "dangle." It doesn't logically hook up to the subject (**bus driver, man,** and **woman**).

You fix this problem by inserting a subject into the sentence—either before the comma (in the modifier):

**Because the bus driver was driving recklessly, the bus went out of control.**
**Since the man was drinking orange juice daily, the cold went away.**
**While the woman was eating lunch in the cafeteria, the computer broke down.**

Or after the comma (in the main statement):

**Driving recklessly, the bus driver caused the bus to go out of control.**
**Drinking orange juice daily, the man made his cold go away.**
**Eating lunch in the cafeteria, the woman learned that the computer had broken down.**

As a rule, **Insert a subject to fix a dangling modifier**.

## 3. Pronoun Shifts

Here's a dramatic example of a common grammar problem:

**One** should try to do **their** best. If **you** don't, **we** as a people will suffer. **I** think that all of **us**, regardless of race, creed, or color, should work together. It's each person's duty to do **their** job to help **us** succeed.

Traditional grammar tells us that

**One** should try to do **their** best.

is a classic case of mixing apples and oranges—with **one**, the apple, being a singular and **their**, the orange, a plural. You can't follow a **singular** with a **plural**. Rather:

**One** should try to do **one's** best.

Or:

**One** should try to do **his** best.
**One** should try to do **her** best.
**One** should try to do **his/her** best.

Traditional grammar also says that a short passage can't contain such a grab bag of pronouns: **one, their, we, you, I, us**. Generally, pick a pronoun and stay with it through a sentence (and a paragraph and the larger project).

Here's a related problem:

A TV **anchorman** frequently buys a toupee to cover **their** bald spot.

Once again you've mixed apples and oranges: **anchorman** = a singular; **their** = a plural. Fix this problem by writing either:

A TV **anchorman** frequently buys a toupee to cover **his** bald spot.
(Use two singulars.)

Or:

TV **anchormen** frequently buy toupees to cover **their** bald spots.
(Use two plurals.)

## 4. Vague Pronoun Reference

What's wrong with these two sentences?

**Milo's father was a lawyer; as a result, Milo wanted to study it.**

**Many American cars are now as reliable as imports, but this surprises the average buyer.**

In the first sentence, the reader probably understands that Milo wants to study law and become a lawyer like his father. But the sentence doesn't specifically say so. Logically, **it** hooks up to **lawyer** and not to the study of law. So you must write:

**Milo's father was a lawyer; as a result, Milo wanted to study <u>law</u>.**

Similarly, **this** in the second example no doubt refers to **this reliability** or **this fact**, but the sentence doesn't specifically say so. To work, it must read:

**Many American cars are now as reliable as imports, but this <u>reliability</u> [or <u>fact</u>] surprises the average buyer.**

As a rule, **A pronoun following a noun\* must specifically refer to that noun**.

## 5. Lack of Parallel Structure

Sentences like to demonstrate predictable structure. What went wrong with the following construction?

**I like to run, to jump, and swimming is one of my favorite activities.**

Here you've set up a construction using infinitives (the word **to** plus a **verb**: **to run**). The first two items are infinitives, but the last is a noun.

The sentence violates parallel structure—you can't write APPLE, APPLE, ORANGE. You must maintain the same form throughout the sentence:

I like **apple, apple,** and **apple**.
I like **infinitive, infinitive,** and **infinitive**.
I like **to run, to jump,** and **to swim**.

Or you can say:

I like **to run, jump,** and **swim**.
(You don't have to maintain the **to** through the sentence.)

If you prefer **running**, turn each item into a noun:

I like **orange, orange,** and **orange**.
I like **noun, noun,** and **noun**.
I like **running, jumping,** and **swimming**.

A writer can use whatever construction he or she likes. The only restriction is to:

**Use the same construction throughout to maintain parallel structure.**

Don't write:

> Once you've read the book, compose an essay; composing the essay, be sure to explore the book's themes.

Rather, construct a parallel structure:

> Once you've read the book, compose an essay; once you've begun the essay, explore the book's themes.

And don't write:

> This book will not only show you the rules but how to use them.
> It is more fun to watch old movies on TV than studying.
> I was told to either shape up or I would be shipping out.
> Neither my friend Paul is going or my friend Sam.
> He wanted money and fame without working hard.
> Mable was a quiet worker but aggressive.
> Elections are both important and a tradition.
> Many of the voters are citizens we contacted and who thanked us for the election material.

Rather, construct parallel structures:

> **This book will show you NOT ONLY the rules BUT ALSO their use.** (Keep "not only/but also" + nouns parallel.)
>
> **It is more fun TO WATCH old movies on TV than TO STUDY.** (Use double infinitives to keep the parallel after "than.")
>
> **I was told EITHER TO SHAPE UP or TO SHIP OUT.** (Use double infinitives to keep the parallel after "either.")
>
> **NEITHER my friend Paul NOR my friend Sam is going.** (Keep the "neither/nor" phrasing parallel.)
>
> **He wanted MONEY and FAME without HARD WORK.** (Keep the noun parallel after "without.")
>
> **Mabel was a QUIET but AGGRESSIVE WORKER.** (Keep the adjective parallel after "but.")
>
> **Elections are both IMPORTANT and TRADITIONAL.** (Keep the adjective parallel after "and.")

> Many of the voters are citizens WHOM WE CONTACTED and WHO THANKED us for the election material.
> (Keep the fragments parallel.)

## 6. Necessary Word Left Out

We hear the next two sentences so often that their problem may not be apparent. Consider their logic:

> **I was so unhappy.**
> **Jane's temperature is higher than Sandy.**

Both share a special parallel problem: They set up situations that demand the writer complete them:

> **I was SO unhappy THAT . . .**
> **I was SO unhappy THAT I ate all the food in the house.**

And the second sentence needs several words to complete the logic, which is that Jane has a higher temperature than Sandy has. As written, the sentence compares an apple with an orange—Jane's temperature is the apple; Sandy is the orange. You can compare:

> **Jane with Sandy**

Or:

> **Jane's temperature with Sandy's temperature**

But you can't write:

> **Jane is higher than Sandy.**
> (This isn't what you originally wanted to say. What happened to "temperature"?)

Rather, accurately:

> **Jane's temperature is higher than Sandy's temperature.**

Or, shorter:

> **Jane's temperature is higher than Sandy's.**

Two rules:

> i. With SO/THAT, keep the structure parallel.
> ii. In a comparison, keep the structure parallel.

## 7. Mismatched Verb Forms

### a. Tenses

If you're writing a sentence in the present, generally stay in the present. And if you're writing in the past, generally stay in the past. So if you write

**The woman hurries forward, grabbed the mugger, and took back her bag,**

you've got a problem: **hurries** = present tense; **grabbed** and **took** = past tense. The solutions are to write:

**The woman hurried forward, grabbed the mugger, and took back her bag.**

Or:

**The woman hurries forward, grabs the mugger, and takes back her bag.**

As a rule, **Generally stay in the same tense**.

But the business can quickly become hairy. What do you do with a sentence like this:

**Every bystander at a crime is suspect, so the police took each one at the bank for questioning.**

You would seem to have another problem: **is** = present tense; **took** = past tense. It would be easy to fix the problem by writing:

**Every bystander at a crime was suspect, so the police took each one at the bank for questioning.**

Yet you can argue that mixing tenses works for this sentence because bystanders are always suspect—just as the sun will always come up and April 15 will always remain tax day.

Some situations stay timeless and hence should stay in the present tense, regardless of an accompanying situation that occurred in the past. The police **took** each one for questioning (a one-shot event that's over and done with), but bystanders at any crime—not just this bank job—will **always** be suspect.

Use common sense in such a situation. You know, for the most part, to **stay in the same tense**. But if a universal comes up, like **every bystander at a crime is suspect**, then there's no reason not to shift temporarily into the present.

THE BASICS OF SENTENCES 63

A related problem shows up in these sentences:

**Doug was with the company for five months before he left.**
**He plans to call her during the week, but he is out of the office most of the time.**
**You left just a few minutes before we arrived.**
**We hike a few miles before we discover the leak in the canteen.**

What's the problem? This is a subtle one.

English verb grammar argues the following: If you have two events occurring in the same time frame but one takes place before the other, you must insert a **have**, **has**, or **had** (whatever's appropriate) before the verb that comes first chronologically.

Confused?

**Doug was with the company for five months before he left.**

Two events here, one taking place before the other:

1. **Doug started work at the company in January.**
2. **Doug left the company in May.**

The event that comes first (January) requires a **had** to set it off from the event that comes second (May):

**Doug had been with the company for five months before he left.**

In the second sentence, the **he** decided to make the call (say, on Monday) before he actually left the office (on Tuesday):

**He has planned to call her during the week, but he is out of the office most of the time.**

In the third, two events happen: Somebody leaves, and somebody arrives. They don't take place at the same time, so you must insert **had** before the one that comes first:

**You had left just a few minutes before we arrived.**

In the last, the **we** start hiking; then they discover the leak in the canteen.

**We have hiked a few miles before we discover the leak in the canteen.**

See the logic? In these four sentences, it's impossible for both events to happen simultaneously; you must move into an earlier tense for the event that comes first.

As a rule, **Use an earlier verb tense for an event that occurs before another.**

### b. Inconsistent active and passive

One last note on the active and passive: Be sure to preserve sentence balance by staying in the active OR the passive within the same sentence. Don't write:

**The committee voted** [active], **and a recommendation was made** [passive].

Or:

**Don was given the ball** [passive], **and he passed it to Frank** [active].

It's better to write:

**The committee voted and made their recommendation.**
(Keep both in the active.)

**Don was given the ball, and it was passed to Frank.**
(Keep both in the passive.)

Or (much better):

**Don received the ball, and he passed it to Frank.**
(Keep both in the active.)

## 8. Wordiness

**Be able to justify every word.** If you can't, get rid of it. **Try to cut as much from a sentence as you can.** Edit for:

a. Bad jargon preferred to plain words (See Key 4, **A Vocabulary of Bad Jargon**, page 83.)
b. The passive (See the discussion, pages 52-56.)
c. Redundancies (See Key 4, **What Words Should I Use?**, pages 111-115.)
d. Sentences with there is/are/were **and** it is

   1. **There were** five cops in the street.
      → Five cops stood in the street.
   2. **It is** necessary for you to go.
      → You must go.

e. Strings of prepositional phrases

> Leonard looked **FOR** a store/**IN** the neighborhood that was a pharmacy.

1. Pull the nouns out of prepositional phrases (**store; neighborhood**).
2. Make one noun describe the other:

    → neighborhood store that was a pharmacy

3. Continue to tighten, moving and deleting words:

    → Leonard looked for a neighborhood pharmacy.

f. Needless repetition

> **Chaucer is an English writer who has written some of the most important works ever written in England.**
>
> → **Chaucer has written some of England's most important works.**

g. Hollow or pompous phrases

> In my own personal opinion, the music of Gustav Mahler, one of the greatest composers of the century, stands at the very summit of musical achievement.
>
> → Mahler wrote great music.
>
> The buildings of Frank Lloyd Wright, who was one of America's finest premiere architects, if not the leading, demonstrate buildings that can be assembled from common materials for the construction.
>
> → Wright's buildings use common construction materials.

9. **Sexist Language**

   a. Change the gender-biased <u>noun</u> and <u>pronoun</u> to **you**:
   Each <u>man</u> is responsible for <u>his</u> time card.
   → **You** are responsible for **your** time card.

   b. Eliminate the gender-biased <u>noun</u> and <u>pronoun</u>:
   Each <u>man</u> is responsible for <u>his</u> time card.
   → Each **worker** is responsible for **the** time card.

   c. Use **the, a,** and **an** instead of <u>pronouns</u>:
   Each man is responsible for <u>his</u> time card.
   → Each worker is responsible for **a** time card.

   d. Use <u>plural nouns</u> and <u>pronouns</u>:
   Each man is responsible for his time card.
   → All <u>workers</u> are responsible for <u>their</u> time cards.

   e. Alternate pronouns—one time use **he**; the next, **she**.

   f. Use <u>gender-free nouns</u>:
   Each man is responsible for his time card.
   → The <u>worker</u> is responsible for the time card.

   g. Use <u>job titles</u>:
   Each man is responsible for his time card.
   → Each <u>police officer</u> is responsible for the time card.

# Key 4

# The Basics of Word Use

- What Is Institutional Language?
- What Are the Characteristics of Bad Jargon?
- What Is the Vocabulary of Bad Jargon?
- What Words Should I Watch Out For?
- What Words Should I Use?

Key 3 claims that one technique for achieving sentence variety is to vary your diction—that is, to vary the words you choose when you write or speak, to choose between words of one syllable and words of more than one syllable.

Such a technique becomes important because, as Key 3 also claims, "a paragraph composed mostly of words of one syllable can deaden the ear (and induce sleep), just as a paragraph made up of words of more than one syllable can have the same effect (and confuse the reader)."

In Key 3, we then looked at a passage from Thoreau's *Walden* to demonstrate how the swing between simple and complex words can be wonderfully satisfying. Though opening up his sentences to complex diction, Thoreau still favors the simple (76 percent of the time). Likewise, your own writing should favor the simple to the complex.

This is not to claim that you should always choose short words over long. The one-syllable word may not do the job; it may not be precise. The word "red" perfectly describes many nouns that are, in fact, **red**. But it shouldn't describe nouns that aren't really red—nouns that are **ruby** (deep red), **cerise** (bright cherry red), **scarlet** (bright red with an orange tinge), **carnelian** (fleshy pink red), **carmine** (purplish red), or even **Titian** (reddish yellow).

But if no real difference exists—as in "utilize" over "use" or "correctional facility" over "jail"—then why not pick the shorter, plainer word?

Indeed, why not? Why do bureaucrats love their long words, their polysyllabic, high-sounding, fancy words?

## What Is Institutional Language?

It's the language of the institution—whether the language of the Internal Revenue Service, the Pentagon, the White House, the FBI, the CIA, the National Rifle Association, the American Medical Association, the American Psychiatric Association, the American Bar Association, the Mafia, Hollywood, the local mayor's office, or the University of Greater Des Moines-Downtown Extension. It's the Official Language of Whoever Wants to Be in Charge. It's jargon.

Jargon—or the vocabulary special to a certain group of people—falls into two groups:

> 1. Good jargon
> 2. Bad jargon

Within our jobs, we all use specific words that people in other jobs don't: Specific words for writers include **adjective, dangling modifier, syntax, semantics, diction,** and **indirect object**.

Words specific to violin makers include **chin rest, fingerboard, f-holes, pegs, sound post, purfle**, and the other fine words used to describe the parts of the violin. Similarly, physicians have their words; butchers have theirs.

All these words serve as the jargon of the trade—and because there's no other word to say precisely **adjective** or **purfle** or **mastoid** or **boning knife**, these are good words. Good jargon.

Good jargon, then, we use to detail an area of human activity, whether it's theology, plumbing, or bookbinding. Good jargon has a precise job: to supply a name when we need a name.

> "What, exactly, do you call that decorative border running around the front and back rims of the violin?"
> "That's the *purfle!*"

**Purfle** is good jargon because it precisely describes the "decorative border running around the front and back rims of the violin." With good jargon, there is probably no other word—no synonym—to replace it, just as there's no other precise, quickly efficient term to replace **purfle** or **adjective**.

With bad jargon, however, you can usually find a shorter, more efficient term to replace the jargon word. For "correctional facility," there's "jail." For "utilize," there's "use."

> Think simple.

Over the years, institutions have properly used their good jargon to describe **purfles** and **scalpels** and **dangling modifiers**. But they've also done something else: They've collected many words that sound important, the "proper" words to "utilize" for a big, important institution like the CIA, the Pentagon, or your local mayor's office.

These words may sound important, but they:

- Lack precision (unlike *purfle* and *mastoid*)
- Replace short words with long words
- Prefer bad jargon to plain words
- Replace particular words with general words
- Create an impersonal, generic tone

Let's read through the parole board memo from Key 3 once more; this time, we'll pay attention to the CAPITALIZED good jargon (language particular to the job) and the underlined bad jargon (language replacing simpler, plainer, clearer, precise words):

---

**PAROLE BOARD ACTION**

(1) A REPORT from your SOCIAL WORKER <u>indicates</u> that a PAROLE PLAN has not yet been <u>developed</u>. (2) Your <u>desire</u> to TRANSFER to the Fond du Lac <u>area</u> has been <u>noted</u> but not <u>facilitated</u> <u>at this point</u> (3) Your CASE is still ASSIGNED to Jefferson County and we have no <u>verification</u> of a residence in the Fond du Lac <u>area</u>. (4) <u>There seems to be some question</u> <u>in regard</u> to the Theresa <u>living situation</u> <u>that should be explored further</u> <u>prior</u> to your next INTERVIEW. (5) A PRE-PAROLE <u>investigation</u> <u>is required</u> <u>prior</u> to your next PAROLE HEARING <u>in order</u> <u>to determine</u> <u>the efficacy of</u> a PLAN in Fond du Lac County.

Attention Social Service: (6) We would <u>appreciate</u> your <u>assistance in providing</u> us with a firm PAROLE PLAN via the <u>inmate pre-parole established procedure and forms</u>. (7) The <u>need</u> for ACCEPTANCE in Fond du Lac County and a RELEASE by the ASSIGNED AGENT in Jefferson County <u>is essential</u> <u>prior</u> to INMATE'S RELEASE.

---

THE BASICS OF WORD USE

## Good Jargon

report, social worker, parole plan, transfer, case, assigned, interview, pre-parole, parole hearing, plan, parole plan, acceptance, release, assigned agent, inmate's release

## Bad Jargon

indicates, developed, desire, area, noted, facilitated, at this point, verification, there seems to be some question, in regard, living situation, area, that should be explored further, prior, investigation, is required, prior, in order, to determine, the efficacy of, appreciate, assistance in providing, inmate pre-parole status procedure forms, need, is essential, prior

Of the bad jargon, you may protest, "But I use these words all the time!"

That is exactly the point. They're so used—so used up—that we've become numb to them. And, word by word, some may not be so terrible. "Noted" and "prior" and "need" are all decent enough words. But overworked and commandeered into almost every piece of institutional writing produced, they've lost their energy and freshness.

Think carefully about the familiar words, the words that first come to mind when you sit down to write. Often we reach for the nearest word—and it will turn out to be a word like "facilitated" or "efficacy" because we hear them so often.

If everybody around you sings the same tune, sooner or later you'll sing it, too.

The **good jargon** in the memo describes precisely the tools and terms of a particular world: **report, parole plan, parole hearing**, and so on. You can't replace that jargon easily or efficiently.

But you **can** replace the **bad jargon** immediately:

indicates = **states** = **says**
desire = **wish**
facilitated = **worked out**
at this point = **now**
in regard to = **about**

# What Are the Characteristics of Bad Jargon?

You've probably noticed that bad jargon has its own special sound. Besides its typical long-winded length, bad jargon likes:

> 1. Turning Verbs into Nouns
> 2. Cramming Nouns Together
> 3. Stacking Prepositional Phrases
> 4. Using Weak Verbs
> 5. Choosing the Passive over the Active
> 6. Choosing Complex Diction over Plain
> 7. Grouping Words and Phrases in Twos and Threes
> 8. Using Words that Echo Other Words

Let's look at each problem in depth:

## 1. Turning Verbs into Nouns

The trick is to find the verb buried inside the noun. Then to set it free using two steps:

> - Remove the verb from the noun.
> - Get rid of the verb/words that precede it.

Thus:

> was able to come to a solution = **solved**
> was in agreement = **agreed**
> performs an investigation = **investigates**
> oversaw the establishment of = **established**

> Sherlock Holmes **was able to come to a solution** regarding the case.
>     TURNS INTO
> Sherlock Holmes **solved** the case.

He **performs an investigation** into the homicide effected in Hollywood.
    TURNS INTO
He **investigates** the Hollywood homicide.

They **oversaw the establishment of an** institution of higher learning.
    TURNS INTO
They **established** a college.

## 2. Cramming Nouns Together

Here's what happens with typical bad jargon, which loves to line up one noun after another:

**The clinic for apprentices in the comic book industry**
    TURNS INTO
**The comic book industry apprentices clinic**

**Photographs of phenomena observed in deep space**
    TURNS INTO
**Deep space observed phenomena photographs**

**Journal records by survivors of Holocaust prison camps**
    TURNS INTO
**Holocaust prison camp survivor journals**

In *Style: Lessons in Clarity & Grace,* Joseph Williams suggests these steps to reduce the number of nouns:

> - Start at the end and rewrite as prepositional phrases.
> - Reduce the prepositional phrases to a reasonable number.

**The comic books industry apprentices clinic**
    MEANS
**The clinic for apprentices in the industry for comic books**
    MEANS
**The clinic for apprentices in the comic books industry**

**Holocaust prison camp survivor journals**
   MEANS
**Journals by survivors of the camps for prisoners in the Holocaust**
   MEANS
**Journals by survivors of Holocaust prison camps**

## 3. Stacking Prepositional Phrases

Prepositions include those small words like **in, out, to, with, under, over, across, by, for, up, down, between**, and **among**. Their role in the sentence is to show direction or location and hook up sentence parts. Once you find the preposition, look for the prepositional phrase, **which begins with a preposition and ends with a noun**. Often one or more adjectives will also appear in the prepositional phrase, so you'll have **a preposition + an adjective + a noun**.

**Prepositional Phrase 1**
Prep Adj Noun
**over the river**

**Prepositional Phrase 2**
Prep     Adj Noun
**through the woods**

**Prepositional Phrase 3**
Prep    Adj       Noun
**to Grandmother's house**

Prepositional phrases love to be stacked together—like a string of nouns or freight cars lined up in a long row behind a train engine. Sometimes the repeated rhythms can sound beautiful:

**Of the people, by the people, for the people**

But often they're as monotonous, one string after another, crammed together, as the cars of a long, slow freight train creeping past a street stop.

Stacked together, prepositional phrases can dull the ear and induce drowsiness. Can't get to sleep at night? Read a batch of prepositional phrases.

You'll find a good collection of prepositional phrases in our parole board memo. For practice, read it out loud, paying attention to the monotony of the stacked phrases. They've been capitalized, and the stacked phrases are set off with a diagonal (/):

> ### PAROLE BOARD ACTION
>
> (1) A report FROM YOUR SOCIAL WORKER indicates that a parole plan has not yet been developed. (2) Your desire TO TRANSFER/TO THE FOND DU LAC area has been noted but not facilitated AT THIS POINT. (3) Your case is still assigned TO JEFFERSON COUNTY and we have no verification OF A RESIDENCE/IN THE FOND DU LAC AREA. (4) There seems TO BE some question IN REGARD/TO THE THERESA LIVING SITUATION that should be explored further prior TO YOUR NEXT INTERVIEW. (5) A pre-parole investigation is required prior TO YOUR NEXT PAROLE HEARING/IN ORDER/TO DETERMINE the efficacy OF A PLAN/IN FOND DU LAC COUNTY.
>
> Attention Social Service: (6) We would appreciate your assistance IN PROVIDING US/WITH A FIRM PAROLE PLAN/VIA THE INMATE PRE-PAROLE STATUS PROCEDURE FORMS. (7) The need FOR ACCEPTANCE/IN FOND DU LAC COUNTY and a release BY THE ASSIGNED AGENT/IN JEFFERSON COUNTY is essential prior TO INMATE'S RELEASE.

(**To transfer, to be**, and **to determine** are really infinitive phrases, but they have the same deadly effect here as the prepositional phrases.)

What's the answer to the monotony of these TWENTY-FOUR phrases? Obviously, it's to avoid them. But as you fix one problem, don't create another by cramming together nouns:

> **Inmate pre-parole status procedure forms**
> MEANS
> **The forms for procedures for the inmate with a pre-parole status**
> MEANS
> **The procedure forms for pre-parole inmates**

A good solution is to strike a middle ground—a few nouns crammed together (**procedure forms**) to avoid too many prepositional phrases lined up on the tracks (**the forms for procedures for the inmate with a pre-parole status**).

**The procedure forms for pre-parole inmates** thus seems preferable to **inmate pre-parole status procedure forms.** It's a sensible mixture of two techniques—stacking prepositional phrases and cramming nouns.

As a rule, **Find the middle ground between stacked prepositional phrases and crammed nouns.**

## 4. Using Weak Verbs

The weak verbs include:

> **is, are, am, was, were, can, could, has, have, had, will, should be, should have been, could be, could have been, make, come, use**

You'll find nothing **grammatically** wrong with these verbs: They just need a rest. Put them out to pasture. True, most writing will automatically rely on **is, are, am, was,** and **were**. You'll find it difficult to avoid them. But as an experiment, each time one shows up, replace it with a verb not on the list. See what happens.

As a rule, **Choose strong verbs over weak verbs.** (See **Strong Verbs,** pages 111-112).

## 5. Choosing the Passive over the Active

**I hit the ball.**
   TURNS INTO
**The ball was hit by me.**
   OR (Worse!)
**The ball was hit.**

Follow these steps to fix the passive:

---
- Figure out WHO or WHAT controls the sentence. If there's no subject, invent one. (WHO hit the ball?)
- Move the subject to the start of the sentence.
- Rewrite as Subject-Verb-Object order.
---

The ball was hit. (**Who** hit the ball?)
   The ball was hit by me. (**Me** = object = real subject, buried inside the prepositional phrase)

**OBJECT - VERB - REAL SUBJECT**
**The ball     was hit   by me.**

TURNS INTO **SUBJECT - VERB - OBJECT**
           I         hit      the ball.

## 6. Choosing Complex Diction over Plain

Some writers and speakers—especially those with a political bent—believe that simple words reveal a simple mind. So they reach for a thesaurus to look for the exotic entry—any word instead of a good, plain word (especially a word of one syllable). Thus:

**be cognizant of** for **know**
**missive** for **letter**
**clandestine** for **secret**
**illicit** for **illegal**
**luncheon** for **lunch**
**employ telephonic communication** for **telephone**
**edifice** for **building**
**remuneration** for **pay**
**transpire** for **become known**
**toilet facility** for **toilet**
**veritable** for **real**

You want to write movie dialogue for a pompous windbag of a senator? No problem. Orate the following out loud in your best pompous, windbag voice:

### SENATOR WINDBAG

> You must make me cognizant by telephonic communication in regards to clandestine illicit remuneration for restroom facility assembly in this edifice; each is a veritable disgrace about which, following luncheon, I shall draft a missive delineating the monetary fraudulences that have variously transpired by the sundry construction agents.

Such pompous euphemisms used to be funny; now we all seem to talk this way, and nobody laughs. What's happened? Why does every aisle at the Kmart have to be called **Cookware Needs** or **Beauty Care Needs Center** instead of **Pots and Pans** and **Makeup**?

Stripped down, Senator Windbag's mouthful means to say:

## SENATOR WINDBAG

> Call me about secret payoffs for toilet construction in this building. They're a real eyesore that I plan to detail in a letter, spelling out the contractors' rip-offs—just as soon as I eat lunch.

So why does the senator prefer the pompous to the plain? Look at the subject: He's talking about **toilets.** Using plain words might make the subject "less serious."

Hyping up the diction also lends a fake sobriety to the situation. People in public—senators, ministers, teachers, the president of the Rotary Club, jail wardens, the head of the FBI or the CIA addressing a congressional watchdog committee—have to sound **serious**. The more money we make, the more we want people to think we deserve our paycheck. So we become a **correctional facilities head administrator** instead of a **jail warden.** And a **gym** becomes a **physical fitness center** and a **hospital** a **health care center** or **health care institution.**

Another possibility may be that many people work at jobs they don't like. Talking about them in plain terms makes the work sound even worse. So we turn up the dial on the language—one syllable up to two or three or ten syllables. "**Employ telephonic communication**" seems a whole lot more important, worth a bigger paycheck, than the modest "**Call me.**"

And if you're tempted to reach for the thesaurus, **Say *No* to** Senator Windbag.

> **Think simple.**

## 7. Grouping Words and Phrases in Twos and Threes

Perhaps because our world so readily falls into patterns of twos (parent and child; husband and wife; teacher and pupil; sun and moon; sunrise and sunset; yin and yang) and threes (father, son, and holy ghost; youth, adulthood, old age; id, ego, and superego; executive, judicial, and legislative branches), so do the words in our sentences. If we're **willing**, we're **able**. If it's **various**, then it's **sundry**. If it's **each**, then it's **every**.

> **Each and every** man is **willing and able** to do **various and sundry** tasks—for the **good and benefit** of all.

By the same token, Cary Grant isn't just **tall** and **dark**. He's **tall, dark**, and **handsome**.

And the bird flew **here, there**, and **everywhere** . . .

The impulse (or craving) to arrange words in sets of two and three can lead your sentences into empty-headed mischief. We often labor over a description, listening to a voice that cries out for a second or third item in a series:

Please call me if you have *questions* or—

Please call me if you have any *questions* or *problems*.

Please call me if you have any *questions, problems*, or—

Please call me if you have any *questions, problems*, or *concerns*.

We're simply plugging a hole to keep some sort of hallucinated symmetry, and the plugs we come up with are **redundant**.

The impulse to be redundant comes naturally. This impulse, joined with words produced in twos and threes, can create some of the gassiest writing around. For every **one** thing, there has to be **another**. For every **first** and **second** concept, there has to be a **third**.

Picture yourself at the keyboard. You type:

**To maintain our budget, we must X, Y . . . and Z.**

**The system is both A . . . and B, while being X . . . Y . . . and Z.**

You're filling in the gaps by sound, not by logic. Your ear says you need a second and third item to complete a series, so, by God, you'll wait till some word shows up—even though the word makes no sense and you don't need it.

As a rule, **Don't trust word pairs**.

(The second word may be redundant with the first.)

As a rule, **Don't trust word triplets**.

(You're probably filling gaps with your ear, not with your brain.)

Travel again through that paragraph from Key 3 of words of more than one syllable. They're broken down by groups of twos and threes:

The agenda legitimized the plan's efficacy in order to (1) present the procedure effectively, (2) underscore the overall intention, and (3) suggest more positive means of interpretation in terms of the (1) protocol for (a) pest-resistant applications and (b-1) structural and (b-2) fiscal considerations to augment the department's image, as well as the (2) protocol for (a) seeking, (b) expanding, and (c) developing a rationale for (i) increased spending and (ii) public awareness.

Or:

The agenda legitimized the plan's efficacy in order to
- (1) present the procedure effectively,
- (2) underscore the overall intention, and
- (3) suggest more positive means of interpretation in terms of the
  - (1) protocol for
    - (a) pest-resistant applications and
    - (b-1) structural and
    - (b-2) fiscal considerations to augment the department's image, as well as the
  - (2) protocol for
    - (a) seeking,
    - (b) expanding, and
    - (c) developing a rationale for
      - (i) increased spending and
      - (ii) public awareness.

Guess what this paragraph "says"?

**Nothing**. It's just a fabrication put together by plugging in bad jargon and patterns of twos and threes. But it **looks** like it means something.

**Moral**: Don't assume you're dumb if you can't penetrate a thicket of jargon. Too often we write off learning a new field, like math or sociology or psychology, because we can't penetrate the prose; the problem may lie with the writer—not with you, the reader. If you can't understand a page in a text, lazy language may be the real issue—not your intelligence.

## 8. Using Words that Echo Other Words

Bad jargon often sounds like bad rhyming poetry. In the parole board memo, certain sounds echo through the sentences like that poetry—or somebody humming along with the radio:

> **PAROLE BOARD ACTION**
>
> (1) A report from your social worker indiCATES that a parole plan has not yet been developed. (2) Your desire to transfer to the Fond du Lac area has been noted but not faciliTATED at this point. (3) Your case is still assigned to Jefferson County and we have no verifiCA-TION of a residence in the Fond du Lac area. (4) There seems to be some quesTION in regard to the Theresa living situaTION that should be explored further prior to your next interview. (5) A pre-parole inVESTtiGA-TION is required prior to your next parole hearing in order to determine the EFfi-CAcy of a plan in Fond du Lac County.
>
> AttenTIon SoCial ServiCe: (6) WE would apprE-CI-ATE your asSIS-TANCE in providing uS with a firm Parole Plan via the inmate PrE-Parole STatuS ProCedure formS. (7) The need for accepTANCE in Fond du Lac County and releaSe by the aSSigned agent in JefferSon County is eSSential prior to inmate'S releaSe.

Two kinds of problems jump out here:

    **a.** **Syllables that echo each other** (indiCATES, verifiCAtion; verificaTION, situaTION, investigaTION, etc.).

    **b.** **Alliteration and assonance** (echoing consonants and vowels).

Listen to the **S** echoes:

    AttenTIon **S**oCial **S**erviCe.

And the **P** echoes:

    **P**arole **P**lan via the inmate **P**re-**P**arole status **P**rocedure

And the **E** echoes:

    vIa the inmate prE-parole status procEdure

What can you do about problems like these?

Probably the best solution is to read everything you write out loud, listening for echoes. You can't do away with all of them—that's impossible. But you can get rid of the worst offenders, those repeated endings like -TION -TION -TION.

Look out for these common endings that signal bad jargon:

**-tion, -ment, -ize, -ly, -ate**

A trick to ridding your prose of repeated endings and echoing patterns is to know that they often appear in bad jargon—appended below for your editing pleasure.

**A word of warning**: These words will look familiar. Of course you can use them; of course you **should** use them.

But sparingly. Compassionately. They're tired and need a rest. (You don't ask somebody on his death bed to run a marathon.)

## WHAT IS THE VOCABULARY OF BAD JARGON?

They're words that we use every day–and that's the problem. They're so common, they don't sound wrong. Why not "utilize" for "use"? Too often we choose the vocabulary of bad jargon because it sounds fancy or sophisticated or "professional." It becomes our default language.

When it's possible, try to choose plain, one-syllable, precise words over the words that follow:

### A Vocabulary of Bad Jargon

| **NOUNS** | | | |
|---|---|---|---|
| absence | communication | empathy | ideology |
| addition | compensation | encounter | impact |
| adjustment | complex | endeavor | increase |
| aggregate (of) | component | enrichment | increment |
| aid | concept | escalation | indication |
| alienation | condition | estimate | indicator |
| alternative | conditioning | evidence | influence |
| appearance | configuration | experience | input |
| application | confrontation | expertise | instance |
| area | conjecture | extent | institution |
| aspect | cooptation | facility | interaction |
| assessment | criteria | fact | interface |
| basis | criterion | factor | interiorizing |
| behavior | critique | feature | interlink |
| capability | data | feedback | involvement |
| capacity | decrease | field | item |
| case | dialectic | fixation | lack |
| category | dialogue | flexibility | level |
| character | dichotomy | formula | line |
| circumstances | dynamics | function | locality |
| class | efficacy | guide | logistics |
| | element | hostility | management |

| | | | |
|---|---|---|---|
| mandate | reference | base | formalize |
| manipulation | relationship | become | fracture |
| matter | request | class | function |
| maximum | response | classify | generate |
| measure | result | communicate | hypothesize |
| medium | role | compense | impact |
| modification | sharing | compose | implement |
| module | situation | comprise | implicate |
| motivation | skills | conceptualize | include |
| nature | solution | concern | increase |
| need | sort | concur | inform |
| needs | speculation | configure | initiate |
| objective | standpoint | confront | insure |
| operation | state | conjecture | integrate |
| option | status | consider | intend to |
| organization | stipulation | contact | interface |
| orientation | tendency | contribute | interiorize |
| outlook | term | converse | interrogate |
| output | termination | critique | involve |
| overreaction | thing | culminate | locate |
| parameter | thrust | customize | maintain |
| participant | totality (of) | decrease | manage |
| participation | trauma | definitize | mandate |
| party | trend | demonstrate | manipulate |
| personnel | type | descend | marginalize |
| perspective | unit | dialogue | modify |
| phase | utilization | donate | motivate |
| phenomenal | value | effect | necessitate |
| phenomenon | value judgment | effectuate | normalize |
| picture | viewpoint | eliminate | obtain |
| policy | | emphasize | operate |
| portion | **VERBS** | encounter | organize |
| posture | accomplish | endeavor | orient |
| preponderance | acquaint | enjoy | orientate |
| presence | acquiesce | ensure | outweigh |
| priority | acquire | escalate | overreact |
| probability | activate | estimate | parent |
| problem | add | eventuate | participate |
| projection | adhere | evince | peruse |
| quality | alienate | exist | position |
| quotient | am | expedite | precede |
| ramification | ameliorate | experience | prioritize |
| rate | apprise | fabricate | project |
| rationale | articulate | facilitate | promote |
| reaction | assist | factor | prove |
| reciprocity | balance | finalize | react |

reference
relate
render
represent
request
respond
result
share
speculate
state
stipulate
strategize
structure
supersede
term
terminate
thrust
transmit
traumatize
typify
utilize
vacillate
value judge
visualize

## ADJECTIVES
absent
additional
adequate
advantageous
alienated
apparent
approximate
available
balanced
better
broad
compatible
confrontational
continuing
counter-
  productive
creative
deliberate
diametrical
digital

dynamic
efficient
equitable
escalating
essential
estimated
existent
expedient
experienced
favorable
feasible
flexible
functional
generational
great
hostile
in-depth
incremental
indicative
initial
insightful
integral
integrated
intentional
interpersonal
involved
logistical
manifest
marginal
maximal
meaningful
minimum
minor
moderate
monitored
multiple
mutual
necessary
numerous
objective
ongoing
operative
optimal
optimum
optional
organizational

orientated
oriented
outstanding
overactive
overall
parallel
parenting
partial
participating
perceptible
preemptive
present
primary
prime
problematic
productive
reactive
reciprocal
relative
relevant
requested
responsive
salient
satisfactory
sharing
situational
so-called
static
substantive
superior
synchronized
systematized
total
transitional
traumatic
ultimate
unilateral
unique
unitary
valid
viable
voluntary

## CONNECTING WORDS
accordingly

along with
antecedent to
as a result of
as regards
as to
as to whether
associated with
basically
due to
due to the fact that
from the stand
  point of
hopefully
in the capacity of
in the case of
in conjunction
  with
in connection with
in the event that
in the line of
in reference to
in regard to
in regards to
in relation to
in such a manner
  that
in terms of
in that
in the event that
in the line of
in the vicinity of
in view of
other than
pertinent to
previous to
prior to
regarding
relative to
subsequent to
to the extent that
with regard to
with a view to
with respect to
with the result that

# What Words Should I Watch Out for?

## 1. A Short List of Individual Words

The words on the *left* pose the problem—the words to keep an eye on for three reasons: (1) The dictionary doesn't recognize the word as a standard form. (2) The dictionary prefers a less awkward form (though it still recognizes the word). (3) Some other problem shows up (like which preposition or particle to use). The words on the *right* offer solutions or correct forms.

acrosst → **across**
administrate → **administer**
affinity to or for → **affinity between or with**
ahold → **hold**
amidst → **amid**
amongst → **among**
and/or → **when possible, use one or the other**
anyways → **anyway**
author (verb) → **write**
ax → **ask**
axed → **asked**
between 1900-1910 → **between 1900 and 1910 or during 1900-1910**
bored with → **bored by**
boughten → **bought**
can't hardly → **can hardly**
cater for → **cater to**
center around → **center on**
complected → **complexioned**
conform to → **conform with**
contiguous with → **contiguous to**
contrast of X and Y → **contrast between X and Y**
contrast with → **contrast to**
convince to → **convince of, convince that**
culminate with → **culminate in**

depending upon → **depending on**
different from → **different than**
disassociate → **dissociate**
dissent with → **dissent from**
doubt if → **doubt that**
drownded → **drowned**
due to → **caused by, because of**
elites → **elite**
enthused → **enthusiastic**
excape → **escape**
firstly, secondly, etc. → **drop the -ly** → **first, second, etc.**
flustrated → **flustered or frustrated**
guesstimate → **guess or estimate**
heighth → **height**
hinderance → **hindrance**
hopefully → **I hope/one hopes**
humans → **human beings**
importantly → **drop the -ly** → **important**
I could care less → **I couldn't care less**
identical to → **identical with**
implant with → **implant into**
in → **within** ("I'm walking in [within] the room.")
in comparison to → **in comparison with**
in contrast with → **in contrast to**
in light of → **in the light of**

incidently → **incidentally**
inculcate with → **inculcate in, into**
independent of → **independent from**
inflict with → **inflicted on** (vs. afflict with;. not "The pain was inflicted on him" but "He was afflicted with pain.")
injected with → **injected into**
instill with → **instill into**
integrate with → **integrate to**
into → **going from here to there** ("I'm walking into [through the door of] the room.")
investigation into → **investigation of**

muchly → drop the **-ly** → **much**
nowheres → **nowhere**
oblivious to → **oblivious of**
off of → **off**
orientate → **orient**
prefer over → **prefer to**
reoccur → **recur**
supposing → **suppose**
thankfully → **I'm thankful**
thusly → drop the **-ly** → **thus**
undoubtably → **undoubtedly**
upmost → **utmost**
whilst → **while**

## 2. A Long List of Word Confusions

**ability** — being able to do something
**capacity** — an amount that can be contained

**abjure** — repudiate or renounce something
**adjure** — command somebody to do something

**about** — approximately ("I made about fifty dollars.")
**around** — circling ("I flew around the house.")

**accede** — comply with ("She acceded to his request.")
**exceed** — go beyond ("His performance exceeded expectations.")

**accent** — emphasize or stress
**ascent** — go up something
**assent** — agree

**accept** — agree to something
**except** — exclude somebody or something

**access** — admittance
**excess** — too much

**adapt** — adjust to a situation
**adept** — skillful at something
**adopt** — borrow or take as your own

**adverse** — opposing ("The drug caused adverse effects.")
**averse** — disinclined, unwilling ("The boy is averse to hard work.")

**advice** — a recommendation
**advise** — make a recommendation

**affect** (verb) — to change
**effect** (noun) — the result

**aggravate** — make worse ("Stress aggravates ulcers.")
**irritate** — be angry with ("I'm irritated with you.")

**THE BASICS OF WORD USE**

**agree on** — share a belief in ("We agree on the path to take.")
**agree to** — consent to ("We agree to those terms.")
**agree with** — hold similar opinion; harmonize with ("I agree with you: Red agrees with blue.")

**all ready** — completely prepared ("He's all ready to go.")
**already** — previously ("He's already gone.")

**all right** — correct form
**alright** — misspelled form

**allot** — distribute
**a lot** — much or many (no such word as "alot")

**allude** — hint at; not say straight out
**elude** — evade or get away
**refer** — say straight out

**allusion** — reference to something
**delusion** — false belief
**illusion** — mistaken impression

**almost** — not quite ("Almost everybody was there.")
**most** — majority of ("Most men agreed.")

**altar** — it's in a church
**alter** — what you do to a pair of pants

**alternate** — one thing after another
**alternative** — available as another possibility

**all together** — together in a group
**altogether** — completely or entirely

**alumna** — female singular graduate
**alumnae** — female plural graduates
**alumnus** — male singular graduate
**alumni** — male and/or female plural graduates

**among** — use for three or more ("Among the triplets, Bob is the smartest.")
**between** — use for two ("Between the twins, Bob is the smarter.")

**amount** — what you measure (like sugar)
**number** — what you count (like coins)

**anecdote** — a story or tale, often funny
**antidote** — what counteracts a poison

**angry at** — use with a situation ("I'm angry at the fact of poverty.")
**angry with** — use with a person ("I'm angry with the president.")

**anticipate** — foresee and prepare for
**expect** — look forward to

**anxious** — worried about something
**eager** — looking forward with enthusiasm

**any one** — a specific person ("Any one of the family")
**anyone** — any person ("Anyone can go.")

**a part** — part of something (like a slice of pie)
**apart** — separate from ("He sat apart from the group.")

**appraise** — estimate the worth
**apprise** — keep somebody up to date about whatever

**apt** — natural inclination for something
**liable** — responsible; obligated by law
**likely** — something will probably happen

**as** — while
**because** — for the reason that

**as** — use when verb follows "as" ("We work as workers DID in the past.")
**like** — use when there's no verb ("We work like dogs.")

**assure** — give a guarantee to somebody
**ensure** — make safe or certain
**insure** — protect against loss (using insurance)

**awhile** (adverb) — use with verb ("REST awhile.")
**a while** (noun) — use with preposition ("Rest FOR a while.")

**balance** — talk about accounting or equilibrium
**remainder** — talk about the rest of something

**because of** — by reason of; on account of
**due to** — attributable to (use with *is/was/were/am/will be*: "It was due to Truman.")

**beside** — next to ("The dog sat beside Sheila.")
**besides** — in addition to ("Besides a dog, Sheila has a cat.")

**biannual** — twice a year
**biennial** — every other year

**big** — use for bulk, weight, mass, volume
**great** — use for showing that something is important
**large** — use for dimensions, quantity, capacity, or extent

**bimonthly** — every two months or twice a month
**semimonthly** — twice a month

**bloc** — group of countries ("the Soviet bloc")
**block** — piece of something (wood, stone, etc.)

**boarder** — somebody who lives in a boarding house
**border** — the line between two states

**born** — what happens to a child
**borne** — to be carried ("She was borne by her servants.")

**bring** — you bring something HERE
**take** — you take something THERE

**callous** — unsympathetic
**callus** — hardened skin

**can** — ability to do something ("I can sing.")
**may** — ask permission ("May I sing?")

**THE BASICS OF WORD USE**

**canvas** — cloth (e.g., a canvas tent)
**canvass** — go door to door ("We canvassed the city.")

**capital** — main, chief; seat of government
**capitol** — statehouse where legislature meets

**cement** — it goes into concrete
**concrete** — a mixture of cement, sand, gravel, water; the concrete road or sidewalk

**censer** — a device in a church for burning incense
**censor** — somebody who judges something
**censure** — what the judge does; to show disapproval

**center around** — wrong use (illogical because you can't be around the center)
**center on** — correct use

**childish** — similar or suitable to a child (a putdown)
**childlike** — like a child (more positive: a compliment)

**cite** — quote a source
**sight** — vision
**site** — a location

**climactic** — deals with a climax
**climatic** — deals with the weather

**coarse** — rough to the touch
**course** — what you take in college

**collaborate** — work with somebody
**corroborate** — confirm something

**compare to** — finding the likeness of one thing in another (comparing the journey of life to a journey down a river)
**compare with** — placing one thing by another to show similarities and differences (Bach with Mozart)

**compel** — forced to act against your will ("The general compelled his troops to fight back.")
**impel** — responding to an inner motive ("Curiosity impelled him to snoop.")

**complacent** — self-satisfied
**complaisant** — willing to do what pleases others

**complected** — no such word
**complexioned** — use this one ("dark complexioned")

**complement** — completing or supplementing
**compliment** — saying something nice about somebody

**compose** — make up or constitute ("The quartet is composed of four cellists.")
**comprise** — include ("The quartet comprises four cellists.")

**connote** — what a word suggests; its associations
**denotes** — the dictionary's specific meaning

**conscience** — what makes you feel guilty
**conscious** — what you are when you're not asleep

**consist of** — to be made up of ("The suite consists of three rooms.")
**consist in** — to have as its main feature ("Success consists in hard work.")

**contemptible** — something that causes contempt/hatred ("Nazi skinheads are contemptible.")
**contemptuous** — shows contempt ("a contemptuous sneer")

**contend for** — try for ("He contended for many prizes.")
**contend with** — put up with ("He contended with headaches.")
**contend against** — protest ("He contended against the unfair courts.")

**continual** — constantly recurrent (like a ringing phone)
**continuous** — uninterrupted (like a whistling teakettle)

**could care less** — wrong form; makes no sense
**couldn't care less** — use this form ("I couldn't care less.")

**council** — group of people
**counsel** — advice or a lawyer
**consul** — an ambassador

**councilor** — a member of a council
**counselor** — a lawyer or advisor

**credible** — believable
**creditable** — praiseworthy
**credulous** — innocent; gullible

**criterion** — the singular ("This criterion is clear.")
**criteria** — the plural ("These criteria are clear.")

**criticize** — use this as the verb ("Criticize the memo.")
**critique** — don't use as a verb ("I'll critique your memo."); use as a noun ("She wrote a good critique.")

**datum** — the singular ("This datum is here.")
**data** — the plural ("These data are here.")

**defective** — having defects in quality
**deficient** — not enough of something

**defer** — put off until later
**differ** — disagree with, over, about

**deprecate** — criticize
**depreciate** — lose value

**desert** — Death Valley
**dessert** — apple pie

**detract** — take away a part; to lessen quantity/value
**distract** — draw away the attention of

**die** — cease living
**dye** — color something

**differ from** — is different from ("Coke differs from Pepsi.")
**differ over** — have a different view of ("Bob and Bill differ over the interpretation.")
**differ with** — disagrees with another ("Bob differs from Bill on abortion.")

**disassemble** — take apart (e.g., a machine)
**dissemble** — pretend or lie

**discreet** — keep your mouth shut
**discrete** — something that's separate

**disinterested** — impartial (like a judge)
**uninterested** — having no interest in something

**disburse** — pay out
**disperse** — scatter

**distinct** — clear
**distinctive** — individual

**do** — accomplish
**due** — owe as an obligation or debt

**dominant** — dominating, controlling ("the dominant male in the herd")
**dominate** — influence or control ("He dominates the herd.")

**each other** — between two people
**eachother** — misspelling of "each other"
**one another** — among three people or more

**effective** — performs its function well
**efficient** — doesn't waste resources

**electric** — produces, carries, or is started by electricity
**electrical** — pertains to but doesn't carry electricity

**elicit** (verb) — draw forth
**illicit** — illegal

**emigrate** — leave a place
**immigrate** — go into a place

**eminent** — prominent ("an eminent lawyer")
**immanent** — existing within a reality ("God was immanent in the world.")
**imminent** — impending ("the imminent storm")

**empty** — containing nothing ("empty can")
**vacant** — unoccupied ("vacant apartment")

**enormity** — great wickedness or very serious crime ("the enormity of his abuse")
**enormousness** — very large or huge ("the enormousness of the warehouse")

**enthuse** — no such word ("I am enthused.")
**enthusiastic** — use this form ("I am enthusiastic.")

**envelop** — enclose or encase
**envelope** — what you put the letter into

**every day** — each day of the week
**everyday** — common, ordinary ("Every day I wear my everyday clothes.")

**every one** — member of a group ("Every one of the group was there.")
**everyone** — means everybody ("I saw everyone.")

**famous** — favorably well known
**notorious** — unfavorably well known

**farther** — refers to distance (i.e., to space)
**further** — refers to the future (i.e., time, degree, addition)

**fewer** — refers to number ("fewer sugar cubes")
**less** — refers to amount/quantity ("less sugar")

**flammable and inflammable** — can catch on fire
**nonflammable** — can't catch on fire

**flaunt** — show off ("She flaunted her wealth.")
**flout** — be disrespectful to authority ("He flouted the law.")

**flounder** — make mistakes; become confused while trying to do something
**founder** — sink (like a ship); fail; stumble and fall

**foreword** — introduction to a book
**forward** — at or near the front

**formally** — something to do with a proper occasion
**formerly** — in the past

**hanged** — what you do to a murderer
**hung** — what you do to a picture

**healthful** — conducive to good health
**healthy** — state of health

**historic** — a memorable event, worth a place in a book
**historical** — any routine event in history

**holey** — full of holes
**holy** — sacred
**wholly** — completely

**holistic** — concerned with a complete system
**wholistic** — wrong spelling

**hopefully** — illogical; avoid this form ("Hopefully, it will rain": Rain comes down with hope?)
**I hope** — use this form ("I hope it will rain.")

**human** — of people
**humane** — compassionate toward people

**if** — introduces a dependent clause in a conditional sentence ("If car manufacturers built safer cars, then we would have fewer accidents.")
**whether** — introduces alternatives ("I didn't know whether it would rain or snow.")

THE BASICS OF WORD USE

**imply** — what the speaker does ("He implied I was an idiot.")
**infer** — what the listener does ("I inferred he thought I was an idiot.")

**impressed by** — be taken with something or someone
**impressed on** — fix firmly in mind ("He impressed on them the need for accuracy.")
**impressed with** — impress one thing with another ("The paper was impressed with a watermark.")

**as regards** — okay to use
**in regard to** — okay to use
**in regards to** — don't use

**incidence** — the rate of which something happens or affects things ("a high incidence of bankruptcy")
**incidents** — events ("several incidents of theft")

**individual** — doesn't mean "people"; means a particular person/thing ("an individual student")
**person** — means people ("She's a helpful person.")

**ingenious** — something that's clever
**ingenuous** — simple or naive

**instance** — an example of something
**instant** — a moment in time

**intense** — strong in degree or quality ("intense cold")
**intensive** — taking effort, concentrated ("intensive review")

**inter** (office, state, etc.) — between offices, states, etc.
**intra** (office, state, etc.) — within offices, states, etc.

**irregardless** — no such word
**disregardless** — no such word
**regardless** — use this one

**it's** — contraction for it is or it has (It's hot today.")
**its** — possessive ("its color")

**later** — a time after this one
**latter** — the last in a list

**lead** — a metal
**led** — guided

**lean** — rest at an angle
**lien** — a claim on something

**lend** — give somebody something
**loan** — what you lend (you lend a loan)

**liable** — responsible; obligated by law
**libel** (verb) — defame
**libel** (noun) — printed defamatory statement

**lie** — recline (used like sit)
**lay** — put something down (used like set)

**loath** — reluctant
**loathe** — to hate

**loose** — free or unfastened ("loose change")
**lose** — misplace something ("Lose your change?")

**luxuriant** — a lot of growth ("luxuriant foliage")
**luxurious** — what rich people have ("luxurious house")

**masterful** — domineering ("a masterful leader")
**masterly** — of a master; skillful ("a masterly performance")

**material** — substances that make up something
**matériel** — equipment, apparatus, and supplies

**may** — use in the present ("We may go.")
**might** — use in the past ("We thought we might go.")

**may be** — a verb showing possibility ("I may be going.")
**maybe** — perhaps ("Maybe I'll go.")

**meantime** (noun) — between times ("in the meantime")
**meanwhile** (adverb) — describes a verb ("Meanwhile he drove his car.")

**militate** — act as a strong influence ("Two problems militated against the governor's success.")
**mitigate** — make less intense, serious, or severe ("His depression was mitigated by winning money.")

**miner** — a person who mines: coal miner
**minor** — somebody who's under age

**moral** — a lesson
**morale** — how you feel

**more than** — "I saw more than twenty eagles."
**over** — don't use when you mean "more than"

**nauseated** — what you are
**nauseous** — thing that sickens

**noisome** — offensive, especially an odor
**noisy** — a lot of noise

**noted** — people famous in a positive way
**notorious** — people with well-known bad reputations

**observance** — celebrating a date
**observation** — paying attention to something

**oral** — what you say out loud ("oral instructions")
**verbal** — of the word, written or spoken

**ordinance** — law
**ordnance** — weapons

**over all** — over an area ("Snow fell over all the town.")
**overall** — taken as a whole ("Overall, I loved the movie.")

**overdo** — do in excess
**overdue** — past due

**peace** — lack of conflict
**piece** — a fragment

**pedal** — a foot lever
**peddle** — to sell

**people** — use when you're talking about big groups
**persons** — use when you're talking about small groups

**persecute** — treat cruelly without cause
**prosecute** — start criminal action against

**personal** — of a person
**personnel** — employees

**petit** — generally means small: petit jury, petit larceny, petit mal, petit point
**petite** — with small, dainty build

**phenomenon** — singular extraordinary occurrence
**phenomena** — plural extraordinary occurrences

**practicable** — feasible; something you can do ("The marathon is practicable.")
**practical** — useful; proved through experience ("practical advice")
**precede** — come before
**proceed** — move forward; advance

**precedence** — established priority ("This has precedence.")
**precedents** — noun plural used for legal example ("The lawyer cited two precedents.")

**at present** — now
**presently** — soon

**principal** — head of something; main person
**principle** — a rule

**prophecy** (noun) — a prediction
**prophesy** (verb) — make the prediction

**prostate** — the gland
**prostrate** — stretched out on the floor

**proved** — use for the past ("It has been proved.")
**proven** — when describing something ("a proven fact")

**purposefully** — with purpose and determination
**purposely** — intentionally

**quiet** — what you want a library to be
**quite** — to a considerable degree

**raise** — lift or bring something up (like children)
**rise** — get up ("I rise at six o'clock.")

**rap** — knock or speak
**wrap** — cover

**rational** — reasonable, sane, able to reason
**rationale** — logical basis for something

**regretfully** — feeling regret ("I regretfully decline.")
**regrettably** — it is to be regretted ("The accident regrettably happened.")

**rend** — tear something apart
**render** — boil something down

**residence** — home
**residents** — inhabitants

**respectfully** — having respect for somebody
**respectively** — in the order mentioned

**right** — correct
**rite** — ceremony
**write** — form words on a surface

**role** — a part to play
**roll** — to tumble; a list

**root** — part of a plant
**rout** — defeat
**route** — a direction to take

**seasonable** — appropriate to a season ("a seasonable fall frost")
**seasonal** — of a season ("I had a seasonal job.")

**sensual** — pleasing to the body (sexual overtones)
**sensuous** — refers to the senses (without sexual overtones)
**sexual** — refers to sex

**shear** — to cut
**sheer** — thin (as of fabric); steep (as of a cliff)

**sit** — what your rear end does; use like lie
**set** — what you do to something; to put something down; use like lay

**stationary** — something that doesn't move
**stationery** — what you write on

**stratum** — singular layers of something
**strata** — plural layers of something

**suit** — a set of clothes or a case in court
**suite** — a set of rooms or furniture

**than** — use to compare things ("I'm taller than Bill.")
**then** — at that time ("I was taller then.")

**their** — possessive ("their house")
**there** — location ("over there")
**they're** — contraction for they are ("They're here.")

**thesis** — singular idea or dissertation
**theses** — plural ideas or dissertations

**to** — shows location ("Go to the store.")
**too** — excessively ("It's too hot.")
**two** — number ("two brothers")

**tortuous** — winding, twisting (like a road)
**torturous** — painful

**toward** — American preference
**towards** — British (or American Midwestern) preference

**turbid** — cloudy, muddy (like water)
**turgid** — inflated, stiff

**venal** — capable of being corrupted (as by bribery)
**venial** — a sin you can excuse

**vice** — wicked conduct; a habit
**vise** — the clamp on a workbench

**waive** — set aside
**wave** — a swell of water; what you do with your hand

**wangle** — get something by manipulating somebody
**wrangle** — bicker with somebody or herd livestock

**weather** — atmospheric conditions
**whether** — introduces alternatives ("I didn't know whether I would go or stay home.")

**where** — use for a place ("a city where I fell in love")
**when** — use for a situation ("a time when I fell in love")

**who's** — contraction for who is ("Who's here?")
**whose** — possessive ("Whose house is that?")

**your** — possessive ("your house")
**you're** — contraction of you are ("You're funny.")

## 3. A Long List of Wordy Phrases

Replace the phrase on the *left* with the word or phrase on the *right*; some phrases you can **CUT**.

a considerable amount of → **much**
a considerable number of → **many**
a decreased number of → **fewer**
a great deal of → **much**
a great number of → **many**
a large number → **many**
a large part of → **many**
a large percentage of → **many**
a large proportion of → **many**
a little less than → **almost**
a majority of → **most**
a number of → **several, many, some**
a period of several weeks → **several weeks**
a small number of → **some, few**
a small percentage of → **some, few**
a sufficient number of → **enough**
absolutely basic fundamentals → **basics, fundamentals**
absolutely essential → **essential**
absolutely exact (perfect, unique) → **exact (perfect, unique)**
according to the law → **legally**
accounted for by the fact that → **because**
ACT test → **ACT, American College Test**
active consideration → **consideration**
actual experience → **experience**
add an additional → **add**
adjacent to → **near**
admit of/to → **admit**
advance forward → **advance**
advance planning → **planning**

advocated that → **advocated**
afford an opportunity → **allow**
all alone by himself → **alone**
all of → **all**
all of a sudden → **suddenly**
along the lines of → **like**
alongside of → **alongside**
already has been → **has been**
alternative choice → **choice**
(five) a.m. in the morning → **(five) a.m.**
an adequate amount/number of → **enough**
an honor and a privilege → **an honor**
and also → **and**
and etc. → **etc.**
anterior to → **before**
anticipate that → **expect**
any and all → **any**
any one of the two → **either**
are in favor of → **favor**
are of the opinion → **believe**
are of the same opinion that → **agree**
arising from the fact that → **because**
as a consequence of → **because**
as a general rule → **generally**
as a matter of fact → **in fact**
as is the case → **as happens**
as of now → **now**
as of this date → **today**
as regards → **about**
as related to → **for, about**
as to → **CUT** or **about**
ask the question of → **ask, question**

assuming that → **if**
as to how → **how**
as to what → **what**
as to whether → **whether**
as to who/whom → **who/whom**
as to why → **why**
at a rapid rate → **rapidly**
at a time when → **when**
at all times → **always**
at an earlier/later date → **before/later**
at an early date → **soon**
at no time → **never**
at present → **now**
at regular intervals of time → **regularly**
at some future point in time → **some time**
at some future time → **later**
at that juncture → **then**
at that time → **then**
at the conclusion of → **after**
at the end of → **after**
at the present time → **now**
at the rear of → **behind**
at the same time as → **when**
at the time when → **when**
at this juncture → **now**
at this (point in) time → **now**
at which time → **then**
ATM machine → **ATM, automated teller machine**
audible to the ear → **audible**
awful atrocity → **atrocity**
balance against one another → **balance**
based on the fact that → **because, due to**
based on X → **X shows**
basically fundamental → **basically**

be beneficial to → **benefit**
be dependent on → **depend on**
be in agreement → **agree**
be in attendance → **attend**
be in possession of → **possess**
be in receipt of → **receive**
be inclusive of → **include**
be supportive of → **support**
because of the fact that → **because**
before in the past → **before**
beyond a shadow of a doubt → **doubtless**
bitter-tasting → **bitter**
blend together → **blend**
both of them → **both**
both X taken together → **both X**
bought and paid for → **bought, paid for**
brought to a sudden halt → **halted**
brought to a sudden stop → **stopped**
but rather → **but**
but though → **though**
by itself → **alone**
by means of → **by**
by reason of → **because of**
by the time that → **when**
by the use of → **by**
by virtue of → **by**
by way of illustration → **for example**
called attention to the fact that → **reminded**
came to a stop → **stopped**
cancel out → **cancel**
cannot be avoided that → **must**
cannot be possible that → **impossible**
cannot help but → **can only**
cash money → **cash, money**
causal factor → **cause**

cause damage to → **damage**
change over time → **change**
close proximity → **close**
closely scrutinize → **scrutinize**
cognizant of → **aware of**
combine into one → **combine**
combine together → **combine**
come to an end → **ended**
comparable to → **the same as**
complete stop → **stop**
completely accurate → **accurate**
completely full → **full**
completely useless → **useless**
component part → **part, component**
concerning the matter of → **about**
conclusion reached → **conclusion**
connect up together → **connect**
consecutive in a row → **consecutive**
consensus of opinion → **consensus, opinion**
considerable amount of → **much**
considering the fact that → **because**
contained in → **in**
contingent upon → **depending on**
continue on → **continue**
cooperate together with → **cooperate with**
copy off → **copy**
cost the sum of → **cost**
could be considered as → **is**
current status → **status**
currently anticipated → **anticipated**
dates back to → **dates to**
decide about this/that → **decide this/that**
decision-making process → **decision-making**

deem it appropriate to → **believe it right**
definite decision → **decision**
definitely proved → **proved**
desired goal → **goal**
despite the fact that → **though**
detailed information → **details**
different varieties → **varieties**
divide up → **divide**
draw to a close → **end**
drop by ten degrees → **drop ten degrees**
due to the fact that → **because**
during the course of → **during**
during the time that → **when, while**
during the winter (etc.) months → **during winter** (etc.)
during which time → **while**
each individual → **each, individual**
early pioneer → **pioneer**
edit out → **edit**
effectuate → **cause**
elucidate → **explain**
employ → **use**
enclosed herewith → **enclosed**
end product → **product**
end result → **result**
endeavor → **try**
endorse the check on the back → **endorse**
entirely eliminate → **eliminate**
equally as important → **as, equally, just as**
equally as well → **equally**
estimated at about → **estimated at**
estimated roughly at → **estimated at**

even more significant → **more significant**
eventuate → **happen**
exact same → **same, exact**
exactly alike → **alike, identical**
examine in depth → **examine**
except in a small number of cases → **usually**
exhibit a tendency to → **tend to**
exhibit the ability to → **can**
expose to elevated temperatures → **heat**
fabricate → **make**
facilitate → **help**
fall by ten degrees → **fall ten degrees**
fatal outcome → **death**
few in number → **few**
fewer in number → **fewer**
fill up → **fill**
final conclusion → **conclusion**
final outcome → **outcome**
final product → **product**
finalize → **end**
finally exhausted → **exhausted**
firmly commit → **commit**
first and foremost → **first**
first began → **began**
first introduction → **introduction**
first met → **met**
first of all → **first**
first priority → **priority**
firstly (secondly, etc.) → **first (second, etc.)**
following on → **after**
for a short space of time → **for a short time**
for the purpose of → **for, to**
for the (simple) reason that → **because**
for this reason → **so**
former alumni → **alumni**
free complimentary → **free, complimentary**
free gift → **gift**
from the point of view of → **for**
from the standpoint of → **for**
from time to time → **occasionally**
fully recognize → **recognize**
fundamentally basic → **fundamentally, basically**
future plans → **plans**
general consensus → **consensus**
geographical location → **geography, location**
give an account of → **describe**
give an indication of → **indicate, show**
give consideration to → **consider**
give rise to → **cause**
give treatment → **treat**
goals and objectives → **goals**
grave emergency → **emergency**
group together → **group**
half of all the → **half the**
has an effect on → **affects**
has an impact on → **affects**
has been engaged in a study of → **has studied**
has been supportive of → **has supported**
has gained much importance in recent years → **CUT**
has got to → **has to, must**
has previously → **has**

has proved itself to be → **has proved**
has reference to → **refers to**
has the ability to → **able, can**
has the appearance of → **appears, looks like**
has the capability of → **can**
has the capacity for → **can**
has the opportunity to → **can**
has the tendency to → **tends to**
have a discussion of → **discuss**
having reference to → **for, about**
having regard to → **about**
help make evident → **make evident**
hereby → **now**
herein → **here, in this**
hereinafter → **after this**
hereof → **CUT**
hereto → **CUT**
herewith → **with this**
highly unlikely → **unlikely**
hitherto → **until now, until then**
HIV virus → **HIV**
hold a meeting → **meet**
hollow cave (cavity) → **cave, cavity**
hollow tube → **tube**
homemade from scratch → **homemade, from scratch**
honest in character → **honest**
honest truth → **truth**
hopefully → **CUT or I hope**
I (etc.) myself (etc.) → **I**
if and when → **if, when**
if at all possible → **if possible**
if it should happen that → **if**
if it should transpire that → **if**
if that were the case → **if so**
immediate vicinity → **vicinity**

implement → **start, put into action**
important essentials → **essentials**
in a confused (etc.) state → **confused (bewildered, unhappy,** etc.**)**
in a number of cases → **many, some**
in a position to → **can, may**
in a satisfactory manner → **satisfactorily**
in a situation in which → **which**
in a very real sense → **CUT**
in accordance with → **by, under**
in addition → **also, besides**
in almost all instances → **almost always**
in an attempt to → **to**
in an effort to → **to**
in anticipation of → **before**
in back of → **behind**
in case → **if**
in cases in which → **if, when**
in close proximity to → **near**
in conjunction with → **with**
in connection with → **about, concerning**
in consideration of the fact that → **considering, because**
in excess of → **more than**
in favor of → **for**
in few cases → **seldom**
in how many cases → **how often**
in instances in which → **if, when**
in length → **long**
in lieu of → **instead of**
in light of the fact that → **because**
in many cases → **often**
in most cases → **often**
in most instances → **often**

THE BASICS OF WORD USE

in my opinion it is not an unjustifiable fact that → **I think**
in my personal opinion → **in my opinion, I believe**
in only a small number of cases → **rarely**
in order to → **to**
in order that X can → **so X can**
in other words → **or, that is**
in rare cases → **rarely**
in reference to → **about**
in regard to → **on, about, concerning**
in relation to → **with, about**
in respect to → **with**
in short supply → **scarce**
in some cases → **sometimes**
in spite of → **despite**
in spite of the fact that → **though**
in support of → **for**
in terms of → **for, with**
in that case → **then**
in the absence of → **without**
in the area of → **in, about**
in the case of → **for**
in the city (etc.) of Detroit (etc.) → **in Detroit** (etc.)
in the course of → **during**
in the environment of → **around, near**
in the event of/that → **if**
in the field of → **in**
in the final analysis → **CUT**
in the first (second, etc.) place → **first** (etc.)
in the form of → **as**
in the foreseeable future → **in the future**
in the instance of → **for**
in the last analysis → **CUT**

in the majority of cases → **usually**
in the matter of → **about**
in the month of January (etc.) → **in January** (etc.)
in the nature of → **like**
in the near future → **soon**
in the neighborhood of → **about, near**
in the not-too-distant future → **soon**
in the past was → **was**
in the possession of → **has, have**
in the proximity of → **near, nearly, about**
in the region of → **near, about**
in the vicinity of → **near, about**
in the month/year of → **in**
in the way of → **in**
in this connection → **about**
in this day and age → **now, today**
in view of → **because**
in view of the fact that → **because**
in width → **wide**
in X different ways → **in X ways**
inasmuch as → **for, because**
incline to the view that → **think**
included in → **in**
infringe on/upon → **infringe**
inherent in → **in**
initiate → **start, begin**
insight into → **idea about**
insofar as (because) → **because**
insofar as (to the extent that) → **so far as**
introduce a new → **introduce**
involves the necessity of → **requires**
is able to → **can**
is because → **is that**
is in the possession of → **has**

is in the process of → **is + verb**
is in a position to → **can**
is of an X nature → **is X**
is of importance → **is important**
is of the opinion that → **believes**
is prepared to → **can, is ready to**
is reported to be → **is**
is tantamount to → **means**
it appears that → **CUT**
it can be stated that → **CUT**
it could be that → **may**
it could happen that → **may**
it goes without saying that → **CUT**
it has been demonstrated that → **CUT**
it has been shown that → **CUT**
it is apparent that → **CUT or apparently**
it is clear that → **clearly**
it is conceivable that → **may, conceivably**
it is critical that → **must**
it is crucial that → **must**
it is doubtful that → **possibly**
it is entirely possible that → **may**
it is evident that → **evidently**
it is found that → **CUT**
it is generally believed → **many believe**
it is generally felt → **many feel**
it is generally thought → **many think**
it is imperative that → **must**
it is important that → **must**
it is important to note that → **CUT**
it is incumbent on → **must**
it is necessary that → **must**
it is obvious that → **obviously**

it is often of interest to note → **CUT**
it is often the case that → **often**
it is plain that → **plainly**
it is possible that → **may, possibly**
it is recognized that → **some believe**
it is suggested that → **some say**
it is the intention of the present writer to → **I intend**
it is unquestionable that → **unquestionably**
it is worth pointing out that in this context → **note**
it is worthy of note → **note**
it may be mentioned that → **CUT**
it may be that → **I think**
it may, however, be noted that → **but**
it must be noted that → **CUT**
it must be remembered that → **CUT**
it should be noted that → **CUT**
it should be remembered that → **CUT**
it will be appreciated that → **CUT**
it would appear that → **CUT**
join together → **join**
keep on eye on → **watch**
keep under surveillance → **watch**
kind of a → **kind of**
lacked self-confidence in myself → **lacked self-confidence**
lacked the ability (capacity, etc.) → **couldn't**
large in size → **large**
large-sized → **large**
last but not least → **last**
last of all → **last**
later on → **later**
lay out (on the table) → **lay (on the table)**

leaving out consideration of → **disregarding**
lengthy → **long**
light snack → **snack**
linkage → **link**
living survivors → **survivors**
located at, in → **at, in**
lose out on → **lose**
luncheon → **lunch**
made an investigation of → **investigated**
made up out of → **made of**
major portion of → **most of**
make a decision → **decide**
make a purchase → **buy**
make application → **apply**
make changes → **change**
make contact with → **meet, contact**
make reference to → **refer to**
many of the → **many**
match up → **match**
may have the effect of increasing → **may increase**
may or may not → **may**
may possibly → **may**
mental frame/state of mind → **frame/state of mind**
mental telepathy → **telepathy**
met with → **met**
might possibly → **might**
militate against → **prohibit**
miss out on → **miss**
mix together → **mix**
more and more → **increasingly**
more often than not → **usually**
more substantial → **greater**
most exact (perfect, unique) → **exact (perfect, unique)**

multitude of → **many**
must eventually → **must**
must inevitably → **must**
must necessarily → **must**
mutual agreement → **agreement**
mutual cooperation → **cooperation**
my personal opinion → **my opinion**
national GNP → **GNP, gross national product**
necessary requirements → **requirements**
necessary requisites → **requisites**
needless to say → **CUT**
new innovation → **innovation**
new trend → **trend**
no later than → **by**
not the same → **different**
notwithstanding → **despite**
notwithstanding the fact that → **though**
null and void → **null, void**
obviously apparent → **obvious, apparent**
of considerable magnitude → **big, large, great**
of long standing → **old**
of no mean ability → **able**
of no small ability → **able**
of the opinion that → **think that**
of very major importance → **important**
of very minor importance → **unimportant**
off of → **off**
old antique → **antique**
on a daily basis → **daily**
on a few occasions → **occasionally**
on a regular basis → **often, regularly**

on a stretch of road ➜ **on a road**
on a weekly basis ➜ **weekly**
on a yearly (year-to-year) basis ➜ **yearly**
on account of ➜ **because**
on an annual basis ➜ **yearly, annually**
on behalf of ➜ **for**
on the basis of ➜ **by**
on the occasion of ➜ **when**
on the grounds that ➜ **because**
on the order of ➜ **about**
on the part of ➜ **by**
on those occasions that/in which ➜ **when**
on two different occasions ➜ **twice**
once in a great while ➜ **seldom, rarely**
one and the same ➜ **the same**
one by one ➜ **singly**
originate from ➜ **come from**
ought to ➜ **should**
outside of ➜ **except**
overall plan ➜ **plan**
owing to the fact that ➜ **because**
past experience ➜ **experience**
past history ➜ **history**
past memories ➜ **memories**
past precedent ➜ **precedent**
pay off ➜ **pay**
perfectly clear ➜ **clear**
period of time ➜ **time, period**
personal belongings ➜ **belongings**
personal friend ➜ **friend**
personal opinion ➜ **opinion**
personally responsible ➜ **responsible**
pertaining to ➜ **about**
pertains to ➜ **is about**

PIN number ➜ **PIN**
place a major emphasis on ➜ **stress, emphasize**
plan ahead ➜ **plan**
plan for the future ➜ **plan**
(ten) p.m. at night ➜ **(ten) p.m.**
(five) p.m. in the afternoon ➜ **(five) p.m.**
pooled together ➜ **pooled**
possibly might ➜ **might**
post-season bowl game ➜ **bowl game**
postponed until later ➜ **postponed**
preliminary to ➜ **before**
present incumbent ➜ **incumbent**
presented in this X ➜ **in this X**
presents a picture similar to ➜ **looks like, resembles**
previous experience ➜ **experience**
previous to ➜ **before**
prior experience ➜ **experience**
prior to ➜ **before**
prior to that time ➜ **before**
probed into ➜ **probed**
proceed to investigate ➜ **study, investigate**
provide a continuous indication of ➜ **continuously show**
provide a summary ➜ **summarize**
provided that ➜ **if**
providing that ➜ **if**
pursuant to ➜ **following**
qualified expert ➜ **expert**
quite exact (perfect, unique) ➜ **exact (perfect, unique)**
RAM memoory ➜ **RAM, random-access memory**
range all the way from ➜ **range from**

rarely (seldom) ever → **rarely (seldom)**
reach a conclusion → **conclude**
reach a consensus → **agree**
real truth → **truth**
red (etc.) in color → **red (etc.)**
reduced to basic essentials → **simplified**
refer back to → **refer to**
referred to as → **called**
regarding → **on, about**
regardless of the fact that → **though**
relates to → **on, about**
relative to → **about**
REM eye movements → **REM, rapid eye movements**
repeat again → **repeat**
reported to the effect that → **reported**
representative cross-section → **representative, cross-section**
resultant effect → **result**
resulting consequences → **results, consequences**
revert back to → **revert to**
revise downward → **lower**
revise upward → **raise**
rich and wealthy → **rich, wealthy**
Rio Grande River → **Rio Grande**
rise up → **rise**
root cause → **root, cause**
rose by ten degrees → **rose ten degrees**
round circle → **circle**
round in shape → **round**
RPMs per minute → **RPMs, revolutions per minute**
same identical → **same, identical**
SAT test → **SAT, Scholastic Aptitude Test**

securely fastened → **secure, fastened**
seems apparent → **seems, apparent**
seldom if ever → **seldom, rarely**
separate and distinct → **separate, distinct**
separate into two equal parts → **halve**
serious crisis → **crisis**
serve as an insulator → **insulate**
should it prove the case that → **if**
simultaneous as → **as**
simultaneously together → **simultaneously, together**
since the time that/when → **since**
situated at, in → **at, in**
small-sized → **small**
so as to → **to**
so as not to X → **to Y** (so as not to die → **to live**)
so far as X is concerned → **for X**
some of the → **some**
somewhere in the neighborhood of → **about**
square in shape → **square**
start off → **start**
started off/out with → **started with**
subject matter → **subject**
subsequent to → **after, following**
sudden crisis → **crisis**
supposing that → **if**
surround on all sides → **surround**
swallow up → **swallow**
take action → **act**
take appropriate measures → **act**
take into consideration → **consider**
taking this factor into consideration → **thus**
terminate → **end**

terrible disaster → **disaster**
terrible tragedy → **tragedy**
than is the case with → **than with**
that is to say → **that is**
that kind (type) of → **that**
that particular → **that**
that specific → **that**
the aforementioned → **that, those**
the concept of → **CUT**
the conclusion reached → **the conclusion**
the costs involved in → **the cost of**
the degree of → **the**
the fact that → **because**
the foregoing → **the, this, these, those**
the fullest possible extent → **mostly, fully, completely**
the great majority of → **most**
the greater proportion → **most**
the issue (question, subject, topic) being addressed → **the issue** (etc.) **is**
the level of → **the**
the magnitude of → **the**
the majority of → **many, most**
the only difference being → **except that**
the opinion is advanced that → **I think**
the possibility exists for → **may**
the predominant number of → **most**
the present X → **the X**
the question as to whether → **whether**
the question of whether → **whether**
the reason for that is → **because**
the reason is because → **because**
the reason why is that → **because**
the sum of five dollars → **five dollars**
the total X → **the X**
the vast majority of → **most**
the volume of demand for → **the demand for**
the X in question → **the X, this X, that X**
there is a chance that → **may**
there is a necessity for → **must**
there is a need for → **must**
there is no doubt that → **doubtless, no doubt**
there is no question that → **no question, unquestionably**
there is now → **there is**
there is reason to believe → **I think**
thereby → **by that**
therefore → **thus**
therefrom → **from it**
therein → **there, in it**
thereof → **its, of it**
thereto → **to that, to it**
thereupon → **then**
therewith → **with it**
these kinds (types) of → **these**
these X in which → **X which**
these X that → **X that, those that**
these X who → **X who, those who**
this kind (type) of → **this**
this particular → **this**
this particular instance → **this instance**
this result would seem to indicate that → **this result shows/indicates or thus**
this specific → **this**
those kinds (types) of → **those**
those X in which → **X which**
those X that → **X that, those that**

those X who → **X that, those who**
through the use of → **by**
time and time again → **time again**
time period → **time, period**
to be cognizant of → **to know**
to summarize the above → **to summarize**
to the extent that → **as much as, so much that**
to the fullest possible extent → **fully**
together with → **with**
total operating costs → **operating costs**
total sum → **sum**
totally useless → **useless**
triangular in shape → **triangular**
true facts → **facts**
truly significant → **significant**
two by two → **paired**
two twins → **twins**
type of a → **type of**
ultimate → **last**
unanimity of opinion → **agreement**
under circumstances in which → **if, when**
unfulfilled vacancy → **vacancy**
uniformly consistent → **consistent**
unless and until → **unless**
unusual in nature → **unusual**
until such time as → **until**
up to now → **formerly**
utilization → **use**
utilize → **use**
utterly unique (perfect, etc.) → **unique (etc.)**
various differences → **differences**

very exact (perfect, unique) → **exact (perfect, unique)**
virtually all → **most**
visible to the eye → **visible**
was in the form of → **was**
was instrumental in → **helped**
was of the opinion that → **believed**
ways and means → **ways, means**
we wish to thank → **we thank**
weekly (week-to-week) basis → **weekly**
went on to say → **added, continued**
what is known as → **CUT**
what is the explanation of → **why**
when and if → **when, if**
when the X is over → **after the X**
when/where X is concerned → **for X**
whereas → **but, though**
whereby → **so that**
wherein → **in which**
whether or not → **whether**
whole entire → **whole, entire**
whole sum total → **sum, total**
will in the future → **will**
will serve to X → **will X**
will take steps to → **will**
with a view to → **intending to**
with full approval → **approve**
with reference to → **about**
with regard to → **about**
with respect to → **about**
with the exception of → **except**
with the object/purpose of → **to**
with the possible exception of → **except**
yearly (year-to-year) basis → **yearly**

## What Words Should I Use?

1. **Strong Verbs** (note how many have one syllable).
2. **The All-Purpose Fancy Word List** (familiar from ACTs, GREs, and crossword puzzles).

**1. Strong Verbs**

abrade
bang
bark
bawl
bite
blare
boil
boom
bubble
bump
burn
burst
buzz
chatter
chime
chirp
clank
clap
clean
clear
click
clink
clutter
color
coo
cough
crack
crash
croak
crunch
cry
cushion
dampen
dazzle
dim
dish
drench

drip
droop
dry
dull
dust
explode
eye
face
feather
fire
fizz
flop
fluff
flush
foam
fog
freeze
fuzz
gab
gag
gasp
giggle
glass
glimmer
glue
goad
gouge
grab
grace
grate
grease
grind
grit
growl
gurgle
gush
haggle
haze
hike

hiss
hone
honk
hug
hurl
hush
ice
jangle
jingle
laugh
lean
load
lob
lop
maim
mat
mess
moan
mud
mumble
murmur
mush
mutter
narrow
numb
oil
pale
pant
peep
pick
pierce
ping
plop
pluck
pock
point
poke
pop
powder

prick
prickle
pulp
puncture
quack
rap
rasp
rattle
raze
ring
rip
rob
rock
roll
round
ruffle
rumble
rustle
sag
sand
sang
scrape
scratch
scream
screen
seal
shag
shake
shimmer
shine
shorten
shout
sing
slam
slap
slop
smell
smooth
snap

snarl
snatch
soap
sparkle
spike
spill
splash
splinter
sponge
spring
sprinkle
square
squash
squawk
squeal
steal
steam
sting
stink
strike
stub
stun
stutter
swell
swipe
tangle
tank
tap
tear
tease
thicken
thin
thud
thump
tidy
tinkle
trick
truck
twinkle
twist
twitter
wane
warble
wave
wax
wet

wheeze
whimper
whine
whip
whisper
whiz
whoop
wire
wound
wrinkle

## 2. The All-Purpose Fancy Word List

a posteriori
a priori
abdicate
abeyance
abhor
abolition
abortive
abrogate
absolve
abstemious
accelerate
acme
acrid
acumen
ad hoc
ad hominem
adage
adept
adroit
adulation
adverse
affable
affluence
aficionado
aggregate
alacrity
alienate
allege
amorphous
analogy
animosity
anomaly

antediluvian
antithesis
apathy
apex
askew
assuage
astute
au courant
augment
aurora
auspicious
autocrat
averse
bacchanal
banal
barrage
beatific
beguile
bellicose
benevolent
benign
benignant
berate
bête noire
blandishment
blasé
boisterous
bon mot
bravado
brazen
bucolic
cabal
cacophony
callous
callus
calumniate
canard
canny
capacious
capricious
carious
carnage
carnivorous
carrion
castigate
caveat emptor

cavil
celestial
celibate
cerebral
chaste
chic
chimera
choleric
clandestine
cogent
colloquy
collusion
commiserate
complaint
compliant
compunction
concur
connote
consensus
contemptible
contraband
coterie
counterfeit
cryptic
cum laude
cupola
cursory
de facto
de jure
dearth
debilitate
debonair
deductive
degradation
déjà vu
demur
demure
denizen
denote
deprecate
depreciate
depredation
desecrate
desultory
dexterous
diffident

| | | | |
|---|---|---|---|
| dilettante | ferret | hoary | lacerate |
| diminutive | fetid | homily | lackey |
| disassemble | fiasco | honorarium | laden |
| disinclined | fiscal | hostelry | lampoon |
| disquiet | flaccid | humane | languid |
| dissemble | flaunt | hybrid | languish |
| dissimulate | flotilla | hypocrite | lascivious |
| dogmatic | flotsam | iconoclastic | lassitude |
| dormant | flounce | idiosyncrasy | latent |
| dotage | flourish | ignoble | laudatory |
| dubious | foible | illicit | lecherous |
| dysfunction | foray | illusory | legerdemain |
| dyspepsia | forensic | imbroglio | lethargic |
| ebullient | forsake | imminent | lexicon |
| eccentricity | fractious | immolate | liaison |
| eerie | fruition | immune | licentious |
| élan | fustian | impeccable | limpid |
| elicit | gainsay | impecunious | literati |
| emaciated | gambol | impolitic | loitering |
| emanate | garish | impugn | lucid |
| embellish | gauche | imputation | lucre |
| emeritus | genial | inchoate | lugubrious |
| émigré | genteel | incognito | macabre |
| emulate | gesticulation | incorrigible | maestro |
| enigma | gist | indolence | maim |
| ennui | gloat | inductive | maladroit |
| equivocate | goad | intaglio | malaise |
| erudite | gratuitous | interim | malevolent |
| eschew | gregarious | ipso facto | martial |
| esoteric | guile | iridescence | martinet |
| euphony | guileless | jaded | masticate |
| ex cathedra | gustatory | jaundiced | maxim |
| exigency | habeas corpus | jettison | mediate |
| expound | haggard | jocose | mélange |
| expunge | halcyon | jocund | mellifluous |
| extravagant | hapless | jovial | mercurial |
| exuberant | harangue | judicious | mete |
| facetious | harass | junket | mettle |
| facile | harbinger | keen | mezzanine |
| factious | hector | ken | militate |
| faculty | Herculean | kin | minute |
| falsetto | hermetic | kiosk | misanthrope |
| fastidious | hiatus | knave | mitigate |
| faux pas | hibernal | knell | mollify |
| feign | hirsute | kowtow | mortify |
| feral | histrionic | labyrinth | mountebank |

| | | | |
|---|---|---|---|
| munificent | paradigm | quibble | sedate |
| nadir | paragon | quintessence | seethe |
| naive | pariah | quixotic | senile |
| necromancy | parody | rabid | sequester |
| nefarious | passive | raconteur | shibboleth |
| nemesis | paucity | ramification | simulate |
| nepotism | peccadillo | rancid | sine qua non |
| nettle | pecuniary | rancor | sinecure |
| nocturnal | pedantic | raucous | sinister |
| non sequitur | pejorative | ravage | siren |
| nonchalant | pelf | raze | slake |
| nonentity | penchant | recalcitrant | sloth |
| nosegay | pendant | reciprocal | solon |
| novice | pensive | rectify | sotto voce |
| noxious | penurious | redress | sporadic |
| nurture | peon | refurbish | spurious |
| obdurate | perdition | regal | status quo |
| obnoxious | perfunctory | regale | stentorian |
| obsequious | permeate | repartee | stipend |
| obtuse | philanthropy | replete | stoic |
| obviate | picaresque | repose | stolid |
| occult | picaro | reprehensible | sub rosa |
| odious | placid | repudiate | subscribe |
| officious | plutocrat | requisite | sunder |
| ogle | polyglot | resonant | sundry |
| olfactory | pommel | resuscitate | superfluity |
| ominous | portfolio | reticence | supernal |
| omnipotent | portly | revocation | surreptitious |
| onerous | post hoc | ribald | suture |
| opportune | précis | riposte | tacit |
| optimum | prescribe | risqué | taciturn |
| ostensible | procrustean | rote | tactile |
| ostracize | progenitor | ruse | talisman |
| paean | prognosticate | sacrilegious | tantalize |
| palate | prolific | saga | tantamount |
| palatial | proscribe | salient | tautology |
| palaver | protean | saline | tawdry |
| palette | proviso | salvo | temerity |
| pallet | puny | sanguine | tempo |
| palliate | putative | saturate | temporize |
| pallid | Pyrrhic victory | saturnine | tenacity |
| palpate | quack | saunter | tenant |
| palpitation | quaff | savant | tenet |
| paltry | quandary | savoir faire | Thespian |
| panacea | quay | scurrilous | timid |
| panegyric | queue | secede | timorous |

| | | | |
|---|---|---|---|
| tirade | ubiquitous | vehement | voracious |
| titan | ulterior | velocity | waive |
| torso | umbrage | vendetta | wastrel |
| travail | unequivocal | vertiginous | wizened |
| trek | unilateral | virile | wont |
| trepidation | untoward | virtuous | yen |
| truculent | usurpation | vitiate | zealot |
| tryst | vacillation | vociferous | zenith |
| turbulent | vacuous | voluble | zephyr |

**Key 5**

# The Basics of Grammar

- Problem 1: Subject Pronouns
- Problem 2: Subject Pronouns in Comparisons
- Problem 3: Subject Pronouns after Verbs of Being
- Problem 4: Object Pronouns after Verbs
- Problem 5: Object Pronouns after Prepositions
- Problem 6: Who or Whom?
- Problem 7: That, Which, or Who?
- Problem 8: Pronoun Agreement
- Problem 9: Subject-Verb Agreement
- Problem 10: Irregular Verbs
- Problem 11: Lie or Lay?
- Problem 12: The Subjunctive*
- Problem 13: The Adverb and -ly
- Problem 14: Adjectives and Linking* Verbs
- Problem 15: Good or Well? (Continued)
- Problem 16: Real or Really? (Sure or Surely?)
- Problem 17: Adjective Comparison
- Problem 18: Where Do I Put the Adverb?
- Problem 19: The Possessive and the Gerund*

Before we look at nineteen basics of grammar, you may want to review the eight parts of speech. If you've forgotten the technical terms to label the words in a sentence, brief definitions follow below. (The **Glossary** adds the less common terms, like **direct object**; see pages 277-280.)

## THE EIGHT PARTS OF SPEECH

1. **Adjective.** Describes a noun or pronoun: the <u>blue</u> shirt; the shirt is <u>blue</u>.
2. **Adverb.** Describes a verb, an adjective, another adverb: <u>slowly</u> ate; <u>too</u> tall; left very <u>quietly</u>.
3. **Conjunction.** Connects words in a sentence (remember them with the mnemonic **FANBOYS**: **f**or, **a**nd, **n**or, **b**ut, **o**r, **y**et, **s**o): The man <u>and</u> woman are here.
4. **Interjection.**\* Breaks up sentence flow; an exclamation/cuss word: <u>Damn</u>! I'm cold.
5. **Noun.** A person, place, or thing: <u>Martha</u>, <u>New Orleans</u>, <u>geometry</u>.
6. **Preposition.** Connects words in a sentence; shows location and direction: I saw the movie <u>in</u> the theater; he ran <u>through</u> the door.
7. **Pronoun.** Takes the place of the noun: Martha = <u>she</u>; New Orleans = <u>it</u>; geometry = <u>it</u>.
8. **Verb**: Shows action or doesn't show action (a state of being): I <u>walk</u>; I <u>am</u> a man.

You can easily remember the parts if you recall that they function in families:

> - Nouns go with verbs.
> - Adjectives go with nouns.
> - Pronouns replace nouns.
> - Adverbs go with verbs.
> - Prepositions go with nouns, pronouns, and verbs.
> - Conjunctions glue together nouns, verbs, pronouns, adjectives, adverbs, and prepositions.

But remember that the **interjection** doesn't function with any word; it's a loner, off on its own in a sentence:

**Damn!**—I cut myself.
I—**damn!**—cut myself.
I cut—**damn!**—myself.
I cut myself—**damn!**

We're going to visit a short list of the most troubling grammar errors. You'll find other grammar problems discussed elsewhere in this book. See, for example, the long section **What Goes Wrong with Our Sentences?** in Key 3 (page 56), which examines dangling modifiers, verb tenses, and related booby traps. Here we'll stick to bare-bones grammar—the most common grammar problems that we face. For less common problems, you'll need to consult a specialty grammar book like *The Gregg Reference Manual*.

We'll examine four sites where the problems most often turn up:
**Pronouns**
**Agreement**
**Verbs**
**Adverbs and Adjectives**

## PRONOUN PROBLEMS

A pronoun takes the place of the noun. Instead of **table**, we say **it**. Instead of **Paul** we say **him**. For our purpose, let's split the pronouns into two groups: **subject pronouns** and **object pronouns**:

| SUBJECT | OBJECT |
| --- | --- |
| I | me |
| you | you |
| he | him |
| she | her |
| it | it |
| we | us |
| they | them |
| who | whom |

Subject pronouns normally come **before** the verb; object pronouns come **after**:

| SUBJECT | VERB | OBJECT |
| --- | --- | --- |
| I | saw | him. |
| We | visited | them. |
| He | kissed | her. |
| It | impressed | me. |
| Who | wrote | it? |
| They | called | whom? |
| She | congratulated | us. |

Famous errors develop from forgetting that subject pronouns come **before** the verb and object pronouns come **after** (with one group of exceptions).

## Problem 1: Subject Pronouns

1. Lou and him went to Utah.
2. Mary and her are working on the report.
3. I'm not sure, but I think Sam and him will sing tonight.
4. Me and him want to see the movie.
5. On the other hand, Alice and them attended the concert.
6. May Jimmy and me leave early?

Each of these presents an error. They should read:

1. Lou and **he** WENT to Utah.
2. Mary and **she** ARE WORKING on the report.
3. I'm not sure, but I think Sam and **he** WILL SING tonight.
4. **He** and **I** WENT to see the movie.
5. On the other hand, Alice and **they** ATTENDED the concert.
6. MAY Jimmy and **I** LEAVE early?

How can you tell? Try the following:

1. Find the verb (which here is CAPITALIZED).
2. Remember the pronoun that precedes the verb has to come from the subject pronoun list.

Or:

3. Leave out the subject up to the pronoun. Read out loud. Sound funny? Choose the other pronoun.

1. Lou and **he/him** WENT to Utah.
2. **He/him** WENT to Utah.
3. **Him** WENT to Utah. (Sounds funny.)
4. **He** WENT to Utah.

Thus logically arriving at the correct answer:

5. Lou and **he** WENT to Utah.

A similar problem arises with comparisons. If you're comparing two things, which pronoun should you choose?

## Problem 2: Subject Pronouns in Comparisons

1. He eats faster than **I/me**.
2. She sings better than **he/him**.
3. She admires Karl more than **I/me**.
4. He talks about food as much as **she/her**.

First find the verb. Then choose the right pronoun.

In **He eats faster than I/me**, where's the verb for the pronoun (**I/me**) in question? You don't see one, so it has to be **me**, right?

Wrong. The verb is there, but it's implied:

**He eats faster than I [eat].**

So the answer is **He eats faster than I eat.** [ = He eats faster than I.]

And:

**She sings better than he [sings].**

In these next two, the answers have to be **I** and **she**. Right?

**She admires Karl more than I [admire Karl].**
**He talks about food as much as she [talks about food].**

Not necessarily. You can certainly read both sentences this way, but there's a second possibility. These are also correct:

**She admires Karl more than me [more than she admires <u>me</u>].**
**He talks about food as much as her [as much as he talks about <u>her</u>].**

**Moral to the story**: Once you learn to choose the correct pronoun in a comparison (and it's usually the subject pronoun that comes before an implied verb), don't fall into the trap of ALWAYS choosing the subject pronoun. Sometimes you may need the object pronoun (which usually follows the main verb—just as it does here).

**And remember the pattern**: Subject pronouns usually come **before** the verb; object pronouns come **after**. So what do you do in the next five examples?

## Problem 3: Subject Pronouns after Verbs of Being

1. It IS **I/me**.
2. Is that you? Yes, **it'S we/us**.
3. The caller WAS **she/her**.
4. The new supervisors ARE **she/her** and **I/me**.
5. Kyle Smith was assumed TO BE **I/me**.

Sticking to the pattern (that object pronouns follow the verb), have you chosen:

1. It IS **me**.
2. Is that you? Yes, **it'S us**.
3. The caller WAS **her**.
4. The new supervisors ARE **her** and **me**.
5. Kyle Smith was assumed TO BE **me**.

If you have, you're wrong. Why?
Here we're dealing with that "one group of exceptions." The problem lies with the verbs—which in every case are verbs of being (verbs like **to be, am, is, are, was**, etc.).

Read these correct forms out loud:

1. It is **I**.
2. Is that you? Yes, it's **we**.
3. The caller was **she**.
4. The new supervisors are **she** and **I**.
5. Kyle Smith was assumed to be **I**. (Seriously? Yes.)

Although the object pronoun does come after the verb, the verbs it follows are action verbs (like **saw, visited, kissed, impressed, wrote, called,** and **congratulated**).

If you have a nonaction verb—that is, a verb of being—you must forget the object pronoun and choose the **subject pronoun**.

Rule: **Subject pronouns come after a verb of being.**

What about a geeky sentence like **Kyle Smith was assumed to be I**? Do you really have to say that? No. Not if you feel foolish letting the correct form escape from your lips. Go ahead and say the wrong form.

But when you **write**, you're obliged to write **I**.

When you speak, you may say whatever you wish. Better to communicate than alienate a listener with geeky grammar. When you write, though, you really have only two choices:

1. **Use the correct form.**
2. **Rewrite if you don't like using the correct form.**

You can certainly write an incorrect form, but if you do, some reader somewhere—one of those anal grammar hotshots—will call you a knucklehead. So cover yourself.

This next bunch is a snap.

## Problem 4: Object Pronouns after Verbs

1. Frank sent Bob and **I/me** a gift.
2. Dan told **we/us** workers the truth.
3. Matt will drive Martha and **she/her** to the mall.
4. Do you know Molly and **he/him** from work?
5. Mrs. Dell urged Humberto and **I/me** to write the report quickly.

No real problem, yet writers commit classic errors:

1. Frank sent Bob and **I** a gift. (Wrong)
2. Dan told **we** workers the truth. (Wrong)
3. Matt will drive Martha and **she** to the mall. (Wrong)
4. Do you know Molly and **he** from work? (Wrong)
5. Mrs. Dell urged Humberto and **I** to write the report quickly. (Wrong)

Many of us, concerned about making an "I/me" error—fearful that somebody out there may call us a knucklehead—will automatically choose **I** over **me**. Regardless. And that's where the famous problem comes knocking at the door.

The subject pronoun comes **before** the verb; the object pronoun comes **after** (usually). Does the pattern work here?

Yes.

1. Frank SENT Bob and **me** a gift.
2. Dan TOLD **us** workers the truth.
3. Matt WILL DRIVE Molly and **her** to the mall
4. DO you KNOW Molly and **him** from work?
5. Mrs. Dell URGED Humberto and **me** to write the report quickly.

The pattern works because each verb is an **action verb**:

**sent, told, will drive, do know, urged**

The pattern also holds for objects of the preposition (that is, the **noun** that comes **after** the preposition in a prepositional phrase).

But guess which form gets chosen—mistakenly? Again, we're often worried that we'll make an "I/me" error and thus shy away from the right form—the "me."

## Problem 5: Object Pronouns after Prepositions

1. She left her estate to Buddy and **I**.
2. That was for **we** women to decide.
3. Between you and **I**, that is pure nonsense.
4. Among Bill, **he**, and **she**, Bill is right.

All wrong.
As a rule, **After a preposition, use an object pronoun**.

The correct forms are (prepositions CAPITALIZED):

1. She left her estate TO Buddy and **me**.
2. That was FOR **us** women to decide.
3. BETWEEN you and **me**, that is pure nonsense.
4. AMONG Bill, **him** and **her**, Bill is right.

## Problem 6: Who or Whom?

The key to using **who** and **whom** is to remember that **who** is a subject pronoun (and thus takes a verb) and **whom** is an object pronoun (and thus doesn't take a verb). So what's the answer to these (verbs CAPITALIZED):

1. The man **who/whom** IS tall IS here.
2. The man **who/whom** I SAW IS here.

3. Dan TOLD Chet **who/whom** to call.
4. I FORGET **who/whom** WON the Super Bowl in 1980.
5. He HAS respect for **who/whom**?

**Who** takes a verb; **whom** doesn't.

That in mind, match up each subject with a verb. If you can't find a verb for **who**, change it to **whom**.

1. The man **who/whom** IS tall IS here.
   a. The man is here. (**Man** goes with the second **is**.)
   b. The first **is** needs a subject. The only possibility is **who**.

So: The man **who** is tall is here. (**Who** goes with the first **is**.)

2. The man **who/whom** I SAW IS here.
   a. The man is here. (**Man** goes with **is**.)
   b. I saw. (**I** goes with **saw**.)

There's no other verb in the sentence. Since **who** requires a verb and there is none, the only possibility is **whom**.

So: The man **whom** I saw is here.

3. Dan TOLD Chet **who/whom** to call.
   a. **Dan** goes with **told**.
   b. **To call** is the infinitive form of the verb, not a verb proper.

Thus: Dan told Chet **whom** to call.

4. I FORGET **who/whom** WON the Super Bowl in 1980.
   a. **I** goes with **forget**.
   b. **Won** needs a subject.

Thus: I forget **who** won the Super Bowl in 1980.

5. He HAS respect for **who/whom**?
   a. **He** goes with **has**.
   b. The preposition **for** takes the object pronoun **whom**.

Thus: He has respect for **whom**?

Given that last sentence, do you choose **who** or **whom** in the following:

He HAS respect for **whoever/whomever** IS in power.

1. **He** goes with **has**.
2. The preposition **for** takes the object pronoun **whom**.
3. Thus: **whomever**

But wait . . . There's another verb in the sentence—**is**—and it needs a subject.

4. Thus: **whoever** (?)

So what's the answer? If there's a preposition, choose **whomever**; if there's a verb, choose **whoever**. But what if you have both?

FOR **whoever/whomever** IS in power

Answer: The **verb** wins:

He has respect for **whoever** is in power.

So what's the answer to this next one:

**Who/whom DO** they RECOMMEND?

The subject pronoun (**who**) comes **before** the verb; the object pronoun (**whom**) comes **after**. Right?
So the answer has to be:

**Who do** they recommend?

Wrong. At least in this special sentence, which is a **question**. And as a question, the sentence inverts the normal SUBJECT-VERB-OBJECT order. You thus have to unwind the sentence to figure out the answer:

They DO RECOMMEND **who/whom**.

1. **They** goes with **do recommend**.
2. With no remaining verb, the only possibility is **whom** (and guess what: It comes **after** the verb, just as the object pronoun is supposed to).

They do recommend **whom**.

And, finally, what about this one:

**Who/whom** DO you THINK IS GOING tomorrow?

Unwound, the sentence reads:

You DO THINK **who/whom** IS GOING tomorrow.

This is another easy one.
1. **You** goes with **do think**.
2. **Is going** needs a subject.
3. Thus: **who**

So: **Who** do you think is going tomorrow?

## Problem 7: That, Which, or Who?

To refer to people, use **that** or **who**.

1. **Who** refers to individual people or groups
2. **That** refers to a type or class:

**Mrs. Sutton is THE ONE STAFF MEMBER who can play canasta.**
**Henrik is THE KIND OF ATHLETE that will turn pro.**

**Which** introduces **nonessential*** fragments; **that** usually introduces **essential fragments*** (see pages 154-155 for a detailed explanation of punctuating essential and nonessential fragments).

**Andy's bike, WHICH HE BOUGHT AT A YARD SALE, works fine.**
**The bike THAT HE BOUGHT AT A YARD SALE works fine.**

Note: With a pair of **that** clauses, change the second **that** to a **which**:

**THAT is a house ~~THAT~~ WHICH I wish I'd bought.**

Now let's turn to what happens when you must make pronouns agree with another word in the sentence. In other words, should you say the following?

**Each person did THEIR job?**

You know the answer from **What Goes Wrong with Our Sentences?** in Key 3: **No**. At least, according to traditional grammar, you shouldn't: **person** = **a singular**; **their** = **a plural**. Since you can't mix singulars and plurals, you should say:

**Each person did his job** or **Each person did her job.**

To address agreement, first we'll examine pronouns; then subjects and verbs.

# Agreement Problems

## Problem 8: Pronoun Agreement

What's the answer to these pronoun agreement problems?

1. A **PERSON** needs to do **his/her/their** own work.
2. **EACH** of these companies had **its/their** employees drug-tested.
3. **ALL** of these companies had **its/their** employees drug-tested.
4. **NEITHER** of the boys was in **his/their** seat(s).
5. **NO ONE** was reassured in **her/their** own mind about the news.
6. Either the **ACCOUNTANT** or the **BOOKKEEPER** left **his/their** work.
7. Either the **BOOKKEEPER** or the **ACCOUNTANTS** left **his/their** work.
8. Either the **BOOKKEEPERS** or the **ACCOUNTANT** left **her/their** work.

As a rule, **A singular subject needs a singular pronoun**. So, with that logic,

1. **PERSON** (singular subject) = **his** or **her** (singular pronoun)
2. **EACH** (singular subject) = **its** (singular pronoun)
3. **ALL** (plural subject) = **their** (plural pronoun)
4. **NEITHER** (singular subject) = **his** (singular pronoun)
5. **NO ONE** (singular subject) = **her** (singular pronoun)

The logic holds for sentences 1-5; each has just one subject. But for sentences 6-8, which have two subjects, use the subject closer to the verb.

6. **BOOKKEEPER** (singular subject closer to the verb) = **his** (singular pronoun)
7. **ACCOUNTANTS** (plural subject closer to the verb) = **their** (plural pronoun)
8. **ACCOUNTANT** (singular subject closer to the verb) = **her** (singular pronoun)

The following pronouns are **always** **s**ingular:

**another, anybody, anyone, anything, each, everyone, everything, no one, somebody, someone**

Thus: Each of them **has/have a** point to make.

And the answer is? **Has.** The word **them** has nothing to do with choosing the right pronoun. If you're foggy about this one, memorize the list of singular pronouns. If your memory isn't so reliable, apply this trick: Cross out the prepositional phrase.

Each ~~OF THEM~~ **has/have** a point to make.

1. **OF THEM** = prepositional phrase
2. Delete prepositional phrase

Each **has/have** a point to make.

Thus: **Each has** a point to make.

One ~~OF THESE APPLES~~ **is/are** poisonous.
**One is** poisonous.

The following pronouns are **always plural**:

**both, few, many, several**

You can memorize these pronouns or apply the deleted prepositional phrase trick:

Few **OF THE MEMBERS is/are** sending their contributions.
**Few are** sending their contributions.

The following pronouns can be either **singular or plural**:

**all, any, none, some**

So which is correct:

None of the lumber **was/were** destroyed.
None of the trees **was/were** destroyed.

For years, many English teachers claimed that **none** always was a singular. In fact, it usually is. Occasionally, though, you'll run across a situation that logically demands to be plural.

Here you shouldn't delete the prepositional phrase. It bears directly on determining singular and plural:

lumber = singular = **was**
trees = plural = **were**

SINGULAR      SINGULAR
**None** of the lumber **was** destroyed.

PLURAL       PLURAL
**None** of the trees **were** destroyed.

Both sentences are correct!

## Problem 9: Subject-Verb Agreement

And what's the answer to each subject-verb agreement problem?

1. My uncle and parents **is/are** here.
2. Neither my uncle nor my parents **is/are** here.
3. Neither my parents nor my uncle **is/are** here.

1. uncle and parents = plural = **are**
2. parents = plural = **are** (with a **neither/nor, either/or** construction, **the subject closer to the verb determines the verb**)
3. uncle = singular = **is**

Here are some tough ones:

There **was/were** a bookcase and a computer in the study.

How many items were in the hall? **Two.** Don't let the opening **there** throw you. The sentence needs a plural verb to accommodate the plural subject (**typewriter** and **computer**):

There **were** a bookcase and a computer in the study.

And:

1. Mumps is among those diseases that **is/are** curable.
2. She is one of the volunteers who **comes/come** to visit.
3. Rosemary is the only one of the women who **has/have** a chance.
4. Bill is the only one of the employees who **wants/want** a raise.
5. Bill is only one of the employees who **wants/want** a raise.

Here's the logic:
1. Mumps is ONE disease that is curable.
2. MANY diseases are curable.
3. Mumps is ONE of those diseases.

Thus:
4. Mumps is AMONG those diseases that **are** curable.

1. She comes to visit.
2. The volunteers come to visit.
3. She's just ONE of the volunteers.
4. But these volunteers come to visit.

Thus:
5. She is ONE of the volunteers who **come** to visit.

1. Rosemary is the ONLY ONE who has a chance.
2. The other women don't have a chance.

Thus:
3. Rosemary is the ONLY ONE of the women who **has** a chance.

1. Bill is the ONLY ONE of the employees who wants a raise.
2. The other employees don't want a raise.

Thus:
3. Bill is the ONLY ONE of the employees who **wants** a raise.

1. The employees want a raise.
2. Bill is ONLY ONE of those employees.

Thus:
3. Bill is ONLY ONE of the employees who **want** a raise.

Collective nouns take singular verbs:

1. A BILLION DOLLARS **was/were** taken.
   a billion dollars = a collective = **was**

2. FENSTER, PIERSOL & COMPANY **is/are** opening a new store.
   FENSTER, PIERSOL & Company = collective = **is**

3. The committee **has/have** asked for a new meeting.
   committee = collective = **has**

4. Two-thirds of the cake **is/are** gone.
   Two-thirds = collective = **is**

In sentence 4, the fraction refers to a collective measurement—hence use a **singular** verb. But when the fraction refers to individual people or things, use a **plural** verb: Two-thirds of the players **are** sinking shots.

Remember that:
**THE number** = singular
**A number** = plural

1. **THE** number of senators **is** small.
2. **A** number of the senators **are** here.

The next one has a wackiness all of its own—although, upon reflection, maybe it's not so crazy. See the logic:

1. What she sees **is** the man.
2. What she sees **are** the men.

Inverted, the sentences reveal the logic:

1. The MAN is what she sees.
2. The MEN are what she sees.

Confronted with a **what** clause, go to the end of the sentence. Is the noun hooked up to the verb singular or plural? If it's singular, choose a singular verb; if it's plural, choose a plural.

Now two more sentences with a similar problem:

1. The key to the show's popularity **is/are** the songs.
2. The best tribute to Shakespeare's plays **is/are** the many yearly performances.

Though you can invert the sentences, that inversion won't determine the verb. Here the CAPITALIZED subject determines the verb:

1. The KEY to the show's popularity **is** the songs.
2. The best TRIBUTE to Shakespeare's plays **is** the many yearly performances.

And if several words separate the subject from the verb, don't let them throw you:

The decision of the park managers, who we know have investigated the matter completely, **was/were** final.

1. Identify the verb: **was/were**.
2. To determine the subject, ask W**hat** was/were final?
3. The **decision** was final.

Thus:
4. The **decision** of the park managers, who we know have investigated the matter completely, **was** final.

The contributions of the home office, despite last year's recession, **is/are** excellent.

1. Identify the verb: **is/are**.
2. To determine the verb, ask W**hat** is/are excellent?
3. The **contributions** are excellent.

Thus:
4. The **contributions** of the home office, despite last year's recession, **are** excellent.

## VERB PROBLEMS

### Problem 10: Irregular Verbs

All verbs in English break into parts to express something that happens today (the **present**), yesterday (the **past**), and in an earlier past, like the day before yesterday (which uses a part called the **past participle**). Luckily for us, most verbs, when they break into their parts, add a regular ending:

Today I **call** my friend.
Yesterday I **called** my friend.
In the past, I **have called** my friend.

Regular verbs add an **-ed** or **-d** to show the past. Irregular verbs, though, do something else:

Today I **sing**.
Yesterday I **sang**.
In the past, I **have sung**.

Today I **swing**.
Yesterday I **swung**. (not **swang**)
In the past, I **have swung**.

Irregular verbs split into groups: the **regular** irregulars (**sing, sang, sung; drink, drank, drunk**), and the **irregular irregulars** (**swing, swung, swung; spin, spun, spun**).

The famous problems using verbs predictably come from errors with the regular irregulars and the irregular irregulars.

For reference, here's a list of the most common regular and irregular irregulars (broken down by principal parts); because of problems with a few regular verbs, they're also included. **Lie** and **lay**, the toughest of the irregulars, we'll save for a bit.

| PRESENT | PAST | PAST PARTICIPLE |
|---|---|---|
| arise | arose | arisen |
| bet | bet | bet |
| become | became | become |
| begin | began | begun |
| blow | blew | blown |
| break | broke | broken |
| bring | brought | brought |
| burst | burst | burst |
| buy | bought | bought |
| choose | chose | chosen |
| cling | clung | clung |
| come | came | come |
| cost | cost | cost |
| dive | dived or dove | dived |
| do | did | done |
| draw | drew | drawn |
| drink | drank | drunk |
| drive | drove | driven |
| drown | drowned | drowned |
| eat | ate | eaten |

| | | |
|---|---|---|
| fall | fell | fallen |
| fly | flew | flown |
| forgive | forgave | forgiven |
| freeze | froze | frozen |
| give | gave | given |
| go | went | gone |
| grow | grew | grown |
| hang (execute) | hanged | hanged |
| hang (a picture) | hung | hung |
| know | knew | known |
| lead | led | led |
| loosen | loosened | loosened |
| lose | lost | lost |
| pay | paid | paid |
| raise | raised | raised |
| ride | rode | ridden |
| ring | rang | rung |
| rise | rose | risen |
| run | ran | run |
| see | saw | seen |
| set | set | set |
| shake | shook | shaken |
| shrink | shrank or shrunk | shrunk or shrunken |
| sing | sang | sung |
| sink | sank or sunk | sunk |
| sit | sat | sat |
| speak | spoke | spoken |
| spin | spun | spun |
| spring | sprang or sprung | sprung |
| steal | stole | stolen |
| sting | stung | stung |
| stink | stank or stunk | stunk |
| swim | swam | swum |
| swing | swung | swung |
| take | took | taken |
| throw | threw | thrown |
| wake | woke or waked | waked or woken |
| wring | wrung | wrung |
| write | wrote | written |

## Problem 11: Lie or Lay?

There's probably no grammar problem as difficult to teach (or, at least, convince students of) as **lie** and **lay**. Before we begin, here's a quick test. See how you do:

1. Today I want to _____ down.
2. The book is _____ on the table.
3. Yesterday the book was _____ on the table.
4. Yesterday I wanted to _____ on the table.
5. Did you _____ the book down?
6. Are you going to _____ the book down?
7. Are you going to _____ down?
8. Did you _____ down yesterday?
9. Did you _____ the book down next to you on the bed?
10. I had been _____ down for a nap when the phone rang.
11. I left the book I'd been reading _____ next to me on the bed.
12. I had _____ the book on the floor, but my dog tried to eat it.
13. The book had _____ there all afternoon.
14. Are you going to _____ down tomorrow?
15. I have _____ down for a nap before.
16. Don't bother _____ the book down.
17. Martha becomes tired easily, so she will _____ in bed to rest.
18. The dog is _____ on the couch.
19. He _____ his bone next to him.
20. Now I _____ me down to sleep; I pray the Lord my soul to keep.
21. I have _____ the book on the desk.

22. The book had been _____ there when I picked it up.

23. Please _____ down and go to sleep.

24. Nancy was tired; she had to _____ down.

25. Finally his friend said, "Get up. Why do you keep _____ there?"

26. "_____ off," Dan said.

27. Dan had shot his friend, and his friend _____ on the floor.

28. Shortly after, the friend was _____ to rest in a cemetery.

29. He's _____ there now.

|  | LIE | LAY |
|---|---|---|
| PRESENT | I lie down.<br>I am lying down. | I lay IT down.<br>I am laying IT down. |
| PAST | I lay down.<br>I was lying down. | I laid IT down.<br>I was laying IT down. |
| PRESENT PERFECT | I have lain down.<br>I have been lying down. | I have laid IT down.<br>I have been laying IT down. |
| PAST PERFECT | I had lain down.<br>I had been lying down. | I had laid IT down.<br>I had been laying IT down. |
| FUTURE | I shall lie down.<br>I shall be lying down. | I shall lay IT down.<br>I shall be laying IT down. |

Promise yourself that no matter how off-key the proper forms may sound, you'll still **memorize** and **use** them. Most of us fail to use **lie** at all, and we let **lay** serve as the generic form for both.

One confusion develops because the past tense of **lie** is the present tense of **lay**: That is, **lay**. We often say, "Yesterday, I was tired, so I **laid** down." Wrong. "Yesterday, I was tired, so I **lay** down."

**THE BASICS OF GRAMMAR**

The verb **lay** (not **lie**) takes a direct object. Just as the chicken lays an EGG (a direct object), so do we **lay IT** down (another object). **Lie**, however, **never** takes an object.

If you're confused, replace **lie** with **sit** and **lay** with **set**.

| LIE = SIT | LAY = SET |
|---|---|
| Today I lie/sit down. | Today I lay/set IT down. |
| Yesterday I lay/sat down. | Yesterday I laid/set IT down. |
| In the past, I have lain/sat down. | In the past, I have laid/set IT down. |
| Tomorrow I shall lie/sit down. | Tomorrow I shall lay/set IT down. |
| I am (was, have or had been) lying/sitting down. | I am (was, have or had been) laying/setting IT down. |

Clearer? Now go back to the quiz and fill in the blanks with a different colored ink. And then grade yourself:

1. lie
2. lying
3. lying or laid
4. lie
5. lay
6. lay
7. lie
8. lie
9. lay
10. lying
11. lying
12. laid
13. lain
14. lie
15. lain
16. laying
17. lie
18. lying
19. laid
20. lay
21. laid
22. lying or laid
23. lie
24. lie
25. lying
26. Lay
27. lay
28. laid
29. lying

How'd you do?

If you missed any, better practice this one over till you know it by heart. Only memorizing the forms will solve the eternal problem of using **lie** and **lay**.

## Problem 12: The Subjunctive

In English, an odd verb construction exists that many of us may be only dimly aware of. To begin, how would you handle these:

1. If I **was/were** you, I'd do that.
2. If he **was/were** younger, he'd try rock climbing.
3. He wishes that he **was/were** tall.
4. She acted as though she **was/were** guilty.
5. The landlord requests that she **pays/pay** a deposit.
6. He recommends that Marie **files/file** her taxes.
7. I know you will suggest that I **am/be** on time.
8. We insist that he **goes/go** to the doctor.
9. The board asks that she **contacts/contact** them.
10. I move that the minutes **are/be** approved.

If you chose the first verb in each sentence, you consistently chose wrong. You should have picked the **subjunctive** form—which may sound as curious as **lie** and **lay**.

Would you ever say any of these:

**I were you**

**He were younger**

**He were tall**

**She were guilty**

Probably not, and that's why we choose the wrong form over the subjunctive. Use the subjunctive for these two situations:

1. In the first instance, you use the subjunctive if you're describing a reality that lies a hundred and eighty degrees away from your present reality: a situation that is day and night from the truth; a situation that can never be.

    **If I were you . . .** (But logically I can never be you.)

    **If he were younger . . .** (But he can never be younger.)

    **He wishes that he were tall . . .** (But he's doomed to being a little fellow.)

    **She acted as though she were guilty . . .** (But she's not; Louie Spottwood confessed.)

2. In the second instance, you use the subjunctive if you're requesting, recommending, suggesting, insisting, or asking. You use the subjunctive because you're requesting, recommending, suggesting, insisting, or asking something **that hasn't yet happened**—and therefore is night and day from the present reality.

> The building manager requests that she **pay** a deposit.
> He recommends that Marie **file** her taxes.
> I know you will suggest that I **be** on time.
> We insist that he **go** to the doctor.
> The board asks that she **contact** them.

> Subjunctive forms:
> am, is, are = **be**
> was = **were**
> singular verbs ending in -s = **drop the -s** (so in the subjunctive, a singular verb like **goes** becomes **go**)

## Adverb and Adjective Problems

### Problem 13: The Adverb and -ly

Adverbs typically end in **-ly**; that means you must remember to include the ending:

> **She drives too quick.** (should be **quickly**)
> **He reads too rapid to understand the content.** (should be **rapidly**)
> **I know this material perfect for the exam.** (should be **perfectly**)

The common exception is **slow**. You can, in fact, drive **slow**, though **slowly** may strike your ear as much better. **Slow** is allowed because of bad grammar perpetuated by road signs:

**DRIVE SLOW**

## Problem 14: Adjectives and Linking Verbs

You know that you must say

> **I sang badly.**
> **She danced well.**

because **sang** and **danced** are verbs, and the words that describe them must be **adverbs**, not adjectives. You can't say:

> **I sang bad** or **She danced good**.

So why, then, are these correct:

1. The handmade dress LOOKS **good**. (not **well**)
2. That SOUNDS **good**. (not **well**)
3. I FEEL **bad**. (and not, as many say, **badly**)
4. The dog SMELLS **good**. (not **well**)
5. The pizza TASTES **good**. (not **well**)

The rule says that a verb requires an adverb; since **looks**, **sounds**, **feel**, **smells**, and **tastes** are verbs, why not use adverbs instead of these adjectives?

Time for another rule: When you have a **linking verb** (a verb that functions like a verb of being—that is, doesn't show action), you use an adjective, just as you do with a verb of being:

> **I am BAD.** (not **badly**)
> **She is GOOD.** (not **well**)
> **The music is LOUD.** (not **loudly**)

Linking verbs include the verbs that handle our senses: **look, sound, feel, taste,** and **smell**.

So does the bloodhound smell **good** or **well**?
It depends . . .
If the dog has rolled around in the woods and picked up a few strong scents, and you have to hose it down before it can enter the house—then, once you've given it a bath, the dog smells **good**.
But if your bloodhound, a good tracking dog, has had a sinus infection, but now, after a trip to the vet, it's able to follow a scent—then the dog smells **well**, since you're describing how the dog's nose functions. You're describing an **action**.

## Problem 15: Good or Well? (Continued)

**Good** is the **adjective**; **well** is the **adverb**.

As an adjective, good describes things:

**a GOOD meal, a GOOD movie, a GOOD car**

But **well**, as an adverb, describes how you **do** things:

**He cooks WELL.**

Is it **She did well/good on her test**? **Well**. Of course! **Well** is the adverb, and the adverb describes the action: how she **did** on her test.
So do you feel good or well?
Again, it depends . . .

Let's say you miss a week from your job with the flu. You've had a fever and headaches, the works. But you gradually recover and return to your desk. A coworker asks how you're feeling. Do you reply, "I feel **good**" or "I feel **well**"?

**Well**—because **well** describes physical health.

But in another scenario, you miss still one more week. During that time, your house burns to a cinder, the dog runs off, the IRS audits your tax returns, you lose the winning lottery ticket, and you discover that the person you've been sleeping with has moved in with your best friend. You're feeling pretty down.

Somehow, though, you get your life back together. You collect on the house, you buy a cat, the IRS says they confused your last name with another, you buy a second winning lottery ticket, and you meet somebody new. The sun comes up in the morning, and life smells sweet. Damn!

You again return to work, and a coworker again asks how you're feeling. Like James Brown, you holler out that you're feeling **good**. No doubt about it.

When you describe the entire psychological and physical package, the holistic good feeling you, you feel **good**.

**Real** good.
Except that . . .

## Problem 16: Real or Really? (Sure or Surely?)

Except that you should say **really** good. Not **real** good. As an adverb, **really** requires the **-ly** (see **Problem 13**). There's no way around this one. You **have** to write (though not necessarily say, if you think you'll sound foolish):

It's really hot.
   NOT
It's real hot.

Thus:

We were really shocked by that news story.
I'm really sad, really happy, really tired, really awake, really sick of "really."

**Real** is the adjective, and it can be used only as an adjective:

a real woman, a real man, a real experience

**Sure** and **surely** work the same way:

I surely am tired, and it surely is hot.
   NOT
I sure am tired, and it sure is hot.

If all these sound odd, substitute **certainly**:

I certainly am tired, and it certainly is hot.

## Problem 17: Adjective Comparison

Another painless rule to master. To compare two things, add an **-er** or **-re** ending:

Floyd is the **taller** of the two boys.
Lilacs smell **more** pleasing than dandelions.

To compare three or more, add an **-st** ending:

Floyd is the **tallest** of the three boys.
Lilacs smell the **most** pleasing of lilacs, dandelions, and carnations.

## Problem 18: Where Do I Put the Adverb?

Which is right—where do you place the adverbs **only**, **even**, and **almost**?

1. **She ONLY needs to sell <u>one more order</u>.** (WRONG)
2. **She needs to sell ONLY <u>one more order</u>.** (RIGHT)

1. **Dad didn't EVEN call me <u>once</u>.** (WRONG)
2. **Dad didn't call me EVEN <u>once</u>.** (RIGHT)

1. **I ALMOST visited <u>every patient</u> in the hospital.** (This could be RIGHT . . . )
2. **I visited ALMOST <u>every patient</u> in the hospital.** (But so could this: Why?)

In the first two pairs, the second sentence shows that there's just one correct placement for the adverb. The third pair shows how correct placement can depend on the word you want to emphasize. As a rule, **Put the adverb next to the word or words it describes**.

## Problem 19: The Possessive and the Gerund

If you add -ING to a verb and use the new word as a noun, it's called a **gerund**, and these nouns can be used as subjects or objects:

sing + -ING = singing; play + -ING = playing
**Gordon's SINGING delighted the audience; they also liked his piano PLAYING.**

When you have a gerund, you normally place a possessive in front of it:

**Gordon's singing; his playing**
**Maggie's complaining; her wrestling with the problem**

If you add -ING to a verb and use it as an adjective, it's called a **participle**; you don't need to show possession:

sing+ -ING = singing; play + -ING = playing
**The man SINGING the song is my cousin. See Tommy PLAYING outside.**

Thus:

**Gordon's singing drove me crazy.** (**singing** = a gerund)
**The picture showed Gordon singing.** (**singing** = a participle)

# Key 6

# The Basics of Punctuation

- What's the Least Punctuation I Need to Know—and Still Survive?
- What Are the Eight Punctuation Patterns?
- How Can Just Eight Patterns Punctuate Almost All the Sentences in the World?
- What Other Punctuation Do I Have to Worry About?
- Is That All? Forty-Nine Basic Punctuation Patterns

## WHAT'S THE LEAST PUNCTUATION I NEED TO KNOW—AND STILL SURVIVE?

Here's a writer reflecting on the mysteries of punctuation:

*When I was a student, no matter how hard I'd labored to clean up a draft, to make sure the punctuation worked correctly, something would go wrong, and back would come my essay, awash with bloody marks. I couldn't keep up with the rules—especially the comma rules. Entering the world of commas was like entering a fun house: a trap door around every corner. A window to fall through. A brick wall to run into.*

*I ran into too many rules—too many comma rules, too many rules ever to learn them. Surely I didn't need all of them.*

*The question that kept me up at nights was,* **What's the least punctuation I need to know—and still survive?**

*For years I punctuated too much, the theory being that it was better to cover my back than leave a hole unplugged—and so in flew a comma where it didn't want to be. My manuscripts resembled novels from the nineteenth century with all their commas and dashes, semicolons. And exclamation points!*

Skim, for example, through any novel by Dickens, and you'll be astonished by the wealth of punctuation that he brings to the page. Modern rules can account for some commas and semicolons, but much of the punctuation in Dickens may seem . . . excessive:

> Posts, and rails, and old cautions to trespassers, and backs of mean houses, and patches of wretched vegetation, stared it out of countenance.

Dickens, like many writers of his time, and like many writers up to the twentieth century, punctuated for the ear as well as for the eye. As you may know, Dickens was a showman who filled halls with his public readings. Today, he'd engage in book tours and signing parties and host his own talk show. At heart, Dickens was an actor, and his punctuation reads dramatically—measured off for effect.

It's easy to imagine Dickens reading the following passage (about the Victorian railroad boom; from *Dombey and Son*, 1848) to a crowd of excited admirers:

---

But as yet, the neighborhood was shy to own the Railroad. One or two bold speculators had projected streets; and one had built a little, but had stopped among the mud and ashes to consider farther of it. A bran-new Tavern, redolent of fresh mortar and size, and fronting nothing at all, had taken for its sign The Railway Arms; but that might be rash enterprise—and then it hoped to sell drink to the workmen. So, the Excavators' House of Call had sprung up from a beer shop; and the old established Ham and Beef Shop had become the Railway Eating House, with a roast leg of pork daily, through interested motives of a similar immediate and popular description. Lodginghouse keepers were favorable in like manner; and for the like reasons were not to be trusted. The general belief was very slow. There were frowzy fields, and cow houses, and dunghills, and dustheaps, and ditches, and gardens, and summer houses, and carpet-beating grounds, at the very door of the Railway. Little tumuli of oyster shells in the oyster season, and of lobster shells in the lobster season, and of broken crockery and faded cabbage leaves in all seasons, encroached upon its high places. Posts, and rails, and old cautions to trespassers, and backs of mean houses, and patches of wretched vegetation, stared it out of countenance. Nothing was the better for it, or thought of being so. If the miserable waste ground lying near it could have laughed, it would have laughed it to scorn, like many of the miserable neighbors.

Read aloud the punctuation makes perfect sense; read silently, with only the eye, the paragraph may seem glutted with commas and semicolons.

Yet, despite its natural drama, Dickens' punctuation resembles that of his contemporaries. Their books materialized in an age when people nightly grouped around the fireplace to listen to the latest installment of *Great Expectations*. When you read a novel orally, you deliver lines with flair, obeying an actor's pauses. Writers knew their prose had to stand up to the scrutiny of both the ear and eye. Since they wrote sentences to be read to an audience, they'd slow down a page with commas and dashes and semicolons. Listen to Dickens as he reads this sentence out loud, bringing to it the rhythms of the voice:

> **Posts, and rails, and old cautions to trespassers, and backs of mean houses, and patches of wretched vegetation, stared it out of countenance.**

Those commas and conjunctions draw out the description, cause us to linger over the particulars. The ear has time to consider each item, to fashion a mental picture. Today we'd hurry through Dickens' slow sentence, deleting conjunctions and losing commas:

> **Posts, rails, cautions to trespassers, backs of mean houses and patches of wretched vegetation stared it out of countenance.**

And in our silent speed, what pictures do we give up?

Punctuation by the twenty-first century has come to be written for the eye, though careful writers still of course punctuate for both the eye and the ear. Read aloud any page by John Updike, and you'll hear sentences written with the ear in mind. And any page of *The New Yorker* will demonstrate punctuation that remembers we have an ear.

But, generally, writers use less punctuation today, and it's quicker and sleeker, eager to hurry the eye along as it races across the page—through our shorter sentences, down our one-sentence paragraphs.

So it may seem like heresy if to suggest that you read your sentences aloud when you punctuate. Many teachers, in fact, believe that punctuating with the ear can be dangerous. Why? What if you're a junior Charles Dickens, ready to pause at every dramatic moment and pop in a comma? Or what if you're in training as a TV anchor? They pause after every word. Think of the extra, unwanted commas.

But it also seems like heresy to suggest that you should punctuate using only your eye. Punctuation from the beginning has been a matter of both eye and ear. You can obviously pause anywhere you like when you read a sentence.

That won't work. You should read sentences in a normal tone, listening to the normal rhythms of your voice.

Most of us understand that our voice reacts when it comes to a break in a sentence. Read aloud both of these sentences:

**Please bring me three items from the store milk bread and eggs.**

Or:

**Although Nancy Joy knew that Brenda would take the nachos to the party she wasn't sure if Brenda would remember to take Howard.**

You hear something, right? Your voice catches, hesitates, because there's something wrong. You probably hear gaps in the first sentence after "store," "milk," and "bread." And in the second sentence after "party":

**Please bring me three items from the store: milk, bread, and eggs.**

**Although Nancy Joy knew that Brenda would take the nachos to the party, she wasn't sure if Brenda would remember to take Howard.**

The first question is, **What do you stick into those gaps?**
And the second: **Can you always trust your ear?**

The second question is easier to answer. **No.** You can trust it only part of the time, for some sentences don't appear to have pauses. To illustrate:

**The woman WHO IS TALL arrived last night**

doesn't need commas for the middle fragment.

But:

**Wanda WHO IS TALL arrived last night** does need commas.
(**Wanda, who is tall, arrived last night.**)

These sentences sound and look the same (almost). Yet one requires commas, and one doesn't. Neither seems to have "pauses," but if they're punctuated alike, you have a problem.

Although the ear can teach a great deal about sentences, it can't solve all your punctuation problems. Nevertheless, you can't rely solely on the eye to punctuate. The eye moves too fast; it will miss punctuation that the ear will hear. And once you hear enough sentences, once you know their bones and sinews, once you internalize the rhythms of many sentences read aloud, you'll become a better writer and editor. Language, after all, consists of words—and words get spoken. How words flow from our lips directly relates to how we punctuate. To pretend that words exist only for the eye is as foolish as to insist that you should punctuate with only your ear.

As a rule, **Use both your eye and ear to punctuate.**

To answer the first question, **What do you stick into those gaps?**, here are eight patterns—"patterns," not rules, although they're "almost rules." Remember that 90 percent of your punctuation marks will be commas and periods. The patterns governing commas and periods thus take on enormous importance.

At the start of this Key, a writer recalled how, as a student trying to punctuate correctly, he could never keep on top of the rules. He'd learn one rule, apply it, and then a new one would pop up. Another rule to learn . . .

> *As a beginning teacher, the torments continued. Now I not only had to know all the rules, I had to teach them all (maybe worth a hundred pages in the handbook)—and in a two-week "unit."*
>
> *So what can you do? What can any reasonable person do who wants to learn to punctuate or wants to teach punctuation to a class, yet can't dodge that brick wall of all those rules?*
>
> *What's the answer?*

The answer is eight punctuation patterns that collapse a hundred pages of rules into six pages of advice that you can learn in about an hour (and that will handle about 90 percent of all sentences).

The eight patterns assume you know the difference between a fragment and sentence. You'll recall from Key 3 what a fragment looks like.

Each fragment needs information either BEFORE it or AFTER it to make sense—to turn it into a complete sentence:

**When it rains** →
**Although the game ended late** →
**If I were you** →
← **because he wanted to do the right thing**
← **since she was available then**
← **which was full of gas fumes**

With information completing the fragment, we get a complete sentence:

When it rains, I GET WET.
Although the game ended late, WE STOPPED FOR SUPPER.
If I were you, I WOULDN'T HESITATE TO CALL WILLY MURDOCH.
RONNIE PAID THE TICKET because he wanted to do the right thing.
I MADE THE APPOINTMENT WITH MY LAWYER since she was available then.
MRS. SNETHEN VACATED HER CABIN, which was full of gas fumes.

## What Are the Eight Punctuation Patterns?

> PATTERN 1: Put a comma after an introductory fragment.
>
> Fragment          Sentence
> AFTER I ATE SUPPER, I washed the dishes.

You'll find three constructions here:

1. The whole sentence (**After I ate supper, I washed the dishes.**)
2. The fragment within the whole sentence (**After I ate supper**)
3. The shorter sentence within the whole sentence (**I washed the dishes**)

In other words, the whole sentence breaks into two parts:

1. **A fragment**
2. **A short sentence**

Pattern 1 says: If you have a whole sentence that begins with an introductory fragment and ends with a shorter sentence, put a **comma** after the fragment.

Let's call this a "pattern" instead of a "rule" because you'll see some introductory fragments that don't need a comma. If the fragment is one or two or three words long, you can omit the comma:

**After supper I washed the dishes.**

Usually, though, once the count hits at least four words, an editor will insert the comma.

**After I ate supper, I washed the dishes.**

Here's another whole sentence with two parts—one a shorter sentence, the other a fragment; this time, however, the fragment comes **after** the shorter sentence. So does it need a comma?

**I washed the dishes AFTER I ATE SUPPER.**

---

PATTERN 2: If the fragment at the end of a sentence COMPLETES the meaning, don't put a comma in front of it.

| Sentence | Fragment |
|---|---|
| I washed the dishes | AFTER I ATE SUPPER. |
| Sentence | Fragment |
| I washed the dishes | BECAUSE THEY WERE DIRTY. |

---

When did the "I" wash the dishes? **After supper**. Is that important?

Yes. It's absolutely **essential**:* Otherwise, you wouldn't know **when** "I" washed them.

**I washed the dishes BECAUSE THEY WERE DIRTY.**

Why did "I" wash the dishes? **Because they were dirty**. Is that important?

Yes. It's absolutely **essential**: Otherwise, you wouldn't know **why** "I" washed them.

However:

---

PATTERN 3: If the fragment at the end of a sentence DOES NOT complete the meaning, put a comma in front of it.

| Sentence | Fragment |
|---|---|
| I washed the dishes, | WHICH IS ALWAYS BORING. |

---

Does the fact that it's always boring to wash the dishes have anything to do with the fact that "I" washed them? No. It's just an afterthought, tacked on for the hell of it. Consider these two:

**THE BASICS OF PUNCTUATION**

**It's hard to understand Tonya.** Compare with: **It's hard to understand, Tonya.**

In the first sentence, Tonya completes the meaning of the main statement: **It's hard to understand this WOMAN [whose name is Tonya]**. In the second, the main statement is already complete: **IT's hard to understand. Tonya** has been tacked on as a **nonessential\*** afterthought.

Next—how do you punctuate two sentences that sit side by side? To begin:

> PATTERN 4: If you connect two sentences by a conjunction, put a comma in front of the conjunction.
>
> Sentence   Conjunction   Sentence
> I ate supper, AND I washed the dishes.

Note that if you don't have a sentence AFTER the conjunction, usually you don't put a comma IN FRONT of the conjunction:

Sentence Conjunction Fragment
**I ate supper AND washed the dishes.**

The shorter the fragment, the more likely the comma will disappear before the conjunction; the longer the fragment, the more likely you'll want it. Recall that this is a "pattern," not a "rule":

**I ate supper, and eventually washed the dishes after I listened to a three-hour opera on the radio.**

You can also use the comma as Dickens did—for dramatic effect:

**I ate supper, and turned deathly ill.**

(Don't forget the seven conjunctions—the **FANBOYS: For, And, Nor, But, Or, Yet, So.**)

A related pattern takes care of a whole sentence that breaks into two shorter sentences— still sitting side by side but separated by a **transition**:

> **PATTERN 5:** If you connect two sentences with a transition, put a period or semicolon in front of the transition and a comma after.*
>
>     Sentence    Transition    Sentence
>     I ate supper. CONSEQUENTLY, I washed the dishes.
>     I ate supper; CONSEQUENTLY, I washed the dishes.
>
> Transitions = consequently, however, accordingly, nevertheless, etc. (See the chart on page 37.)
>
> *Five exceptions don't require a comma after the transition: hence, next, now, then, thus.

Either a period or semicolon will work: a period = a semicolon. Use a semicolon if the sentences show a relationship that you want to emphasize:

**I ate <u>supper</u>; CONSEQUENTLY, I washed the <u>dishes</u>. (<u>supper</u> leads to <u>dishes</u>)**

A similar pattern takes care of a whole sentence that breaks into two shorter sentences, but this time nothing separates them but space—there's no transition.

So what do you do?

> **PATTERN 6:** To avoid a run-on, connect two related sentences with a period or semicolon.
>
>     Sentence    Sentence
>     I ate supper. I washed the dishes.
>     I ate supper; I washed the dishes.

**Note:** A run-on has nothing to do with wordiness. You can have a run-on as short or as long as wanted. Punctuation defines a run-on—not word count. A run-on just means that you've jammed together two sentences with either a comma or no punctuation.

    **Wrong:** I ate supper, I washed the dishes.
    **Wrong:** I ate supper I washed the dishes.

You can fix a run-on in four ways:

## Four Ways to Fix a Run-on Sentence

| **Use a Period**<br>I ate supper. I washed the dishes. | **Use a Comma + a Conjunction**<br>I ate supper, and I washed the dishes. |
|---|---|
| **Use a Semicolon**<br>I ate supper; I washed the dishes. | **Turn One Sentence into a Fragment and Connect**<br>After I ate supper, I washed the dishes.<br>I ate supper before I washed the dishes. |

The two final patterns handle a single sentence that has a fragment inserted into its center. The problem becomes how to punctuate the fragment inserted into that center—do you put commas around the fragment?

---

**PATTERN 7: Don't put commas around a fragment if the sentence subject isn't identified.**

    S---      Fragment               ---S

The man WHO WASHED THE DISHES ate supper with me.

---

Because the subject, **man**, is not identified in any way (for example, by a name), you need the fragment to tell **which man ate supper with me**. Lacking this fragment, you can't identify the man.

Likewise:
**The coach WHO GOT FIRED was my friend.**

Which coach was my friend? The coach **WHO GOT FIRED**. Without that ID, you wouldn't know which coach. If you need the fragment to identify the subject, don't use commas. This kind of fragment is called **essential** (because you need it).

However:

---

**PATTERN 8: Put commas around a fragment if the sentence subject is identified.**

                S---    Fragment               ---S

Bob, WHO WASHED THE DISHES, ate supper with me.

The basic sentence is **Bob ate supper with me**. Into that sentence, you're inserting the fragment **WHO WASHED THE DISHES**.

Because the subject, **Bob**, is identified with a name, you DO NOT need the fragment to tell you **WHICH man ate supper with me**. Without the fragment, you'll still be able to identify Bob. Such a fragment is called **nonessential** (because you don't need it).

**Warning:** The topic of using fragments came up in Key 3, but this caution bears repeating: Use them carefully. Used carelessly, they'll stamp you as an amateur. They're fine for certain kinds of writing, but in formal projects you'll probably want to write nothing but sentences.

**And remember:** If you're worried that you may be writing fragments, look for them in the most obvious place—after a main statement. That's where they often get stranded.

Sentence          Fragment
**I went to the movies. BECAUSE I LIKE ARNOLD SCHWARZENEGGER.**

Connect the fragment to the sentence. You don't need a comma before the fragment because it tells WHY you went to the movie (Pattern 2):

**I went to the movie because I like Arnold Schwarzenegger.**

Sentence       Fragment
**I washed the dishes. WHICH IS REALLY BORING.**

Fix this by connecting the fragment to the sentence with a comma (Pattern 3):

**I washed the dishes, which is really boring.**

Again, you need the comma because the fragment is an afterthought, tacking on interesting but not essential information.

Sentence         Fragment
**I went to the movies. ALTHOUGH MY SISTER DIDN'T GO.**

And since the fragment offers no essential information about the main statement, connect it with a comma (Pattern 3):

**I went to the movies, although my sister didn't go.**

# How Can Just Eight Patterns Punctuate Almost All the Sentences in the World?

That's exactly the right question to ask. Logic demands to know how eight patterns can take care of 90 percent of your punctuation.

**The Eight Patterns**

| |
|---|
| 1. F,S |
| 2. SF |
| 3. S,F |
| 4. S,CONJ S |
| 5. S./;TRANS,S |
| 6. S./;S |
| 7. S-F-S |
| 8. S-,F,-S |

You can punctuate almost all the sentences in the world by **plugging together** the eight patterns.

Memorize the eight patterns in this shorthand. Only eight patterns—but you can combine them in an infinite number of ways. For example, how would you punctuate:

**Although Harry S Truman irritated many Americans with his bluntness he still charmed the great share of voters we'll never see his like again I daresay.**

As a first step, read the sentence out loud, marking each gap:

**Although Harry S Truman irritated many Americans with his bluntness / he still charmed the great share of voters / we'll never see his like again / I daresay.**

Then decide if each part is a fragment or a sentence:

1. Although Harry S Truman irritated many Americans with his bluntness = **fragment**

2. he still charmed the great share of voters = **sentence**
3. we'll never see his like again = **sentence**
4. I daresay = **sentence** (but an awfully short sentence, and one that works like a tacked-on, nonessential fragment)

Then ask yourself:

1. What do I put after a fragment that starts a sentence? According to Pattern 1, a **comma**.
2. What do I put after a sentence that's followed by a sentence? According to Pattern 6, a **period**. Or, if they're related, a **semicolon**.
3. What do I put before a tacked-on fragment at the end of a sentence (or at least a tacked-on sentence that functions like a fragment)? According to Pattern 3, a **comma**.

Thus: I want the following construction:

**FRAGMENT, SENTENCE; SENTENCE, FRAGMENT = F,S;S,F**

But there's no pattern that says F,S;S,F. True, but Pattern 1 = F,S. And Pattern 6 = S;S. And Pattern 3 = S,F.

So, combined, these three patterns take care of one whole sentence that happens to have four parts: **whole S = F + S + S + F = F,S;S,F.**

                                                      F,S

**Although Harry S Truman irritated many Americans with his bluntness, he**

                     S;S                                           S,F

**still charmed the great share of voters; we'll never see his like again, I daresay.**

But what if you have five parts? Or six? Or twenty? In theory, you can endlessly combine the patterns, but common sense says that sooner or later, you'll want to employ periods instead of semicolons. The key is to know the difference between the fragment and the sentence.

1. If a fragment comes at the **beginning** of a sentence, follow it with a **comma**:

    **FRAGMENT sentence = comma (F,S)**

2. If a fragment splits a sentence in the **middle**, check the subject: Is it identified? If it is, **use two commas**; if it isn't, **don't use any commas**:

    **first part of sentence split FRAGMENT split last part of sentence =**

    a. **if subject has no ID, no commas (S-F-S)**
    b. **if subject has ID, two commas (S-,F,-S)**

**Remember**: These patterns mean one sentence split through its center—not two joined sentences, as in Patterns 4, 5, and 6.

3. If a fragment comes at the **end** of a sentence, **DON'T** use a comma if you NEED the fragment; DO use a comma if you DON'T NEED the fragment.

sentence FRAGMENT =
a. if fragment needed, no comma (SF)
b. if fragment not needed, comma  (S,F)

If you know how the fragment functions in these patterns, you won't have a problem with most commas.

And if you remember that sentences placed next to each other follow just three patterns, you should have no difficulty punctuating any number of sentences:

**SENTENCE conjunction SENTENCE** = comma (S,CONJ S)

**SENTENCE transition SENTENCE** = period/semicolon + comma
(S./;trans,S)

**SENTENCE SENTENCE** = period/semicolon (S./;S)

Armed with these eight patterns, you can go into the world, dismantle just about any sentence, and plug in the punctuation. Always remember to ask **fragment** or **sentence**? **Comma** or **period** (that is, a **semicolon**)?

## WHAT OTHER PUNCTUATION DO I HAVE TO WORRY ABOUT?

Not much. Just the basics—which means knowing how to handle:

> Other comma uses
> Other semicolon uses
> The dash
> The colon
> The apostrophe
> Quotation marks

Specifically, you should worry about:

1. **A Few More Patterns that DO Need a Comma**
   a. Commas with a series
   b. Commas with interrupters
   c. Commas with dates
   d. Commas with adjectives
   e. Commas with deleted words
   f. Commas with quotations

2. **Patterns that DON'T Need a Comma**
   a. To separate a subject from its verb
   b. To separate a verb from its object
   c. Before AND + a fragment
   d. After ALTHOUGH, EVEN THOUGH, SINCE, WHILE, IF, AS, BECAUSE, BEFORE, and AFTER
   e. After the FANBOYS: FOR, AND, NOR, BUT, OR, YET, SO
   f. After HENCE, NEXT, NOW, THEN, and THUS
   g. Before a title

3. **The Semicolon with a Series**

4. **The Dash**
   a. After an introductory fragment
   b. In the middle of a sentence
   c. At the end of a sentence

5. **The Colon**
   a. After a verb of being
   b. After a preposition

6. **The Apostrophe**
   a. To show possession
   b. To show something left out

7. **Quotation Marks with Periods, Commas, Your Own Title, and Emphasis**

## 1. A Few More Patterns that DO Need a Comma

### a. Commas with a series: the X, Y, and Z pattern

With a series of three or more items, separate each with a comma:

X, Y, and Z

Remember that the final comma is optional (business writing, journalism, and advertising frequently omit the final comma).

**Cary Grant was tall, dark(,) and handsome.**

Either style works, though occasional ambiguities will appear if you delete the final comma; to be safe, use it throughout. Whichever style you choose, stay consistent.

### b. Commas with interrupters

As a rule, **Don't use commas with ESSENTIAL fragments.**
And as a second rule, **Use commas with NONESSENTIAL fragments.**

**Mrs. Yoder, MY BARBER'S FRIEND, called last night.**

The fragment is **nonessential** because we can identify the subject by name—**Mrs. Yoder.**

**My barber's friend FROM ALABAMA left a message.**

The fragment is **essential** because we don't know which friend of the barber left the message. So we need **from Alabama** to identify her.

The situation becomes tricky with fragments like the following:

**My son, Aaron, likes to play pool.**
**My son Aaron likes to play pool.**

How many sons does the speaker have? By using those commas, the first sentence announces that the speaker has one son—and only one son. In the second sentence, however, "I" can have any number:

**My son Aaron likes to play pool.**
**My son Henry likes to race motorcycles.**

Do you see the job those commas perform? This can become embarrassing with:

**My wife Carol likes to read novels.**

Dropping the commas will turn the speaker into a bigamist. He needs commas to stay out of jail:

**My wife, Carol, likes to read novels.**

If there's more than one of something (sons, wives, books, etc.), don't use commas. If there's only one, use commas.

**Salinger's novel,** *The Catcher in the Rye,* **has become a classic.**

This sentence accurately uses commas because Salinger has published only one novel. Compare that with:

**Salinger's book,** *The Catcher in the Rye***, has become a classic.**

This makes no sense because Salinger has published four books. You should thus write:

**Salinger's book** *The Catcher in the Rye* **has become a classic.**

c. **Commas with dates**

Do this:

**Iona saw Cassie McGuire on July 7, 1894, in St. Louis.**

Not:

**Iona saw Cassie McGuire on July 7, 1894 in St. Louis.**

If you have both the month and day of the week, you must enclose the year in commas.

But:

**Iona saw Cassie McGuire in July 1894 in St. Louis.**

This means, for example, that newsletter dates lacking the day of the week (December 5, 1951) should appear on the masthead as:

December 1951    Volume 1, Number 1

d. **Commas with adjectives**

I saw an old, tired man at the park.
I saw an old stone fence at the park.

**THE BASICS OF PUNCTUATION**

Why use commas for the first but not for the second? Easy:

1. The man is both old AND tired.
2. The man is both tired AND old.

Thus:

3. I saw a tired, old man at the park.

But:

1. I saw an old and stone fence at the park. (?)
2. I saw a stone and old fence at the park. (?)

Thus:

3. I saw a stone, old fence at the park. (?)

If you can

(1) replace the comma with **and**

Or:

(2) invert the adjectives without losing sense, you probably need the comma. But if you can't ("an old and stone fence"; "a stone, old fence"), you probably don't need the comma.

The difference is that, in the first sentence, both adjectives **equally** describe the man: He's **old and tired, tired and old**. Hence **I saw an old, tired/tired, old man at the park**.

In the second sentence, "old" describes the phrase "stone fence." You don't need the comma. Hence **I saw an old stone fence at the park**.

Compare these two:

**I studied the colorful annual migration of the Canadian geese.**
**I studied the colorful annual report.**

Which one needs the comma? It's the first because you can invert **colorful** and **annual**:

**I studied the annual, colorful migration of the Canadian geese.**

e. Commas with deleted words

If you leave out words in a parallel series, fill in the gap with a comma:

**Sarah is my daughter; Aaron IS my son. Sarah is my daughter; Aaron, my son.**

Deleting "is" from the second sentence requires the comma to fill in the gap. Likewise:

> Brando said he could have been somebody AND could have been a contender.
> Brando said he could have been somebody, could have been a contender.

### f. Commas with quotations

Here's a familiar one. If you introduce a quotation, most of the time use a comma; read about the colon to introduce quotations on pages 171 and 178.

> **Jack said, "I won't go to your party."**

> **"I won't go to your party," Jack said, "because Marie will be there."**

But (note the new sentence):

> **"I won't go to your party," Jack said. "Marie will be there."**

## 2. A Few Patterns that DON'T Need a Comma

### a. To separate a subject from its verb

If there's only one comma in a sentence, don't let it separate the subject and verb:

SUBJECT ^ VERB
    **I,           HIT the ball.**

Rather:

> **I hit the ball.**

SUBJECT------------------------------------------------^ VERB

> **All that my grandmother Harrington claims, IS that she won't vote for any Republican.**

Rather:

> **All that my grandmother Harrington claims is that she won't vote for any Republican.**

Be on the lookout for sentences with **is** and **was**: They attract unnecessary commas.

SUBJECT ^ VERB
**The point, IS that Kenny read the article. (WRONG)**
**The point is that Kenny read the article. (RIGHT)**

SUBJECT-------------------------------- ^ VERB
**The person with the bag of books, WAS my brother. (WRONG)**
**The person with the bag of books was my brother. (RIGHT)**

If you place an interrupter after a subject—and interrupters call for two commas—then you can separate the subject from the verb:

**The point, however, is that Kenny read the article.**

It's better, though, not to separate the subject and verb with anything. Thus:

**However, the point is that Kenny read the article.**

b. To separate a verb from its object

Nor do you want to separate a verb from the object that follows:

SUBJECT VERB ^ OBJECT
**I          hit, THE BALL.**

Rather:

**I hit the ball.**

SUBJECT                                    VERB ^ OBJECT
**All that my grandmother Harrington claims is, THAT SHE WON'T VOTE FOR ANY REPUBLICAN.**

Rather:

**All that my grandmother Harrington claims is that she won't vote for any Republican.**

SUBJECT                    VERB ^ OBJECT
**The person with the bag of books was, MY BROTHER. (WRONG)**
**The person with the bag of books was my brother. (RIGHT)**

SBJ  VERB ^ OBJECT
**The point is, THAT KENNY READ THE ARTICLE. (WRONG)**
**The point is that Kenny read the article. (RIGHT)**

c. **Before AND + a fragment**

You'll recall this one from Punctuation Pattern 4 (page 152):

If you don't have a complete sentence after the conjunction, usually you don't put a comma in front of the conjunction:

SENTENCE CONJUNCTION FRAGMENT
**I ate supper AND washed the dishes.**

However, with a long fragment, you may want a comma:

**I ate supper, and eventually washed the dishes after I listened to a three-hour opera on the radio.**

d. **After ALTHOUGH, EVEN THOUGH, SINCE, WHILE, IF, AS, BECAUSE, BEFORE, and AFTER**

Never write:

**Although, it may be cold, I won't take my parka.**
**Even though, she'd paid the bill, cable service stopped.**
**He bought the new car because, he got a good deal.**

Rather:

**Although it may be cold, I won't take my parka.**
   = Pattern 1: F,S
**Even though she'd paid the bill, cable service stopped.**
   = Pattern 1: F,S
**He bought the new car because he got a good deal.**
   = Pattern 3: SF

The comma becomes proper only when you follow these words with an **INTERRUPTER**:

**Although, AS I RECALL, it may be cold, I won't take my parka.**
**Even though, ACCORDING TO TOM, she'd paid the bill, cable service stopped.**
**He bought the new car because, AFTER ALL, he got a good deal.**

e. **After the FANBOYS: FOR, AND, NOR, BUT, OR, YET, SO**

Never write these:

**Bob caught a fish, but, Brian caught a cold.**
**Bob caught a fish but, Brian caught a cold.**

I like to ride my bike, and, I ride it every day.
I like to ride my bike and, I ride it every day.
I like to ride my bike, and ride it every day.

Rather:

Bob caught a fish, but Brian caught a cold.
I like to ride my bike, and I ride it every day.
I like to ride my bike and ride it every day.

### f. After HENCE, NEXT, NOW, THEN, and THUS

Omit the commas in the following:

Hence, the president is overjoyed.
Next, the president will visit the United Nations.
Now, is the time to deliver such a speech.
Now, the president will deliver his speech.
Then, he will deliver a major speech.
Thus, the Israelis signed the peace pact.

Rather:

Hence the president is overjoyed.
Next the president will visit the United Nations.
Now is the time to deliver such a speech.
Now the president will deliver his speech.
Then he will deliver a major speech.
Thus the Israelis signed the peace pact.

### g. Before a title

Here's an odd one. What makes the comma wrong in front of this title?

**I love Hemingway's short story, "The Three-Day Blow."**

Remember what such a comma signifies: It would mean that Hemingway has produced only one short story—and, in fact, he published one hundred and eight. You should write:

**I love Hemingway's short story "The Three-Day Blow."**

Odder still is this construction:

**I read Hemingway's novel, *The Old Man and the Sea*.**

Since Hemingway wrote more than one novel, the sentence should say:

**I read Hemingway's novel *The Old Man and the Sea*.**

Why do those commas show up? Perhaps we see them because writers are recalling that commas can introduce quoted dialogue:

**Jack said, "I won't go to your party."**
**"Please don't buy avocados," Denise said, "unless they're on sale."**

And they mistakenly transfer the comma from the quoted dialogue to the title:

**I love Hemingway's short story, "The Three-Day Blow."**

## 3. The Semicolon with a Series

If you're composing a sentence with a series of items, each of which has a comma, then set off each item with a semicolon:

Item 1 = **New York, New York**
Item 2 = **Chicago, Illinois**
Item 3 = **San Francisco, California**
Item 4 = **Austin, Texas**

                                                          Item 1
**Last year, I visited my four favorites cities: New York, New York;**
        Item 2                       Item 3                      Item 4
**Chicago, Illinois; San Francisco, California; and Austin, Texas.**

## 4. The Dash

Writers tend to undervalue the dash. It's a powerful tool for slowing down a sentence so that readers will pay attention—like this. You can use dashes generally where you'd position a comma:

> a. After an introductory fragment
> b. In the middle of a sentence (around an interrupter)
> c. At the end of a sentence

**a. After an introductory fragment**

**New York, Chicago, San Francisco, and Austin—these are my four favorite cities.**

This is a special kind of fragment: You set up an idea; then elaborate after the dash with a complete sentence. The colon works the same way:

**New York, Chicago, San Francisco, and Austin: These are my four favorite cities.**

(Remember not to capitalize after the dash; only after the colon.)

The dash acts with greater force; by comparison, the colon seems tame. Dashes typically reveal emotions. A writer, for example, who wants to show fear may use the dash:

**The flickering gaslight, the creak on the stairs, the eerie howl across the moor—I slammed shut the shutters and secluded myself in Master's library. How my heart raced!—how my poor fingers trembled!—how alone I felt! Would there be no relief from this horror? Was I to suffer an ignominious death—a fate far worse than any I could have foretold just the fortnight back—when the wicked spectre of Lancelot Grigben first appeared at Bertram Manor?**

b.  **In the middle of a sentence**

Let's consider one sentence written three ways:

**Mr. Braithwaite (who finally won the lottery after buying 2,545 tickets) celebrated with his family.**

**Mr. Braithwaite, who finally won the lottery after buying 2,545 tickets, celebrated with his family.**

**Mr. Braithwaite—who finally won the lottery after buying 2,545 tickets—celebrated with his family.**

What differences do you see? What messages do parentheses, commas, and dashes send to the reader?

In the first sentence, there's just one piece of information that the sentence really wants to tell us: that Mr. Braithwaite celebrated with his family. But almost as an afterthought, we're slipped some background information **(who finally won the lottery after buying 2,545 tickets)**.

Parentheses tend to whisper: (By the way, just in case you wanted to know, let me add this). Material that isn't important often ends up inside the parentheses.

Commas, on the other hand, treat all parts of the sentence democratically. Commas don't whisper; they speak in a normal tone of voice:

**Mr. Braithwaite, who finally won the lottery after buying 2,545 tickets, celebrated with his family.**

Dashes, though, turn up the volume. They urge you to pay attention. They shout into the ear—you there, listen up!

**Mr. Braithwaite—who finally won the lottery after buying 2,545 tickets—celebrated with his family.**

Hear how, from the first sentence to the third, the emphasis has shifted? In the first, the main piece of information is that Mr. Braithwaite celebrated with his family. In the second, both parts seem equally important.

But in the third—thanks to those dashes—the main piece now has become the fact that Mr. Braithwaite won the lottery after buying all those tickets, all 2,545!

Dashes can also help sort out a complicated sentence like this one:

**My four favorite cities, New York, New York; Chicago, Illinois; San Francisco, California; and Austin, Texas, offer the visitor many tourist attractions.**

Don't these dashes considerably clarify the sense?

**My four favorite cities—New York, New York; Chicago, Illinois; San Francisco, California; and Austin, Texas—offer the visitor many tourist attractions.**

**Thus:** If you're confronted with a middle section that's cluttered or has items demanding special punctuation, set the middle off with dashes. The reader will thank you.

### c. At the end of a sentence

Like the dash at the beginning or in the middle of a sentence, the dash at the end functions to slow down the eye and make you pay attention to each word.

Now listen to the difference:

**Like the dash at the beginning or in the middle of a sentence, the dash at the end functions to slow down the eye—and make you pay attention to each word.**

Without a dash, the eye keeps reading. Business as usual. But with the dash, the eye knows something is up—time to get serious.

The dash magnificently shines a spotlight on the most important part of the sentence—the part that you don't want the reader to miss. A dash, then, works as a fine tool to help the reader through a tough explanation.

Commas (or worse, parentheses) don't yell at the reader to wake up and pay attention—the way a dash can. A dash sticks out and signals to the reader—**hey, here's the important stuff!**

## 5. The Colon

The colon functions like a dash: to call attention to the important stuff that follows. So what's the difference?

The colon behaves less obtrusively than the dash. It also brings a kind of seriousness to the sentence. A dash suggests emotion; a colon feels cooler, less spontaneous. At the end of a sentence, the dash typically introduces a summing-up afterthought, pregnant with feeling:

**I lost my wallet, my keys, my job, and my humor—what a day!**

The colon, however, attends to more serious business, and that's why formal writing admires it; the colon typically leads the reader from one idea to the next:

**J.S. Bach's influence reaches far beyond the baroque period: Later composers as diverse as Brahms, Stravinsky, and Schoenberg all learned from him.**

The colon carries you from Side A (Bach) to Side B (composers he influenced). The colon thus guides the reader into a logical connection; it's another powerful tool to have in your arsenal: one of the best transition devices known to good writing.

You can group the colon's main functions under two heads (see the **Forty-Nine Basic Punctuation Patterns**, on page 175, for a detailed look at these functions):

- To list
  Please bring me three items from the store: milk, bread, and eggs.
- To introduce, explain, or elaborate
  Dear Dr. Smith: (introduction to a letter)

**JFK once said: "Ask not what your country can do for you; ask what you can do for your country."** (introduction to a famous quotation; use the colon to introduce famous quotations; the comma for introducing all other quotations)

**J.S. Bach's influence reaches far beyond the baroque period: Later composers as diverse as Brahms, Stravinsky, and Schoenberg all learned from him.** (explanation or elaboration of an idea)

**Remember**: Don't use a colon with the following:

    a. **After a verb of being** (am, is, was, were, are, shall be, will be, could be, should be, should have been, etc.)

**The biggest city in New York is: New York City.** (WRONG)

    b. **After a preposition** (of, with, to, in, out, by, from, etc.)

**This book is by: Alice Munro.** (WRONG)

The exceptions come with lists that run down the page. If you set up a list with a verb of being or a preposition, then you can use the colon.

| The problems ARE: | Please send the magazine TO: |
|---|---|
| 1. | 1. |
| 2. | 2. |
| 3. | 3. |
| 4. | 4. |
| 5. | 5. |
| 6. | 6. |

Not sure about when you should leave out the colon? Experiment. Try leaving it out. If the sentence doesn't sound odd, you probably don't need it; if it sounds odd, you do.

**Please bring me three items from the store milk bread and eggs.**

That definitely sounds odd. But these don't:

**The biggest city in New York is New York City.**
**This book is by Alice Munro.**

Thus:

**Please bring me three items from the store: milk, bread, and eggs.**

## 6. The Apostrophe

Given the missing apostrophes on signs and in print, this may be a losing battle, but so that you get your money's worth, here's the scoop on the apostrophe:

**You still need to use it.**

It's easy to become pretty pessimistic about the future of the apostrophe. You see inconsistent apostrophe use everywhere–text messages to formal letters. Or public signs that shamelessly declare:

**Walgreens**
**Bills Market**
**St. Marys Hospital**
**Mens Shoe's**
**Application's Now Being Accepted at McDonalds**

And those—of course!—should read:

**Walgreen's** (it's Walgreen's drugstore)
**Bill's Market**
**St. Mary's Hospital** (how could those nuns abandon the apostrophe?)
**Men's Shoes**
**Applications Now Being Accepted at McDonald's**

Or emails that sign off with:

**Thats all for now. Hope its not too cold there.**
**(That's all for now. Hope it's not too cold there.)**

---

The apostrophe has two primary uses:

a. To show possession
b. To show something left out

---

**a. To show possession**

In English, to show possession, we add an apostrophe to **all** words except seven—**his, hers, ours, theirs, yours, its** (when you don't mean to contract **it is**), and **whose** (when you don't mean to contract **who is**).

The rule works like this:

**Say a noun, and where the noun stops, add the apostrophe.**

To show that one cat (a singular cat) has fur, say the word:

**cat**

The word ends with **-t**; add the apostrophe + **-s** after the **-t**:

**cat's fur**

To show that two cats (**plural** cats) have fur, say the word:

**cats**

The word ends with **-s**; add the apostrophe after the **-s**:

**cats' fur**

What's the problem? None—except maybe with a few words that don't add **-s** to make their plurals. But you can learn these words in a hurry:

**man = man's**
**men = men's**
**woman = woman's**
**women = women's**
**child = child's; children = children's**
**ox = ox's; oxen = oxen's**
**deer = deer's; deer = deer's** (singular and plural = same)
**sheep = sheep's; sheep = sheep's** (singular and plural = same)

Most other words simply add an **-s** (**-es** or **-ies**). Don't let these confuse you:
**city = city's; cities = cities'**
**baby = baby's; babies = babies'**

### b. To show something left out

If you leave out a letter to contract a verb, fill up the gap with an apostrophe:

**that is = that's; you are = you're**
**I am = I'm; do not = don't**
**does not = doesn't**
**it is = it's**

Now hold up your right hand and swear:

> I promise never, EVER to confuse it's and its.

**It's** is the contraction for **it is**; **its** is the **possessive**\* (and one of the seven exceptions to the apostrophe rule—you don't need the apostrophe).

**It's raining outside. Its color is green.**

## 7. Quotation Marks with Periods, Commas, Your Own Title, and Emphasis

In a few pages, you'll meet several patterns that show how to use quotation marks. The box below points out four problems connected with quotation marks:

1. **Place quotation marks OUTSIDE the period, regardless of how short or long the quotation.**
   She said, "Hello."
   She said, "I'd really like to get together and talk, but my schedule is full."
   I love the round sound of "rotunda."

2. **Place quotation marks OUTSIDE the comma, regardless of how long or short the quotation.**
   "Hello," she said.
   "I'd really like to get together and talk, but my schedule is full," she said.
   I love the round sound of "rotunda," which means "a round hall with a dome."

3. **Don't put quotation marks around the title of something you write.** (And don't underline your own title, either.)

4. **Don't overdo quotation marks.** There's nothing "worse" than a "writer" who thinks they're "cute" and "fills" a sentence with them "every" "other" "breath."

The forty-nine patterns that follow include a number of handbook rules like the one that says you have to put the quotation marks OUTSIDE the period. The rules have no or few exceptions. That's why they're rules.

## IS THAT ALL?

Most of the time, you won't need much more punctuation than we've looked at in Key 6. But in case you do, keep the following handy for reference:

## FORTY-NINE BASIC PUNCTUATION PATTERNS

### The Apostrophe

1. **Use an apostrophe to show possession.**

    Bill's book
    everybody's answer
    the men's tires
    the man's tires
    the woman's tires
    the women's tires
    the hostess's plans; the hostesses' plans
    Mrs. Phillips' answer (if adding an extra "s" makes theword hard to pronounce, add only the apostrophe)
    Athens' tourist attractions
    for goodness' sake
    Bob Smith's house; the Smiths' house
    Tom and Bill's book (the one book belongs to both Tom and Bill)
    Tom's and Bill's books (each owns a book)

**Warning: Don't use the apostrophe with seven pronouns: YOURS, HIS, HERS, OURS, THEIRS, ITS, and WHOSE.**

   This book is yours; the car is his; the book is ours. Its color is green. (BUT: It's raining outside.)

2. **Use the apostrophe to show something left out.**

    shouldn't = should not
    they're = they are
    the class of '51 = the class of 1951

3. Use the apostrophe to show the plural for letters, numbers, symbols, and numbers used as words.

   Mind your P's and Q's.
   The A's won the pennant.
   He crosses his 7's.
   I saw +'s and -'s in the grade book.
   He often talks of the 1960's. (But it's better to write the **1960s**; leave out plural apostrophes if there's no danger of a misreading.)

**Warning: Don't forget that the ONLY plurals formed with the apostrophes are letters, numbers, symbols, and numbers used as words.**

In other words, don't write a goofy illiteracy like:

**Mens Shoe's**

## Quotation Marks

4. Use double quotation marks (" ") to set off direct quotations.
   Harvey wrote: "It's good to travel in Wyoming. The land is beautiful."

5. Use single quotation marks (' ') to set off a quotation inside a quotation.
   Lou wrote: "My brother says 'hello' to you."

6. Put quotation marks around titles of short stories, short plays, short poems, and songs; articles in newspapers, magazines, and journals, book chapters; and episodes of TV shows.
   I read an article called "Miracle Cure for Cancer" in *Reader's Digest*.

But:

**Italicize titles of books, long plays, long poems, newspapers, magazines, journals, movies, TV shows, and CDs.**

I read the novel *War and Peace*. (I read the novel War and Peace.)

Italics = underlining. Underline if you're writing in longhand.

7. **Use either quotation marks or italics (= underlining) to set off a special word.**

    We often use the word "really."
    We often use the word *really*. (We often use the word really.)

## The Comma

8. **Use the comma to separate three or more items in a series; last comma = optional.**

    Cary Grant was tall, dark(,) and handsome.

9. **Use the comma before FOR, AND, NOR, BUT, OR, YET, SO to join two sentences.**

    The man came into town, for his wife wanted some groceries.
    The man came into town, and the dog barked at him.
    The man came into town, but nobody paid any attention.

10. **Don't use a comma before the second part of a compound verb (which means only ONE subject but TWO verbs).**

    The man LIKES to jump and LIKES to run. (two "likes" = compound verb)
        NOT
    The man likes to jump, and likes to run.

11. **Use a comma after an introductory word or phrase at the start of a sentence.**

    Nevertheless, I think you're right about that.
        NOT
    Nevertheless I think you're right about that.

12. **Use commas to set off a nonessential fragment.**

    Dr. Smith, WHO IS AN EXCELLENT TEACHER, is also a good doctor.
        NOT
    Dr. Smith WHO IS AN EXCELLENT TEACHER is also a good doctor.

13. **Use a comma to separate items in dates and addresses.**

    December 7, 1941, is an important date.
           NOT
    December 7, 1941 is an important date.

    He lives at 221 South Maple Street, Lamoni, Iowa 50140.
           NOT
    He lives at 221 South Maple Street, Lamoni, Iowa, 50140.

## The Colon

14. **Use a colon to start a formal letter.**

    Dear Dr. Smith:

15. **Use a colon to start a series.**

    I visited four cities: New York, Chicago, San Francisco, and Austin.

16. **Use a colon to start a famous quotation.**

    Shakespeare said: "To be or not to be."

17. **Use a colon in time references, scriptural references, and explanations/elaborations.**

    3:47 p.m., Luke 4:12
    Angela was proud of her mother: CEO of a major company.

18. **Ordinarily, do not use a colon after a VERB OF BEING (am, are, is, were, was, will be, shall be, etc.) or after a PREPOSITION.**

    WRONG: Her favorite subjects are: math and English.
    RIGHT: Her favorite subjects are math and English.
    WRONG: I want to major in: English and math.
    RIGHT: I want to major in English and math.

## The Semicolon

19. **Use the semicolon to separate related sentences.**

    I bought a car; it's an old VW.
    There is a dog; listen to it bark.
    My daughter was born in San Francisco; my son was born in Madison.

20. **Use a semicolon in front of a transition if there's a sentence on either side of it. (See the chart on page 37.)**

   I went to Paris; consequently, I tried out my French.
   Mary's father is a doctor; nevertheless, he no longer practices.

## Capitalization

21. **Capitalize the first word of a sentence and the first word of a sentence (but not a fragment) after a colon.**

   Here's the book.
   Please bring me three items from the store: You should buy milk, bread, and eggs.
   Please bring me three items from the store: milk, bread, and eggs.

22. **Capitalize the pronoun "I" and the interjection "Oh!"**

   Martha and I simultaneously exclaimed "Oh!" when the phone rang.

23. **Capitalize proper nouns and adjectives (many come from foreign countries and ethnic groups).**

   October
   the House of Representatives
   the Dark Ages
   French horn
   the English horn
   Chinese food
   Senator Ted Kennedy
   Harvard University
   Saturday
   the White House
   Fifth Avenue
   an African-American woman
   Chicano short stories

24. **Capitalize compass directions when they refer to a part of the world or a region of the country.**

   the Near East
   North Africa
   the South
   He moved back East.

**But remember:** We headed south to North Carolina. (Don't capitalize "south" because it isn't a specific region, unlike the South—the southern United States.)

## The Question Mark

25. **Use a question mark after a DIRECT question.**

    Where are you going?
    What does this mean?

26. **Don't use a question mark after an INDIRECT question (which means that the question does not directly address its audience).**

    Betsy wanted to know if she was going.
    LaVerne asked Lola Mae if she wanted to come with him.

27. **If there's a direct question within a sentence, put the question mark INSIDE the quotation marks.**

    WRONG: The boss asked, "Are you asking for time off"?
    RIGHT: The boss asked, "Are you asking for time off?"

28. **Use a question mark after questions within a sentence, but don't capitalize the first word of each question because the questions are part of one sentence.**

    Can you tell me what the fare is? when the flight leaves? what gate I should show up at? what stops it makes?

29. **Put the question mark INSIDE the quotation marks when it applies only to the quoted matter; OUTSIDE when it applies to whole sentences.**

    John asked, "Where's my brother?" (Question mark applies only to what John asks.)
    Do you know if John asked where his brother is? (Question mark applies to whole sentence.)
    Juanita asked, "What is truth?" (Applies only to quoted matter.)
    What is the meaning of the term "half truth"? (Applies to whole sentence.)

## The Exclamation Point

30. **Don't overuse the exclamation point. Don't stick it in at every chance.**

    WRONG: Oh! Come on! Do you really mean that?!
    RIGHT: Oh, come on! Do you really mean that?

31. **Use the exclamation point after an interjection or emphatic statement.**

    You definitely may not go alone!
    Thief! Murderer!
    Look out—oh damn!—here comes my brother for his money.

32. **Don't use more than one exclamation point.**

    WRONG: Oh, no!!!
    RIGHT: Oh, no!

33. **Put the exclamation mark INSIDE the quotation marks when it applies only to the quoted matter; OUTSIDE when it applies to the whole sentence.**

    They chanted, "Four more years! Four more years!"
      (Applies only to quoted matter.)
    Stop whistling "Dixie"!
      (The whole sentence, not just the song title, is an exclamation; the exclamation point applies to the whole sentence.)

## The Period

34. **Use a period after abbreviations unless they're acronyms (that is, a word formed from the first letters or syllables of words).**

    Mr.      Ph.D.
    Mrs.     Sept.
    Dr.      Ms.

**But not:** NATO (North Atlantic Treaty Organization = **acronym**)

35. **Use a period at the end of a sentence.**

    The dog barks.

36. **Use three periods in a row (ellipsis) to show something has been left out of quoted material. Use a fourth period to show the end of a sentence.**

   The president said: "We must all try to help the poor . . . by giving our share."
   The governor promised to "establish a task force, crack down on welfare abuse, and send the guilty to jail. . . . Then we will have a state to be proud of," he added.

## The Hyphen

37. **Hyphenate spelled-out numbers from twenty-one through ninety-nine and with spelled-out fractions.**

   forty-four
   thirty-third anniversary
   one-half inch
   two-thirds of the assembly

38. **Hyphenate certain family relationships.**

   son-in-law BUT stepson
   great-grandmother BUT grandmother
   great-aunt BUT second cousin

39. **Hyphenate to connect compound words with all-, ex-, self-, and -elect.**

   all-American
   all-purpose
   ex-wife
   self-contained
   president-elect

40. **Hyphenate to connect compound modifiers before the noun they modify or words that act as a unit. But DO NOT hyphenate when three or more modifiers follow the verb.**

   up-to-date styles
   eighteenth-century novel
   how-to-do-it book
   secretary-general
   Johnny-come-lately
      BUT: Those styles are up to date.
         The book shows how to do it.

BUT: She is the secretary-general.
(Both words form a new unit and need the hyphen.)

41. **DO NOT hyphenate compound modifiers if they come after the <u>verb</u>.**

    the ever-changing weather BUT the weather <u>is</u> ever changing
    a well-known fact BUT the fact <u>was</u> well known

42. **DO NOT hyphenate if the first word of the compound modifier is an adverb ending in -ly. However, DO hyphenate an adjective ending in -ly in compound modifiers.**

    a frequently quoted book (**adverb**)
    our rapidly dwindling oil supplies (**adverb**)
     BUT: a friendly-appearing dog (**adjective**)
     BUT: a kindly-looking doctor (**adjective**)

43. **Hyphenate between a prefix and a capitalized root word.**

    anti-Communist
    post-Civil War
    trans-Siberian
    non-American
    un-American

**But don't hyphenate:**

nonstop, nonstick, nonviolence and other *non* words that don't precede a proper noun (like **American** and **German**—thus: **non-American** and **non-German**).

44. **Hyphenate between certain\* prefixes and root words to separate vowels.**

    semi-antique
    anti-inflammatory
     BUT: semiannual
     BUT: antiimperialism

*See a recent dictionary to sort out these puzzles.

45. **Hyphenate verbs that might be misconstrued.**

>    re-create (meaning "create anew")
>    			vs.
>    recreate (meaning "refresh")
>
>    re-cover (meaning "cover again")
>    			vs.
>    recover (meaning "regain")

46. **Hyphenate when two or more compound adjectives share a common word and modify the same noun; here the hyphen replaces the common word every time but the last.**

>    The newsletter printed the names of the first- and second-place winners.
>    Many tutors prefer two-, three-, and four-hour sessions with their students.

47. **Hyphenate a word consisting of a letter and another word.**
>    A-OK
>    U-boat
>    H-bomb
>    X-ray

## Parentheses and Brackets

48. **Use parentheses to enclose a parenthetical or nonessential remark.**

>    The snow had blanketed the driveway (a blizzard had blown in over the night), but we managed to back the car out.

**Note:** Though the parentheses enclose a complete sentence, the enclosed sentence does not begin with a capital letter, and there is no period within the parentheses.

**But:** When an enclosed sentence stands completely separate from another sentence, start the enclosed sentence with a capital letter and place the period INSIDE the final parenthesis:

>    The snow blanketed the driveway. (A blizzard had blown in over the night.)

**49.** **Use brackets to enclose unquoted material in a direct quotation and to enclose the Latin word *sic* (which you also italicize) to show an error in the original quotation.**

"The defendant [Lloyd Turner] was acquitted of burglary." Here the name of the defendant, which was not in the original quotation, clarifies the reference—you learn who the defendant is.

"We reached our destanation [*sic*] after many wrong detours." Here you want to show that the misspelled word (should be "destination" instead of "destanation") was in the original quotation.

# Key 7

# The Basics of Revision

- How Should I Revise?
- Nineteen Sentence-Editing Suggestions
- What Usually Goes Wrong?
- Forty-Four Editing Reminders
- How To Revise a Problem Manuscript: A Case Study
- How Should I Proofread?
- Nineteen Proofreading Strategies

## HOW SHOULD I REVISE?

Mysteriously, other than professionals, most writers don't really revise.

That is, serious, top-to-bottom revision of both content and language. Some writers even claim that revision somehow damages the truth and spontaneity of what they produce. They sincerely believe that minor tinkering—like inserting an apostrophe—takes care of "revision." They believe that the first draft, with only slight modification, is ready to go—to the supervisor, professor, or big New York publishing house.

Unfortunately, too many teachers hand back essays and exams marked with red and never ask for a revision—a revision that follows up on those red marks and asks for a clearer statement of the Big Picture and reworked Main Sub-points and individual sentences.

If there's no revision, why bother to mark up the writing at all?

Such casual disregard for revision teaches the bad lesson that revisions don't really matter. And thus we journey through our schooling, jobs, and life with one more piece of misinformation about how to write.

Revision isn't just a final cleaning up of the text, something you do if you have the time. It's the **second half** of the writing process.

> - First half: Writing the first draft
> - Second half: Revising

Repeat the following as your mantra:

> **I'm not done till I revise.**
> **I'm not done till I revise.**
> **I'm not done till I revise.**

Revision usually takes these three stages:

---

### STAGE ONE—Checking for Content

1. Read over the first draft. **Do not correct your grammar or punctuation.** Just read for the Big Picture.
2. When you're done, write down the Big Picture. If you can't find it, rewrite until you can jot it on a three-by-five card.
3. Number each paragraph.
4. Write down the Big Picture for each paragraph. Each paragraph should have a topic-sentence Big Picture; if it doesn't, rewrite until it does.
5. Put all the apples with apples; all the oranges with oranges.
6. Make sure the Setup sets up the material, the Development develops, and the Wrap-up wraps up. If you don't need a Wrap-up, get rid of it.
7. Go back to the computer and fix the content problems.
8. Print out.
9. Read over one more time for content. If it hangs together, go to Stage Two.

---

### STAGE TWO—Checking for Style

1. Read over the language: sentences, word use, grammar, and punctuation. (See the **Nineteen Sentence-Editing Suggestions**, below.)
2. Check all headings, numbered listings, etc. (everything that isn't content and language—all the stuff that packages your material). Are they spaced properly, etc.? Fix problems.
3. Run computer spelling checks/grammar checks/style checks.
4. Print out.
5. Proofread. This is different from reading for content revision. Now you're checking for mechanical problems, from spacing to missing letters and commas. (See the **Nineteen Proofreading Strategies** at the end of this Key.)

> **STAGE THREE—Double-Checking for Content and Style**
>
> 1. Give your manuscript to three people (although one will do). Ask them to:
>    - Write down the Big Picture
>    - Write down the Main Sub-points
>    - Put a check beside any problem
> 2. If their comments seem valid (if all three fumble identifying the Big Picture or check the same paragraph, you've got a problem), revise again, following Stages One, Two, and Three.
> 3. At some point, pull the plug, trust yourself, and hand in or send off the manuscript. During Stage Two, when you're working over the sentences and language, apply the **Nineteen Sentence-Editing Suggestions**.

## NINETEEN SENTENCE-EDITING SUGGESTIONS

1. Avoid prepositions:

   The man **With the hat From the store By the road Across the river Near the house With shutters** is my brother.

2. Avoid these weak verbs:

   **am, are, is, was, were, be, been, being, should have been**, etc.

3. Use strong action verbs. (See the list of **Strong Verbs**, pages 111-112.)

4. Don't use bad jargon (if you can help it). (See **A Vocabulary of Bad Jargon**, pages 83-85.)

5. Don't use too many nouns stacked up next to each other:

   **The mechanics illustration clinic was held at the factory self-improvement lounge.**

6. Don't repeat unimportant words too often.

7. But don't go out of your way to find synonyms (especially odd ones) for a repeated word.

**THE BASICS OF REVISION**

8. Avoid slang, though occasional slang will work if you use general words ("okay," "cool," "buns") rather than particular and dated words ("bee's knees," "swell," "neat," "groovy," "out of sight," "rad," "ice"), which have a short shelf life (and thus become incomprehensible).

9. Don't start every sentence with a subject-verb:

   **BARB HIT the ball.**

10. Avoid passives:

    Write **I hit the ball** instead of **The ball was hit by me** or **The ball was hit**.

11. Don't repeat word patterns (starting every sentence the same way; putting the same pattern in every middle, etc.).

12. Don't make every sentence the same length.

13. Avoid long sentences that take up a whole paragraph.

14. Combine too many short sentences into longer sentences; break too many long sentences into short sentences.

15. Don't write one long paragraph. Break up long paragraphs at sub-points.

16. Don't be cute:

    **No cute words, quotation marks around "cute" words, or multiple exclamation marks.**

17. Don't beat around the bush. Say what you mean plainly and directly.

18. Obey every rule of grammar and punctuation unless you have good reason for breaking it.

19. Don't write any sentence you don't understand:

    **You can't expect your reader to figure it out for you.**

## What Usually Goes Wrong?

Anybody who's edited for a few years probably needs a rubber stamp to mark problems that just won't go away. You see them from page to page, manuscript to manuscript, and after a while, most editors can predict what will go wrong:

> **What's the Big Picture?**
> *It's* **or** *its*?
> *Than* **or** *then*?
> *Affect* **or** *effect*?
> **The quotations go OUTSIDE the comma and period!**
> **Italicize book titles!**
> **Vague Wrap-up!**

And so on. Below are forty-four problems that just won't go away. They're probably the most common editing errors that we make—problems with content and paragraphs, sentences, words, grammar, and punctuation. In other words, they summarize problems examined in this book, from Key 1 through Key 6.

Memorizing all forty-four will change your life.

## Forty-Four Editing Reminders

### Content and Paragraphs

1. Don't write long introductions: In the first paragraph, set up the Big Picture.
2. In the Setup, briefly set up your Main Sub-points (Main Sub-points 1, 2, 3, etc.).
3. In the Development, develop your ideas in the order set up in the Setup (Main Sub-point 1, 2, 3, etc.).
4. Don't write long Wrap-ups that exactly repeat your Setup: Finish up in new words, in as few words as possible.
5. In formal writing, don't write too many one- or two-sentence paragraphs.
6. Don't call your essay by the title of what you're writing about—don't call it *Hamlet* if you're writing about *Hamlet*.
7. Make your title refer to your Big Picture: An Analysis of Character Types in *Hamlet*.

## Sentences

8. Keep your sentences parallel:

    WRONG: I like to run, to jump, and swimming is one of my favorite activities.
    RIGHT: I like to run, to jump, and to swim.

## Words

9. Remember the difference between **than** and **then**:

    **Than** = the comparison; **then** = next
    She's older than I am.
    Then he decided to visit his brother.

10. Remember the difference between **affect** and **effect**:

    **Affect** is usually the verb. **Effect** is usually the noun.
    **Affect** = change. **Effect** = result.
    WRONG: How does this effect you?
    RIGHT: How does this affect [change] you?
    WRONG: What is the affect?
    RIGHT: What is the effect [result]?
    WRONG: How does the affect effect you?
    RIGHT: How does this effect affect you?

11. Remember the difference between **to** and **too**:

    **To** = showing location; to do something
    I'm going to the store.
    I'm going to work hard.

    **Too** = also; in addition; a lot of something
    I want to do that, too.
    It was too hot to go to town.

12. Remember the difference between **it's** and **its**:

    **It's** = It is (It's raining) or It has (It's been raining).
    **Its** = the possessive (Its color is green).

13. Remember the differences among **there/their/they're**:

19. If the fragment at the end of the sentence DOES NOT complete the meaning, put a comma in front of it:

    **S,F (Sentence, Fragment)**
    I washed the dishes, WHICH IS ALWAYS BORING.
    You washed the dishes, DIDN'T YOU? (question at end)

20. If you connect two sentences by a conjunction, put a comma in front of the conjunction (**FANBOYS: for, and, nor, but, or, yet, so**):

    **S,CONJ S (Sentence, Conjunction Sentence)**
    I ate supper, AND I washed the dishes.

21. If you don't have a complete sentence after the conjunction, don't put a comma in front of the conjunction:

    I ate supper AND washed the dishes.

22. If you connect two sentences with a transition, put a period or semicolon in front of it and a comma after (remember that **hence, next, now, then,** and **thus** don't need commas):

    **S./;TRANS,S (Sentence./; Transition, Sentence)**
    I ate supper. CONSEQUENTLY, I washed the dishes.
    I ate supper; CONSEQUENTLY, I washed the dishes.

23. To avoid a run-on, put a period or semicolon (but never a comma) between two sentences:

    **S./;S (Sentence./; Sentence)**
    I ate supper. I washed the dishes.
    I ate supper; I washed the dishes.

24. Don't put commas around a fragment if the sentence subject isn't identified:

    **S-F-S (Sentence-Fragment-Sentence)**
    The man WHO WASHED THE DISHES ate supper with me.

    Here the subject, **The man,** is not identified with a name like Bob, so you don't use commas.

25. Put commas around a fragment if the sentence subject is identified:

    **S-,F,-S (Sentence-,Fragment,-Sentence)**
    **Bob,** WHO WASHED THE DISHES, **ate supper with me.**

Here the boldfaced part is the basic sentence—**Bob ate supper with me**. The capitalized part is the fragment—WHO WASHED THE DISHES.

Because the subject has a name, **Bob**, you use commas.

26. Don't write fragments when you should write sentences:

    I washed the dishes. WHICH IS REALLY BORING.

    Fix this one by connecting the fragment to the sentence with a comma:

    **I washed the dishes, which is really boring.**

    I went to the movies. BECAUSE I LIKE WILL FERRELL.

    Again, connect the fragment to the sentence, but this time don't use a comma because the fragment completes the meaning:

    **I went to the movies because I like Will Ferrell.**

But:

    I went to the movies. ALTHOUGH MY SISTER DIDN'T GO.

    This time you do need a comma; the fragment adds tacked-on information that doesn't complete the meaning:

    **I went to the movies, although my sister didn't go.**

27. Put quotation marks around titles of short stories, short plays, and short poems; articles in newspapers, magazines, and journals; book chapters; episodes of TV shows; and songs.

    > I like Hemingway's "The Three-Day Blow."
    > I read "Obama Names Court Nominee" in *The New York Times*.
    > I saw a *60 Minutes* episode called "Welfare Fraud in Chicago."
    > Chapter Three of the book *Writing to Learn* is called "A Liberal Education."

28. Italicize (or underline if you're writing in longhand) titles of books, long plays, long poems, newspapers, magazines, journals, movies, TV shows, and CDs.

29. Don't italicize (or underline) or put quotations around your own title.

THE BASICS OF REVISION

30. Put quotation marks OUTSIDE the period and comma:

    WRONG: I read "The Three-Day Blow".
    RIGHT: I read "The Three-Day Blow."
    WRONG: I read "The Three-Day Blow", which is by Hemingway.
    RIGHT: I read "The Three-Day Blow," which is by Hemingway.

31. Put quotation marks INSIDE the semicolon and colon:

    WRONG: I read "The Three-Day Blow;" it is by Hemingway.
    RIGHT: I read "The Three-Day Blow"; it is by Hemingway.
    WRONG: I read "The Three-Day Blow:" Have you?
    RIGHT: I read "The Three-Day Blow": Have you?

32. Don't put a comma before a title, as in:

    I read Hemingway's, *The Old Man and the Sea*.

Or:

    I read Hemingway's, "The Three-Day Blow."

33. Don't put a comma after a conjunction (FANBOYS: **for, and, nor, but, or, yet, so**) in sentences like these:

    WRONG: But, what I didn't like was the movie.
    RIGHT: But what I didn't like was the movie.
    WRONG: And, I hope that you'll write me a letter.
    RIGHT: And I hope that you'll write me a letter.

34. Don't put a comma after these words (which start fragments)—**although, even though, though, since, while, if, as, because, before,** and **after**—in the following sentence pattern:

    WRONG: Although, I'm glad that you spoke up, you're wrong.
    RIGHT: Although I'm glad that you spoke up, you're wrong.

35. Sentence interrupters: Be sure to put the commas on either side of the fragment inserted into the sentence in situations like these:

    My brother, FRANK, is here.
    My brother, ON THE OTHER HAND, is here.
    Mrs. Smith, MY SECRETARY, is a good typist.
    You, OF COURSE, are a good student.
    One thing I'd like to talk about, IF I HAVE TIME, is sex.

36. Don't put a comma before a verb when there's no other comma in the sentence:

> WRONG: What I really wanted to tell you, WAS I like you.
> RIGHT: What I really wanted to tell you was I like you.
> WRONG: All I can see, IS that gas station up ahead.
> RIGHT: All I can see is that gas station up ahead.

37. Don't put a comma or a colon after **such as** (but do put a comma before it):

> WRONG: I like many books, such as, *War and Peace.*
> RIGHT: I like many books, such as *War and Peace.*
> WRONG: I like many books, such as: *War and Peace.*
> RIGHT: I like many books, such as *War and Peace.*

38. Don't put a colon after a **preposition (to, with, by, in, out, of, under, over,** etc.):

> WRONG: This novel is by: Ernest Hemingway.
> RIGHT: This novel is by Ernest Hemingway.

39. Don't put a colon after verbs of being (**am, is, are, was, were, will be, shall be,** etc.):

> WRONG: The three cities I saw are: Paris, New York, and Chicago.
> RIGHT: The three cities I saw are Paris, New York, and Chicago.

40. Use the apostrophe to show possession or contraction:

> WRONG: Bobs house. Im going to Bobs.
> RIGHT: Bob's house. I'm going to Bob's.
> WRONG: I cant do that. It wont work. Dont do that.
> RIGHT: I can't do that. It won't work. Don't do that.

## Grammar

41. Don't write dangling modifiers. CURE: Put in a subject:

> WRONG: DRIVING DANGEROUSLY, the bus went out of control.
> RIGHT: BECAUSE THE BUS DRIVER WAS DRIVING DANGEROUSLY, the bus went out of control.
> WRONG: DRINKING ORANGE JUICE DAILY, my cold went away.
> RIGHT: SINCE I DRANK ORANGE JUICE DAILY, my cold went away.

WRONG: WHILE EATING LUNCH IN THE CAFETERIA, the computer broke down.
RIGHT: WHILE THE WOMAN WAS EATING LUNCH IN THE CAFETERIA, the computer broke down.

42. Pronoun agreement: Make the pronoun (**he, she, it, their**) agree with the **SUBJECT**:

    WRONG: Each **PERSON** should do **their** work.
    RIGHT: Each **PERSON** should do **his** work.
    RIGHT: Each **PERSON** should do **her** work.
    RIGHT: All **PEOPLE** should do **their** work.
    WRONG: Every **MAN** knows **their** job.
    RIGHT: Every **MAN** knows **his** job.
    RIGHT: All the **MEN** know **their** jobs.
    WRONG: Each **WOMAN** knows **their** job.
    RIGHT: All the **WOMEN** know **their** jobs.

43. Starting a sentence with **There is** or **There's**: If you have a plural subject after these, shift to **There are**:

    WRONG: There's a DESK and COMPUTER in my office. (**two** things in the office)
    RIGHT: There are a desk and computer in my office.

## Tenses

44. Don't jump from **past tense** into **present** or from **present tense** into **past**. Be consistent and stay in the tense you started in.

    WRONG: I saw [PAST] my friend, and he waves [PRESENT].
    RIGHT: I saw my friend [PAST], and he waved [PAST].
    WRONG: I see [PRESENT] my friend, and he waved [PAST].
    RIGHT: I see [PRESENT] my friend, and he waves [PRESENT].

**Remember**: When you write about the arts (fiction, poetry, drama, movies, dance, visiting an art gallery, etc.), stay in present tense. *End*

# How To Revise A Problem Manuscript: A Case Study

We're going to revise a manuscript from the Big Picture down to the sentence and word levels; then do an edit for grammar and punctuation.

This memo comes from, let's say, a state agency; it's mailed to several thousand employees around a large state. The costs for time spent writing the memo, photocopying, and mailing presumably add up to a considerable sum.

---

TO: SWPS Customers
FROM: Earl Dale Diehl, SWPS Business Manager
SUBJECT: SWPS Rate Reduction
DATE: October 12, 2010

Notification of substantial rate reductions in the Statewide Phone System rates which took affect September 22, 2010 were recently distributed to all current user's of SWPS. Affective cost control measures in the operation of the Network and increased statewide calling volume are the primary reasons for the savings that you will experience.

In order to aid your agency or department in assessing the positive impact that this will have on your Fiscal Year 9 budget a summary of August SWPS usage at the New Rates, is enclosed. This summary can be compared to the actual August bill that was calculated using the Old Rates.

Although, the impact of the reduction results in a savings of 28.6% for the entire SWPS user group pool the savings for individual SWPS user's will vary depending on: the pattern of SWPS calls.

Rate Summary information giving a breakdown of SWPS calls by Zone and Time of Day will become a permanent addition to the Summarized Usage Report which is produced with the bill each month, this information should be helpful in future months to more fully understand the impact of the rate reduction.

Please pass this memo on to your Budget, Fiscal, and Telecommunications staff.

If you have any questions please call me at 111-111-1111.

---

What's the Big Picture? Hard to say. So that's where we have to start. A further problem is determining the **audience** of the memo. Should the memo go out blindly to all SWPS customers? Or only to those responsible for paying the office bills?

## STEP ONE
## What Does It Say?

To arrive at the Big Picture, we need to "translate" each paragraph—a paragraph-by-paragraph boiled-down version of the original (whose bad jargon makes translation nearly impossible).

**Paragraph One:**
1. News about reduced SWPS rates that went into effect on September 22, 2010, was sent to all SWPS users.
2. Two reasons for savings: cost control; increased calling volume.

**Paragraph Two:**
3. A summary of August SWPS calls at the new rates is enclosed.
4. You can see how money will be saved by comparing the August bill calculated at the old rates.

**Paragraph Three:**
5. Overall, users as a group will save 28.6%; savings for individual users will vary according to call patterns.

**Paragraph Four:**
6. From now on, a rate summary that breaks calls down by zone and time of day will be attached to the use report that's part of the monthly bill.
7. You can use this summary to "more fully understand the impact of the rate reduction" (plan your budget -?-).

**Paragraph Five:**
8. Pass the memo on.

**Paragraph Six:**
9. Call me if you have questions. (And that's one of the ironies of the memo: Who won't be calling after wading through this unfocused gobbledygook?)

**Thus:**

- What's the main reason to write this memo?

**Big Picture:**

- To tell readers to use the new SWPS rates to calculate their next budget.

## STEP TWO
## What Content Order Makes Sense?

Given the Big Picture, the order should probably be:

1. **Memo Subject Line**: SWPS Rate Reduction and Fiscal Year 9 Budget
2. **Paragraph One**: Big Picture: Use the new SWPS rates to calculate budgets.
3. **Paragraph Two**: The new rate reduction will have an impact on the next budget. You can see the difference the reduction will make by comparing old and new rates for last August's phone bill. The group reduction is 28.6%; savings for individual users will vary according to calling patterns. The reductions have resulted from:

    (a) cost control

    (b) increased calling volume

4. **Paragraph Three**: In the future, the bill will include a breakdown of SWPS calls by zone and time of day; this breakdown will help in figuring the budget.
5. **Paragraph Four**: Pass the memo on. Call me.

## STEP THREE
### The Revision

TO: Accounts Payable Managers
FROM: Earl Dale Diehl, Statewide Phone System Business Manager
SUBJECT: SWPS Rate Reduction and Fiscal Year 9 Budget
DATE: October 12, 2010

As of this date you must use a new set of rates to figure the monthly SWPS phone bill for your office.

On September 22, 2010, substantial reductions in Statewide Phone System rates, went into affect. Although, group savings for SWPS user's are 28.6% savings for individual user's will vary depending on: the calling pattern.

To help determine the impact the new rates will have on your Fiscal Year 9 budget we're enclosing a summary of the August bill calculated at both the old and new rates, in the future you'll notice that each month your bill will break down SWPS calls by zone and time of day, this information will help in planning your budget.

If you have questions call me at: 111-111-1111.

## STEP THREE, Continued
### The Final Revision (Corrected for Style—Punctuation, Grammar, Etc.)

TO: Accounts Payable Managers
FROM: Earl Dale Diehl, Statewide Phone System Business Manager
SUBJECT: SWPS Rate Reduction and Fiscal Year 9 Budget
DATE: October 12, 2010

As of this date, you must use a new set of rates to figure the monthly SWPS phone bill for your office.

On September 22, 2010, substantial reductions in Statewide Phone System rates went into effect. Although group savings for SWPS users is 28.6%, savings for individual users will vary, depending on the calling pattern.

To help determine the impact the new rates will have on your Fiscal Year 9 budget, we're enclosing a summary of the August bill calculated at both the old and new rates. In the future, you'll notice that each month your bill will break down SWPS calls by zone and time of day. This information will help in planning your budget.

If you have questions, call me at 111-111-1111.

**STEP FOUR**
**What Can You Learn from This Revision?**

1. Clearly state the Big Picture; don't imply it.

2. State the Big Picture as early as possible in the Setup (paragraph one); don't delay it.

3. Use the Development (paragraphs two and three) to develop the Main Sub-points.

4. Keep the Wrap-up short.

5. Don't forget the reader:
    a. Keep the Big Picture up front.
    b. Use short paragraphs (with 5-6 sentences per paragraph as the limit).
    c. Don't write all short, all medium, or all long sentences; use a mixture (averaging 15-20 words for your medium sentence).
    d. Keep the language free of bad jargon, wordiness, and sexism.
    e. Keep the punctuation and grammar free of problems.

6. If necessary, rewrite each paragraph and sentence.

# How Should I Proofread?

Carefully.

Several times. The key to effective proofreading is to read in stages:

**Stage One: Read the body** (all the text except the heads, titles, page numbers, etc.).

**Stage Two: Read everything EXCEPT the body** (everything you didn't read in Stage One).

Within both stages, try the following:

## NINETEEN PROOFREADING STRATEGIES

1. If possible, ask a colleague to proofread your manuscript. (But he or she must know the rules.)
2. If you work with more than one proofreader, ask them to initial each page read to cut down errors.
3. Keep a log of problems. Problems from one project tend to show up on a later, similar project.
4. Keep a log of names, special spellings, company word use, etc.
5. Lots of numbers? Ask your colleague to read those out loud to you as you follow along from the original.
6. Use one of these techniques to keep your concentration:
    a. With hard copy, use a ruler to move from line to line. Don't worry about sentences; worry about **lines**.
    b. At the computer screen, start at the bottom and scroll up, **line by line by line**.
    c. Read **out loud**.
7. Check titles, heads, etc., against the table of contents.
8. Check page numbers against the table of contents and index (if there is one).
9. If you're interrupted or stop to rest, mark your place.
10. If you find a mistake, look for mistakes nearby:

    **Mistakes tend to cluster in the same location.**

11. Check all sequential matter:
    a. Page numbers
    b. Numbered heads
    c. Numbered tables, charts, and graphs
12. If you write "see page 12," make sure that page 12 presents the referenced material.

13. Check all mechanics that come in pairs: commas, parentheses, brackets, quotation marks, and dashes. It's easy to lose one half a pair.

14. If you have columns of figures, make sure they line up.

15. If you have numbered items, make sure they line up.

16. If you change the page spacing, make sure to wrap it properly from one page to the next (that is, that the text goes all the way to the bottom of the page).

17. If you change the page spacing, make sure that one paragraph hasn't been sucked into another: Check that you've indented each new paragraph. Make sure that the indents remain at the same tab.

18. Don't listen to music or watch TV when you proofread.

19. If you're proofing at the computer screen, you still must print up hard copy to proofread: You're not finished until you've examined the print on the page.

*

To wrap up this Key—and this book—one last reminder: You have a reader out there who trusts that you'll bring your best to the page. Honor that trust. Never forget what we owe the reader.

# EDITING EXERCISES

**Key 1**  209
    Exercise 1—Finding the Big Picture  209
    Exercise 1—Sample Revision  210

**Key 2**  211
    Exercise 2—Revising Paragraphs  211

**Key 3**  213
    Exercise 3—Misplaced and Dangling Modifiers  213
    Exercise 4—Effective Sentences  215
    Exercise 5—Wordy Sentences  217

**Key 4**  219
    Exercise 6—Redundancy  219

**Key 5**  221
    Exercise 7—Editing Test  221

**Key 6**  225
    Exercise 8—Run-on Sentences  225
    Exercise 9—Essential and Nonessential Fragments  227
    Exercise 10—Colons  229
    Exercise 11—Apostrophes  231
    Exercise 12—Dictation  233
    Exercise 12—Dictation Answers  237

**Key 7**  241
    Exercise 13—The Forty-Four Reminders Quiz  241
    Exercise 14—Final Revision  249

# Key 1: Exercise 1—Finding the Big Picture

**Revise this letter for a clarified Big Picture. Don't be afraid to strip it down; the streamlined revision follows on the next page.**

## A Response Letter with Information and Directions (and a Few Problems . . .)

---

January 3, 2010

R.J. Smith
Smith and Associates
1212 Elm Street
Madison, WI 53705


Dear Mr. Smith:

On the issues regarding your professional practice, we recently discussed with your receptionist the information that we will automatically require each month to update your financial records and prepare the necessary tax returns. The information will include the canceled checks from both checking accounts, a summary of charges and receipts for both offices and the canceled checks and bank statement from your bank.

We would also like to see a copy of last year's personal federal and state income tax returns.

We will notify you as soon as possible regarding our next scheduled visit to your office.

Thank you again for the trust you have placed in us by allowing us to assist you with your professional practice and your personal financial affairs. We will look forward to our next meeting.

Very truly yours,


Harrison M. L. Jones, CPA
Jones Enterprises

# Key 1: Exercise 1—Sample Revision

This revision gives a bare-bones treatment to the material. You may wish, for example, to expand the last sentence so that it's not so blunt. But this draft serves as a good model of an efficiently introduced and supported Big Picture.

## Revision of the Response Letter

January 3, 2010

R.J. Smith
Smith and Associates
1212 Elm Street
Madison, WI 53705

Dear Mr. Smith:

Each month we need the following to update your financial records and prepare your tax returns:

1. Canceled checks from both accounts

2. Bank statements

3. Charges and receipts for both offices

We also need last year's personal federal and state income tax returns.

We will notify you about our next visit.

Sincerely,


Harrison M. L. Jones, CPA
Jones Enterprises

# Key 2: Exercise 2—Revising Paragraphs

**Both paragraphs present many editing problems. First work on the sense of the passage; then clean up the language.**

"Adoption Should Not Be Base On Race!"

Many politicians are is asking the federal government to increase the number of children in foster care for adoption over the next six years, the House of representatives have created a tax credit adoption program that will give 5,000 dollars to the family that is adopting kids, it also makes it easier to adopt from other races. In the foster care program there are 450,000 children that are waiting to be adapted by some family. Of the 440,000 children in foster care, 100,000 have no parents to go back to so they must be put in permanent homes. Being adopted could have happen to anybody no matter who you are; like Tommy Davidson who was a great comedian on the show, "In Living Color. Tommy was adopted by Barbara Davidson in 1963. She was not what you expect; black, she was white. Barbara got Tommy when he was only 18 months old, the reason she got Tommy was because her mother was in danger and Tommy was always getting sick. He was raised with two other kids, one was a girl the same age as Tommy and another boy who was a gay activist who died of AIDS. Barbara wanted him to grow up in an integrated place, but could not get him a way from racism. Tommy talks about how both sides of the world hated him. In the case where he was hanging with some black people, when they saw his sister, would look at him differently. In another case where he was with some white people, they would also start looking at him differently. On May 1 the House and Means Committee approved a new bill that will make adoption easer. It was voted by voice on the Floor in May 6. There are 49% of minorities that are in the 480,000-500,000 children in foster, this new bill is suppose to stop the denying of adaptation by their race or color of the parent or children in which the government is giving money to that program (Alissa J. Rubin. p. 1226)

Kristin was born in 1992 from a mother part Native American and part white, her father was black. When she was only six, her mother gave birth. And then putting Kristin up for adoption. Judy and Nicholas were looking to adopt a girl. Kristin is proud of her background, happy to have such a great family, that has told her the truth from the beginning that she was not their biological daughter. In other cases like this case in Texas, two kids in foster care were going to be adopted by the foster care parents and were denied. When this happened they filed a law suit against the agency for discrimination against their race. Of the 100,000 children 50% of them are black. (Ronnie Polaneczky p. 137-107).

# Key 3: Exercise 3—Misplaced and Dangling Modifiers

**Rewrite to fix the modifier problem:**

**Misplaced**: Loping across the path, we saw two moose.
**Revised**: We saw two moose loping across the path.
**Dangling**: At the age of five, my family moved to Iowa.
**Revised**: When I was five, my family moved to Iowa.

1. Creeping across the dusty road, I saw a bull snake.

2. Looking over his new clothes, the blue suit and white shirt pleased him the most.

3. Staying up all night, the project for Senator Dix was finished by hearing time.

4. After asking three or four people, the right house was finally located.

5. After washing the window, my dog wanted to go for a walk.

6. Leaning against the barn, Harry saw the shotgun.

7. Needing a bath, I chased the dog into the basement.

8. After playing pool with Uncle Jack, my taxes didn't get mailed on the 15th.

9. I saw that the serial murderer had been captured on my new TV.

10. I bought a motorcycle from a Hell's Angel with a leak somewhere.

11. Happily cavorting in the garden, we watched the rabbits.

12. Except when pickled, I don't care for hot peppers.

13. She put the cheese into the garbage that she hadn't yet had time to eat.

14. When visiting the museum, the painting by Picasso was stolen and the police alerted.

15. The sheriff warned the man not to give a firearm to his friend that was loaded.

# Key 3: Exercise 4—Effective Sentences

**Read out loud and listen carefully: Choose the best sentence. Problems: Dangling and misplaced modifiers, verb tense consistency, pronoun agreement and vague pronoun reference, and parallel sentence parts. Be able to defend your choice.**

1a. Planning to visit the Grand Canyon, maps came that Tom Drake ordered from the travel association.

1b. Maps came from the travel association that Tom Drake ordered, planning to visit the Grand Canyon.

1c. Planning to visit the Grand Canyon, Tom Drake ordered maps from the travel association.


2a. The Frankenstein monster quickly got to his feet but staggering as he learned to navigate the laboratory.

2b. The Frankenstein monster quickly got to his feet but staggered as he learned to navigate the laboratory.

2c. The Frankenstein monster learned to navigate the laboratory but staggering as he quickly got to his feet.


3a. Hollywood used to shoot many cheap westerns in less than a week, and this surprises many of us.

3b. Many cheap westerns were shot by Hollywood in less than a week, and they surprise many of us.

3c. Hollywood used to shoot many cheap westerns in less than a week, and this speed surprises many of us.


4a. Of course, some cats grew as big as a stuffed footstool and weighed as much as a dog.

4b. Of course, some cats grew as big as a stuffed footstool, weighing as much as a dog.

4c. Of course, some cats, having a dog's weight, grew as big as a stuffed footstool.

5a. During the classical period, many composers had similar practices that musicologists group with Mozart.
5b. Many composers had similar practices during the classical age that musicologists group with Mozart.
5c. During the classical period, many composers that musicologists group with Mozart had similar practices.

6a. Crying as much as an hour, two boxes of Kleenex were not enough to handle her tears.
6b. Crying as much as an hour, she needed more than two boxes of Kleenex to handle her tears.
6c. Crying as much as an hour, her tears could not be handled by two boxes of Kleenex.

7a. Thus a bird spends most of their life on the lookout for food and other birds.
7b. Thus birds, on the lookout for food and other birds, spend most of their lives.
7c. Thus a bird spends most of its life on the lookout for food and other birds.

**There** = place. I'm going there.
**Their** = possessive. I'm going to their house.
**They're** = contraction. They're going to their house, over there.

14. Don't forget **-d** on the end of **supposed** and **used** and other past tenses:

    WRONG: I'm suppose to go.
    RIGHT: I'm suppose**d** to go.
    WRONG: I use to do that.
    RIGHT: I use**d** to do that.

15. Don't forget **-s** on the end of plural words that end in **-st**:

    WRONG: I saw two psychologist.
    RIGHT: I saw two psychologist**s**.
    WRONG: I read about the early colonist in America.
    RIGHT: I read about the early colonist**s** in America.

16. Don't write the following as one word:

    | WRONG: alot | RIGHT: a lot |
    |---|---|
    | WRONG: eventhough | RIGHT: even though |
    | WRONG: highschool | RIGHT: high school |
    | WRONG: inorder | RIGHT: in order |
    | WRONG: infact | RIGHT: in fact |
    | WRONG; incase | RIGHT: in case |

## Punctuation

17. Don't forget to put a comma after an introductory fragment:

    **F,S (Fragment, Sentence)**
    AFTER I ATE SUPPER, I washed the dishes.

18. If the fragment at the end of a sentence completes the meaning, don't put a comma in front of it:

    **SF (Sentence Fragment)**
    I washed the dishes AFTER I ATE SUPPER.

# Key 3: Exercise 5—Wordy Sentences

**Trim these to the bone: Make sure, though, that you don't leave out essentials.**

1. I wanted to pay a visit to New York over Christmas in December, but I didn't have the time or money or resources for the flight out to the east coast.

2. There were many customers at the local bank who were among those who received great benefit from the new IRA updates.

3. The neutral Swiss, who are very private by nature, have always maintained their neutrality and privacy.

4. Due to the simple fact that she was able to visit with the alder person about the consequences of removing the stop sign, Mrs. Thompson, the chair of the committee, was thus in a position to convince him of the merits of the petition.

5. It is a fact that the gas station that sells Mobil stands on the corner of Franklin and State next to the factory that manufactures bicycles for children.

6. The vague, harassing phone calls had no rhyme or reason to them and confused us all; they were made by psychologically upset people who needed therapy.

# Key 4: Exercise 6—Redundancy

**Edit these phrases to the fewest possible words:**

obviously apparent

consensus of opinion

mix together

combine together

noticeable to the eye

visible to the eye

audible to the ear

alone all by himself

during the winter months

a minor who has not yet reached the age of 19

endorse the check on the back

in the month of May

in the city of Detroit

past experience

honest truth

final conclusion

bought and paid for

round circle

whole entire

winning another victory

two twins

resulting consequences

absolutely basic fundamentals

awful atrocity

no living survivors

free gift

simultaneously together

new innovation

true facts

old antique

hollow cavity

real truth

advance forward

advance planning

and etc.

ask the question

before in the past

end product

important essentials

mutual cooperation

expired and terminated

personal opinion

plan ahead

plan for the future

postponed until later

qualified expert

same identical

seems apparent

# Key 5: Exercise 7—Editing Test

A. **SENTENCE COMPLETION. Determine if the following groups of words are complete sentences. If they are, write C by the number. If they are not, rewrite and complete the meaning.**

   1. As long as you have signed up for the workshop.

   2. Having seen the men rob the bank, John called the cops.

   3. The person with the merchandise from Macy's.

   4. Vivian hoping that the day would be challenging.

   5. Al was relieved when he finished the last page.

B. **VERBS AND PRONOUNS. Circle the appropriate form used in standard English.**

   6. There **was/were** only one boy and one girl in the hall.

   7. The role of broadcasters, especially in an age with so many technological advances, **is/are** changing almost daily.

   8. Either the Brewsters or Helen **plans/plan** on buying the resort.

   9. Affirmative Action will assist any woman who believes that **she is/they are** facing discrimination.

   10. I **was/had** been in the car for three hours when I reached Chicago.

   11. Barack Obama and **she/her** live in the White House.

   12. My sister Marge invited Ben and **she/her** over for supper.

   13. I like to **lay/lie** down for a nap after I have **set/sat** up watching TV.

   14. The jury has decided to release **its/their** finding.

   15. Henrietta, who's taller than **I/me,** declared yesterday that she likes Wilfred better than **I/me** [i.e., Henrietta likes Wilfred better than she likes the speaker].

C. **PUNCTUATION. Place the necessary punctuation in the following sentences.**

16. Rowena was formerly a professional softball player now she is a sportscaster.

17. Has Billy Smith who lives near Sams farm announced that he will quit the familys grocery business.

18. Men who put down women are called chauvinists.

19. They were no ordinary family however they carried on the activities of daily life.

20. It's a great day for the childrens picnic.

21. Watch out for that low-flying helicopter Bob shouted.

22. Bring me the following items milk bread and eggs.

23. Although the police arrested Pat Evans was the real culprit.

24. Its been a long time since I read the novel The Sound and the Fury.

D. **EFFECTIVE SENTENCES. Revise the following.**

25. This morning Bud left instructions for me to water the lawn, to repair the hinge, and for cleaning the garage.

26. Filling the tank in Boston, the gas lasted until he reached Connecticut.

27. Chewing on the hay, I sat down to milk the cow.

28. When Carol gave Tina a gift, she was surprised.

**E. CAPITALIZATION. Circle the letters that need capitals.**

29. the letter written by professor holman on may 1 was addressed to senator kohl and ended up at the french pub, a famous restaurant in milwaukee.

30. as a senior at east high school, I took typing, french, german, and music.

31. we drove south to visit the south; last year we headed west to visit the west.

32. if I were governor, I would try to be a better governor than governor smith.

# Key 6: Exercise 8—Run-on Sentences

**Don't rewrite: Just supply punctuation and/or conjunctions.**

1. There used to be fish in the pond I remember catching them when I was a boy.

2. "Here's the TV guide" he said "now choose the program you want and I hope it's an exciting one."

3. We were pleased with our choice of a day for the vacation though it had been snowing at supper the weather cleared by ten.

4. The troop had no coffee no cheese no bread and the milk had begun to spoil as a result lunch consisted of popcorn.

5. Eileen calls that junker of hers a "car" but "reject" would describe it better wouldn't it?

6. Tuberculosis was the most terrible killer of the nineteenth century however cancer has replaced it in the twentieth.

7. The Nebraskan Willa Cather was one of the first women writers to explore plains life by writing O Pioneers! and other novels she helped to start America's literature of the Midwest.

8. If Jay's batting eye had been a little sharper for example he could have been the best player in the county.

9. On top of the peak is a silo after you pass that you will spot the old village in the valley below.

10. I explored the church carefully Father O'Brien led me up to the bell tower which had been replaced in 1934.

11. Wilma has formed her opinion nothing you can say will change it.

12. We have enough money we can build a supermarket.

13. I asked Chief Sears about the burglary ring he said that so far as he knew the case was under investigation.

14. "If you go to the store after you drop me off" he told his son "be sure to buy batteries for the flashlight I'm pretty sure we're out of them."

15. Frank says that the food spoils rapidly it shouldn't be left outside in the sun.

16. When you come to a red brick school across from a gas station turn left you should then go exactly one block.

# Key 6: Exercise 9—Essential and Nonessential Fragments

**Review the Eight Punctuation Patterns; pay special attention to Patterns 7 and 8. Then punctuate the following sentences (and some may not need commas):**

1. My mother who bakes the best pies in Murray got a prize at the county fair.
2. The woman who got second prize is a friend of my mother.
3. The book that I was telling you about is now on the best-seller list.
4. Several works by Thomas McGuane a twentieth-century Montana author have been made into movies.
5. Sandy who thinks she looks like a movie star is taking dancing lessons.
6. Have you ever read, "Nobody's Angel" a novel by Thomas McGuane?
7. Paula who is the youngest in the group is always late.
8. This is the suit that I bought before Easter.
9. This suit which I bought before Easter is now too small.
10. The preacher sat down on the chair that was minus one leg.
11. The preacher sat down on the chair which was minus one leg.
12. The diet that I am following allows all the sweets you want.
13. The New York Lose-It-All Diet which I am following allows all the sweets you want.
14. The city that was damaged most by the flood was Dubuque.
15. Dubuque which is an historic city sits on the banks of the Mississippi.
16. We entered the White House which was being closed for the day and tried to find the office that Ralph had told us about.
17. Her doctor who usually made house calls said that she would have to come into the clinic.
18. Dr. Hutchinson who usually made house calls said that she would have to come into the clinic.
19. The doctor who usually made house calls said that she would have to come into the clinic.

# Key 6: Exercise 10—Colons

**Where needed, supply colons** (*but no other punctuation mark*):

1. My three favorite cities are San Francisco, New York, and Chicago.
2. I like three cities San Francisco, New York, and Chicago.
3. I'll tell you whom I see Ralph, Lou, and Bill.
4. He threw a ball at Bill and Lou.
5. I like the following people Martha, Jane, and Sam.
6. JFK once said "Ask not what your country can do for you; ask what you can do for your country."
7. Joan ate a big supper seven courses, including salad, soup, the central dish, vegetables, and apple pie.
8. I told her the following life has many mysteries.
9. Look out here comes the helicopter.
10. Don't worry I'll be home by next week.
11. I am a man, a teacher, and a father.
12. I am the following a man, a teacher, and a father.
13. The problems of the house are that it needs paint, a new roof, and new plumbing.
14. Here are the house's faults it needs new paint, a new roof, and new plumbing.
15. The guys who caught the ball are Bob and Bill.
16. The following guys caught the ball Bob and Bill.
17. I read many books by Stephen King such as *Carrie* and *Misery*.
18. Be sure that you take pictures of Nancy, Will, and Tom.
19. Be sure that you take pictures of my friends I mean Nancy, Will, and Tom.

# Key 6: Exercise 11—Apostrophes

**Supply the missing apostrophes:**

1. Bills coats collar (singular coat)
2. Bills coats collars (plural coat)
3. *Websters Dictionary*s definitions (proper name)
4. Websters dictionaries definitions (dictionaries published by the same publisher)
5. Lloyds brothers houses roof (singular brother)
6. Lloyds sisters houses roof (plural sister)
7. Everybodys duties
8. The bulls horns (plural bull)
9. The bulls horns (singular bull)
10. Hell attend school; she cant because shes sick.
11. Its snowing again; hes singing into that tape recorder of theirs.
12. Ralphs not at his aunts house. (singular aunt)
13. Theyre at Toms.
14. Whos at the doctors office? (singular doctor)
15. Whats Bills dads phone number?
16. Boys dormitory (plural boys)
17. Boys dormitory (singular boy)
18. The mans jobs duties (singular job)
19. The mens jobs duties (plural job)
20. The girls purses (singular girl)
21. The girls purses (plural girl)
22. The womans cars hoods paint (singular car)
23. The womens clubs rules (singular club)
24. The childs toys directions (singular toy)

25. The childrens toys directions (plural toy)
26. The deers tracks indentations in the snow (plural tracks)
27. The sheeps smell
28. The citys bright lights; the cities bright lights
29. The oxens stables straw (singular stable)
30. The teachers pupils homework (singular teacher/pupil)
31. The teachers pupils homework (plural teacher/pupil)
32. The babys coats buttons (singular coat); the babies coats buttons (plural coat)
33. The spys secret codes message (plural code)
34. The spies secret codes message (singular code)
35. The Supremes first records album covers design (singular record)
36. The Beatles famous songs lyrics (singular song)
37. A months leave of absence; two weeks vacation
38. Three days sick leave; one weeks vacation
39. One days sick leave; twelve months leave of absence
40. Louies aunts paycheck (singular aunt)
41. The nurseries children; the nurserys childrens lockers
42. Whose house is that? Thats the Smiths.

# Key 6: Exercise 12—Dictation

These sentences will test primarily for punctuation, but you'll also discover some usage problems (like IT'S vs. ITS). Ask a friend to read the sentences out loud to you—four or five sentences at a time. Listen carefully to the punctuation. (Ask your friend not to take dramatic pauses; just to read normally.)

You can also practice by filling in the punctuation—be sure, though, to read out loud to yourself (again, no dramatic pauses allowed).

The corrected sentences follow on pages 237-240. You'll find more than one way to punctuate some of the sentences.

1. Although the mans car was parked across the street from McDonalds he wasnt in the car
2. I saw Richards mother at St Marys Thrift Shop she was buying childrens clothing
3. Mr Smiths secretary a speed typist or so I've heard can type this insurance companys documents faster than anyone elses secretary right
4. Martha saw Mr Smiths brother who was the mailman run down the street but the man whom she saw yesterday didnt run down the street did he
5. Although I was sick in the evening I was well enough in the morning to jog five miles eat a healthy delicious breakfast and go to my job at Arbys
6. Jane do you like my car No I don't Well I don't care
7. Ralph said to Max Have you seen Mikes brothers car
8. The man was born at 420 South DeWitt Street Topeka Kansas 63301 on July 4 1980 or so I think
9. After eating the dog ate somebody elses food
10. Bill asked Leo Wheres my grandmothers uncles TV
11. Sam saw Leo at 118 East Williamson Madison WI 53703 on July 3 2010 with his sisters friend I think
12. When it stops raining please send this package to Mr Smiths garage afterwards well talk about business

13. Can Leos brother however survive a trip to 426 East 44th Street New York New York 10059 on August 4 2010 in your opinion
14. If therefore I meet you at Bills youll bring that friend of Franks wont you
15. Sandra who was born in Chicago a city in Illinois will as a result sell her fiances house if I'm not mistaken
16. Although Leos mothers house was old nevertheless she sold it if Im not mistaken for a large sum didnt she
17. The evenings entertainment was moreover overpriced however everybody and I mean everybody enjoyed the four musicians performance
18. Los Angeles home of Hollywood delighted me consequently I plan to return in Leos friends van
19. I believe that Leo however left to visit Chicago as a result Tim his friend stayed in Cleveland with Tims only friend Nancy at Nancys
20. Edward visited New York I however visited three other cities Paris France Rome Italy and Des Moines Iowa
21. Mary ate a vanilla ice cream cone her husband a chocolate neither however had popcorn if I have my facts straight
22. John F Kennedy thirty fifth president of the United States b 1917 died didnt he in 1963
23. If you can Martha get your dads car for the weekend if you can't although I hate to think of this well take the bus okay
24. The man who is tall is here and ready to help the man who is short and also here
25. I like to run and swim and have often done both to keep in shape and see my friends
26. Dear Mom

    Although you just sent me $259.00 Im broke again and as a result I need some more money Heres why tuition books and money lent to my roommates boyfriend Leo whos from Chicago Illinois I promise I wont spend it all at once and will never bother you or call or write or ask for money again,

    Love Brenda

27. The woman who is talking to the dog that I bought last week in New York and that is a pit bull is my sister

28. After you eat your breakfast however it would be a good idea Leo to go to Nancys to see your friends car wouldnt it

29. Here are two famous assassinations Abraham Lincoln sixteenth president b 1809 shot if I recall this properly in 1865 John F Kennedy thirty fifth president b 1917 shot if I recall this one also properly in 1963

30. The man who left New York last week to see the woman who was driving to Chicago arrived last night

31. The car and the bike you bought last week and paid a lot of money for are here and in the garage and basement

32. Leo and Martha and Bill want to fly or take the train to see their friends and to visit New York and Chicago and Madison

33. The boy who was running saw the dog that was barking and also saw the cat that was eating the meat and drinking its water and meowing

34. Lou who was running saw the dog Spot that was barking and he also saw the cat Martha that was eating the meat drinking its water and meowing

35. I saw Chicago and New York and Los Angeles on my trip and visited museums in all three cities

36. I saw Chicago New York and Los Angeles on my trip and I visited museums in all three cities

37. The sheriff arrested three criminals Smith Jones and White

38. The three criminals the sheriff arrested are Smith and Jones and White

39. Please buy me a new TV I hope it's a good one like a Sony

40. Please buy me a new TV and I hope it's a good one a Sony

41. The woman who saw her friend and bought the bread returned to her home and turned on the TV and ate supper didnt she

42. Martha who saw her friend and bought the bread returned to her home turned on the TV and ate supper right

43. Mr Smith my teacher grew up in Chicago Illinois 60637 where he was born b 1970 his wife Judy b.1971 is also a teacher

44. Where Doug is Leos house in Chicago or in Milwaukee and where is Leo now that I think of it

45. Spike Lees movie Do the Right Thing will be shown this weekend at the Majestic Im going with Nancys friend

46. The man who made Do the Right Thing is currently making a movie whose title I don't know

47. Spike Lee has made at least three classic feature films Shes Gotta Have It School Daze and Do the Right Thing hasnt he

48. Sam who lives next door to Mr Wilsons only friend Jason the kid who wears the hockey mask read Newsweek last week

49. The kid who lives next door to Mr Wilsons friend who wears the hockey mask read Newsweek last week I think

50. If you can Martha watch the episode called Lucy Kills Ricky on the rerun of I Love Lucy one of my favorite shows

51. The article called Meet Coach Smith was in last Saturdays Wisconsin State Journal wasnt it

52. Look out she shouted That plane is going to hit Sams new house

53. Do you know whos going to the farm Jack to give the farmer whose milk we buy some money

54. Martha said First look at its color however be sure that it's a color that we read about in our science text Beginning Science

55. Theyre over there Ralph said in their house Go to their house to see if the two men theyre taking care of are there too

55. Brian whose grandma read the article called The Atlantic Ocean in The National Geographic also saw an episode of Nightline called The Pacific Ocean

57. If you can Ralph look at the chapter called The Dead Pig in The Butchers Handbook

# Key 6: Exercise 12—Dictation Answers

1. Although the man's car was parked across the street from McDonald's, he wasn't in the car.
2. I saw Richard's mother at St. Mary's Thrift Shop; she was buying children's clothing.
3. Mr. Smith's secretary, a speed typist, or so I've heard, can type this insurance company's documents faster than anyone else's secretary, right?
4. Martha saw Mr. Smith's brother, who was the mailman, run down the street, but the man whom she saw yesterday didn't run down the street, did he?
5. Although I was sick in the evening, I was well enough in the morning to jog five miles, eat a healthy, delicious breakfast, and go to my job at Arby's.
6. Jane, do you like my car? No, I don't. Well, I don't care.
7. Ralph said to Max, "Have you seen Mike's brother's car?"
8. The man was born at 420 South DeWitt Street, Topeka, Kansas 63301 on July 4, 1980, or so I think.
9. After eating, the dog ate somebody else's food.
10. Bill asked Leo, "Where's my grandmother's uncle's TV?"
11. Sam saw Leo at 118 East Williamson, Madison, WI 53703 on July 3, 2010, with his sister's friend, I think.
12. When it stops raining, please send this package to Mr. Smith's garage; afterwards, we'll talk about business.
13. Can Leo's brother, however, survive a trip to 426 East 44th Street, New York, New York 10059 on August 4, 2010, in your opinion?
14. If, therefore, I meet you at Bill's, you'll bring that friend of Frank's, won't you?
15. Sandra (who was born in Chicago [a city in Illinois]) will, as a result, sell her fiancé's house, if I'm not mistaken.

16. Although Leo's mother's house was old, nevertheless, she sold it, if I'm not mistaken, for a large sum, didn't she?

17. The evening's entertainment was, moreover, overpriced; however, everybody—and I mean everybody—enjoyed the four musicians' performance.

18. Los Angeles (home of Hollywood) delighted me; consequently, I plan to return in Leo's friend's van.

19. I believe that Leo, however, left to visit Chicago; as a result, Tim, his friend, stayed in Cleveland with Tim's only friend, Nancy, at Nancy's.

20. Edward visited New York; I, however, visited three other cities: Paris, France; Rome, Italy; and Des Moines, Iowa.

21. Mary ate a vanilla ice cream cone; her husband, a chocolate; neither, however, had popcorn, if I have my facts straight.

22. John F. Kennedy (thirty-fifth president of the United States [b. 1917]) died, didn't he, in 1963?

23. If you can, Martha, get your dad's car for the weekend; if you can't—although I hate to think of this—we'll take the bus, okay?

24. The man who is tall is here and ready to help the man who is short and also here.

25. I like to run and swim and have often done both to keep in shape and see my friends.

26. Dear Mom,

    Although you just sent me $259.00, I'm broke again, and, as a result, I need some more money. Here's why: tuition, books, and money lent to my roommate's boyfriend, Leo, who's from Chicago, Illinois. I promise I won't spend it all at once and will never bother you or call or write or ask for money again.

    Love, Brenda

27. The woman who is talking to the dog that I bought last week in New York and that is a pit bull is my sister.

28. After you eat your breakfast, however, it would be a good idea, Leo, to go to Nancy's to see your friend's car, wouldn't it?

29. Here are two famous assassinations: Abraham Lincoln (sixteenth president [b. 1809]), shot, if I recall this properly, in 1865; John F. Kennedy (thirty-fifth president [b. 1917]), shot, if I also recall this one properly, in 1963.
30. The man who left New York last week to see the woman who was driving to Chicago arrived last night.
31. The car and the bike you bought last week and paid a lot of money for are here and in the garage and basement.
32. Leo and Martha and Bill want to fly or take the train to see their friends and to visit New York and Chicago and Madison.
33. The boy who was running saw the dog that was barking and also saw the cat that was eating the meat and drinking its water and meowing.
34. Lou, who was running, saw the dog, Spot, that was barking, and he also saw the cat, Martha, that was eating the meat, drinking its water, and meowing.
35. I saw Chicago and New York and Los Angeles on my trip and visited museums in all three cities.
36. I saw Chicago, New York, and Los Angeles on my trip, and I visited museums in all three cities.
37. The sheriff arrested three criminals: Smith, Jones, and White.
38. The three criminals the sheriff arrested are Smith and Jones and White.
39. Please buy me a new TV; I hope it's a good one, like a Sony.
40. Please buy me a new TV, and I hope it's a good one: a Sony.
41. The woman who saw her friend and bought the bread returned to her home and turned on the TV and ate supper, didn't she?
42. Martha, who saw her friend and bought the bread, returned to her home, turned on the TV, and ate supper—right?
43. Mr. Smith, my teacher, grew up in Chicago, Illinois 60637, where he was born (b. 1970); his wife, Judy (b. 1971), is also a teacher.
44. Where, Doug, is Leo's house—in Chicago or in Milwaukee—and where is Leo, now that I think of it?
45. Spike Lee's movie *Do the Right Thing* will be shown this weekend at the Majestic; I'm going with Nancy's friend.

46. The man who made *Do the Right Thing* is currently making a movie whose title I don't know.
47. Spike Lee has made at least three classic feature movies—*She's Gotta Have It*, *School Daze*, and *Do the Right Thing*—hasn't he?
48. Sam, who lives next door to Mr. Wilson's only friend, Jason, the kid who wears the hockey mask, read *Newsweek* last week.
49. The kid who lives next door to Mr. Wilson's friend who wears the hockey mask read *Newsweek* last week, I think.
50. If you can, Martha, watch the episode called "Lucy Kills Ricky" on the rerun of *I Love Lucy*, one of my favorite shows.
51. The article called "Meet Coach Smith" was in last Saturday's *Wisconsin State Journal*, wasn't it?
52. "Look out!" she shouted. "That plane is going to hit Sam's new house."
53. Do you know who's going to the farm, Jack, to give the farmer whose milk we buy some money?
54. Martha said, "First look at its color; however, be sure that it's a color that we read about in our science text, *Beginning Science*."
55. "They're over there," Ralph said, "in their house. Go to their house to see if the two men they're taking care of are there, too."
56. Brian, whose grandma read the article called "The Atlantic Ocean" in *The National Geographic*, also saw an episode of *Nightline* called "The Pacific Ocean."
57. If you can, Ralph, look at the chapter called "The Dead Pig" in *The Butcher's Handbook*.

# Key 7: Exercise 13—The Forty-Four Reminders Quiz

For each problem:
- Fix what's wrong
- Write the reminder (there may be more than one) BELOW the problem.

1. The title of a student essay.

    <u>"Hamlet"</u>

**Reminder:** An Analysis of Ghost Imagery in <u>Hamlet</u>.
Don't title your essay something somebody else has used. Underlining, but don't use quotations for a play title.

2. I really enjoyed the book, "Great Expectations".

    I really enjoyed the book <u>Great Expectations</u>.

**Reminder:** No comma, quotation marks for the title.
Delete the unnecessary comma.

3. I went to bed early; and I got up around four, I brushed my teeth then.

   OC ✓

**Reminder:**

4. I hope its not to early for me to go, have you seen its' new color since they painted?

**Reminder:**

5. There going to they're house, over their.

**Reminder:**

6. After the party we walked home.

    If you study hard you'll probably get good grades.

**Reminder:**

7. I think the problem, is that you didn't prepare.

    All I knew then, was that you were coming to see me.

**Reminder:**

8. This movie was directed by: Steven Spielberg.

    Send our letter of thanks to: your mother.

**Reminder:**

9. The primary problems were: organization and proofreading.

   The places I want to go are: New York and Chicago.

**Reminder:**

10. While eating lunch, the computer broke down.

    Driving recklessly, the bus went out of control.

**Reminder:**

11. The secretary, who types fast, will get a raise.

    Mr. Brown who types fast will get a raise.

**Reminder:**

12. All of us down at the factory knew in point of fact that she would help us.

    Every night of the week he studied and accordingly got good grades.

    Come over and see me and if I have time I'll help you.

**Reminder:**

13. For entertainment I enjoy reading, playing the piano, and I attend a lot of movies.

**Reminder:**

14. I use to work at the store, now I'm suppose to get a job at McDonalds.

**Reminder:**

15. Each person should do their job. Every husband saw their wife. Each wife saw their husband.

**Reminder:**

16. There's many laws to worry about. There's a lot wrong with that isn't there?

**Reminder:**

17. Eventhough I'm tired I'm still going to highschool everyday.

**Reminder:**

18. I read that article called "sick a lot".

    I read that short story called "Big Top", and then I saw it on TV.

**Reminder:**

19. When you're done you can read, "Big Top;" its good. I read, "big top:" have you?

**Reminder:**

20. But, I'm not sure about that.

    And, he's not sick if I remember correctly.

**Reminder:**

21. Although, I'm glad that you came to my house, it was to late.

**Reminder:**

22. I hope we can visit Nancys parents. Thats her parents house is'nt it?

**Reminder:**

23. How does this affect effect you?

    It was a very affective presentation.

**Reminder:**

24. I like many movies such as: Citizen Kane.

    I like many movies, such as, Citizen Kane.

**Reminder:**

25. I read the article Relief in Somalia in The New York Times, I saw a show about Somalia called Will There Be Relief on 60 Minutes.

**Reminder:**

26. I went to the movie however I didn't like it.

**Reminder:**

27. I went to the movie I didn't like it.

**Reminder:**

28. It was to hot for the too men to go to town, to.

**Reminder:**

29. I read about two psychiatrist who claimed that three musicologist all had the same problem.

**Reminder:**

30. I went to Helen C. White Hall. Which is across the street.

**Reminder:**

# Key 7: Exercise 14—Final Revision

**As a final exercise, revise this passage from the Preface. Handle it in every way necessary, from reorganizing the paragraph to editing sentences.**

In my estimation our political leaders don't seem too notice what we all want, there head is in the clouds, as its to plain to see. How are you suppose to vote with enthusiasm when the choice is between a Republican and a democrat eventhough, in theory their different from each other. I don't like like politics and won't vote in the future if some politician says something like "Trust me;" thats an insult to: our intelligence. Well something is really wrong. The problem with politics is that its' goal, aren't allways alot like the common mans or women. What I want to know is: why isn't Newsweek and Time and other magazines publishing articles, such as: What Wrong with Americas politics? Theres many things that make me angry. Also I do'nt think TV use to be as bad as it is. Each tv station now has their own political bias. Watching t.v. daily T.V. dosen't tell one much about political truth, as an of, 60 Minutes, called "How politics on TV Effects You", a good title pointed out.

# Twenty-Three Writing Projects

Project 1: Writing a Profile: The Writer  253
Project 2: Compiling a Journal of Ideas  253
Project 3: Looking Inside Yourself for Ideas  253
Project 4: Looking Outside Yourself for Ideas  254
Project 5: Looking Outside Yourself for Ideas: Eavesdropping  254
Project 6: Brainstorming in a Group  254
Project 7: Identifying Thirteen Logical Fallacies  254
Project 8: Summarizing One Source (Not Stating Opinion)  257
Project 9: Summarizing One Source (Stating Opinion)  258
Project 10: Summarizing Sources (Not Stating Opinion)  258
Project 11: Summarizing Sources (Stating Opinion)  258
Project 12: Summarizing Sources: The OED—"Air," "Earth," "Fire," and "Water"  258
Project 13: Writing a Research Paper: Popular Culture  259
Project 14: Writing a Position Paper: The Environment  264
Project 15: Writing a Second Position Paper: Social Issues  265
Project 16: Writing a Personal Essay  266
Project 17: Writing a Second Personal Essay  270
Project 18: Writing an Argumentative Essay: Alice vs. Humpty  270
Project 19: Writing a How-To Essay  271
Project 20: Writing a Book Review  271
Project 21: Writing a Movie Review  272
Project 22: Writing Literary Analysis Using Comparison and Contrast  273
Project 23: Writing about the Ideal Job (with a Résumé and Cover Letter)  275

## Project 1: Writing a Profile: The Writer

Imagine that you've been hired to write a profile of your favorite writer.

Your article will describe the writer's work (the kinds of work he or she produces) and talk about the writer's writing habits (where ideas come from; where and when the writer likes to write; the number of drafts; whether the writer composes in longhand or at the computer, etc.). You'll ask about problems your writer has to deal with and about favorite kinds of projects to write. Favorite books to read? Advice for young writers?

Be sure to find out if your writer liked to write as a child (why or why not?). Did the writing experience change for the better or worse in high school (why?).

Also: How did his or her family feel about writing and reading (were there many books in the house?). Can you think of anything else the reader should know?

Model your article after an interview-article you might see in any popular publication (print or online). If you wish, you might include a picture of the writer at work.

By the way: That writer you're interviewing is **you**. (But write the interview in third person: "She says that . . ." "He believes that . . .") In other words, you're writing a third-person profile of yourself as a writer.

## Project 2: Compiling a Journal of Ideas

After you've completed Project 1, circle the ideas (the interesting points) that came up in the interview with yourself.

Buy a notebook or open a computer file, write "Journal of Ideas" across the first page, and record these ideas. Promise yourself that every day you'll enter new ideas: stuff that jumps into your head about absolutely everything. Funny things that you've noticed. Stuff that upsets you. Ideas from TV news or print/online sources. Ideas from books you're reading. Promise, too, that you'll write a sentence or two (or more) about each idea; elaborate why you're interested in it.

## Project 3: Looking Inside Yourself for Ideas

Go into a room where you can be by yourself and lock the door. Make yourself comfortable—coffee, music, whatever it takes (but no TV, please). On a blank page or computer screen, write a few words identifying an idea that you feel strong about—you either love or hate it. Now turn to pages xx-xxiv and follow brainstorming strategies 1, 3-7 (as needed).

## Project 4: Looking Outside Yourself for Ideas

Open a dictionary. Put your finger down on a word. Then turn to pages xxi-xxiv and follow brainstorming strategies 2-7 (as needed).

## Project 5: Looking Outside Yourself for Ideas: Eavesdropping

Position yourself in a public area (hidden behind a potted plant, the salad bar, a couple of old-timers drinking beer) and eavesdrop on a conversation. Jot down all the ideas that come up—no matter how off the wall.

Choose one to write about, turn to pages xxi-xxiv, and follow brainstorming strategies 2-7 (as needed).

## Project 6: Brainstorming in a Group

In a class or writing group, come up with a word or idea. Jot it across the top of a card. Now pass the card to the person on the right. Triggered by the key word, that person should write down the first thing that comes to mind. No censorship allowed: Anything goes. The point here is to build a chain of ideas, A through Z.

After three trips around the group, someone should write the original word on the blackboard; then place the brainstormed words around the original (i.e., the blackboard will show a sun and sun rays—the original word hooked up to the brainstormed words).

Then write a thirty-minute essay on the original word that includes **all the terms** on the board. (Try to take the exercise seriously.) When you're done, read the essay out loud to your group.

## Project 7: Identifying Thirteen Logical Fallacies

For over two thousand years, logicians have identified a common collection of fallacies (a fallacy is some predictable flaw in thinking that weakens your argument).

Perhaps the best-known fallacy is the (1) **argumentum ad hominem**. Here you attack the person rather than deal logically with an issue at hand: **You'd be smart if you wore better clothes** or **It's hard to believe him because he smiles all the time.**

A related fallacy, the (2) **red herring**, avoids the real issue by drawing attention to an irrelevant issue (that is, like the **argumentum ad hominem**, it ignores the question): **Why worry about terrorists when we ought to do something about the environment?**

Another common fallacy, especially in advertising and on college campuses, is the (3) **bandwagon**—everybody's doing it, so why shouldn't you? **Go ahead and cheat. Everybody else does**.

Still another common fallacy, (4) **begging the question**, restates a point you've just made without answering *why*—in other words, you're begging a question to be answered. (Because this fallacy restates the main point, professors sometimes call it a "circular argument.") **He's lazy because he doesn't like to work**. Here you finish where you started, answering little in the process.

A fifth fallacy assumes that because two things resemble each other in some way, they therefore have to be alike in other ways—hence, the (5) **false analogy: Since I saw** *The Transporter*, **I don't need to see** *Transporter 2* **or** *Transporter 3*.

We hear a lot of the next fallacy on TV talk shows. In (6) **false authority**, the assumption is that an expert in one field can necessarily serve as an expert in another. Thus you hear famous people voicing all kinds of gas about any topic on the menu—regardless of their expertise. **School loans must be cut, as the country's leading lawyer said**.

Another political favorite is the (7) **false cause**, the assumption that because one event follows another, the first causes the second: **Because the Democrats have taken office, government spending has gone up**.

An argument that you often hear from friends and family poses only two solutions for a problem (and there may be many more). This is the (8) **false dilemma**, which states that only two alternatives exist: **We have just two choices—to vote Democrat or to vote Republican**.

And a common fallacy we make judging friends and families is (9) **guilt by association**, an unfair attempt to blame person A for the beliefs or actions of person B: **He must be a thief because his brother went to jail**.

The fallacy you see most in college essays is the (10) **hasty generalization**, a broad statement based on little evidence: **Teenagers are reckless drivers** or **All Germans love dark beer**.

Still another favorite fallacy of the essay is the (11) **non sequitur**. Here statement B doesn't logically follow statement A: **Billy Pierce has a high school diploma; therefore, he will get a good job**. Right . . .

And a third essay favorite is (12) **oversimplification**, a statement or argument that leaves out relevant issues: **People who become movie stars have lots of luck**.

The final fallacy is the (13) **slippery slope**, which assumes that if you let something happen, it will be the first step to disaster: **Handgun control will lead to a police state.**

This project has three steps:

**Step One**: In a group or on your own, identify the following kinds of fallacies:

1. He claimed that either path would lead to unfortunate consequences—whether we cut down the forest or go without lumber to build houses.
2. You should drink Pepsi-Cola because all cool people drink it.
3. I don't want to hear his new CD; the old one was terrible, so I know this one will be, too.
4. He cheats because he doesn't like to play fair.
5. As the DNA expert testified at Waldo Hill's trial, strangulation was the obvious cause of death.
6. That's the stupidest argument I ever heard, but I'm not surprised because you're stupid.
7. "If you smoke marijuana," my mother warned, "you'll become a crack addict."
8. If we don't enact capital punishment, criminals will take over and the entire country will go to hell.
9. My professor likes me; therefore, he will give me a good grade.
10. You can't trust Bob. His whole family is worthless.
11. All people believe in God.
12. If you want to become a great basketball player, all you have to do is practice.
13. The congressman believes that we shouldn't spend money to help the Mexican earthquake victims because we've got our own problems at home.

**Step Two**: Buy a newspaper and turn to the editorial page. Using either a staff editorial or a letter to the editor, analyze it for fallacies. (Longer letters to the editor are pregnant fields for analysis.)

**Step Three**: Compose a one-page, double-spaced essay that identifies and discusses the fallacies you found on the editorial page.

## Project 8: Summarizing One Source (Not Stating Opinion)

A summary is a brief, neutral statement of a larger work's main points. A summary can be as skimpy as a cable blurb for an old *Seinfeld* episode ("Jerry, George, Elaine, and Kramer wait to get seated in a Chinese restaurant") or as long as the table of contents at the start of this book. Summaries can take many forms, from a preview of a coming movie to a cover letter introducing a report. Before you write a summary, you must consider the **kind** you want to write; try to find a model.

If you're summarizing other writing, decide, first, how many pages you want to write (finding a model will help here). Then, as you read:

1. Underline the Big Picture.
2. Underline the topic sentence in each paragraph (if you can't find a topic sentence, write your own).

Then, starting with the Big Picture:

1. List each topic sentence.
2. Decide which topic sentences are Main Sub-points. Keep those.
3. Do a second list, keeping just the Big Picture and Main Sub-points.
4. Write a draft, using sentences and paragraphs, that discusses the Big Picture and Main Sub-points.
5. Use occasional quotations from the text—but probably no more than two or three.
6. The order of the summary should follow the order of the source. That is, in your Setup, discuss the Big Picture and Setup of the source; in your Development, discuss the Development of the source; and in your Wrap-up, discuss the conclusions stated in the Wrap-up of the source.

Remember these formalities in writing a summary:

1. In the first sentence, mention the title and author of the source.
2. The first time you refer to the author, use the complete name; thereafter, the last.
3. Stay in present tense: "The author says . . . " "He believes . . . "
4. Don't state your own opinion anywhere in the summary. Just give the facts.

This project has nine options to choose from:
1. Summarize a chapter in a novel.
2. Summarize a chapter in a textbook.
3. Summarize an article in a popular magazine.
4. Summarize an academic article in a journal.
5. Summarize a long article in a newspaper.
6. Summarize a chapter in a software manual.
7. Summarize a section in an Internal Revenue publication.
8. Summarize a long set of directions (from any "how-to" publication).
9. Summarize an encyclopedia article that's more than a page.

## Project 9: Summarizing One Source (Stating Opinion)

Follow the directions in Project 8, but at the end of the summary, state how you feel about the topic. Discuss any logical fallacies (taking care not to commit your own fallacies).

## Project 10: Summarizing Sources (Not Stating Opinion)

Follow the directions in Project 8, but summarize **two** or more sources.
1. In the first paragraph, state the sources' titles, authors, and Big Pictures.
2. Summarize the sources in the order introduced in the Setup.
3. In the Wrap-up, compare and contrast ideas; avoid stating your opinion.

## Project 11: Summarizing Sources (Stating Opinion)

Follow the directions in Projects 8 and 10, but at the end of the summary, state how you feel about the topic. Mention any fallacies that you see in the logic (taking care not to commit your own fallacies).

## Project 12: Summarizing Sources: The OED—"Air," "Earth," "Fire," and "Water"

The *Oxford English Dictionary* stands as one of the world's great intellectual treats: Multivolumed, with various supplements, the OED was issued in 1928 after over fifty years' work; just about every word in the English language appears in the original volumes or the supplements, in glorious detailing. The editors view their dictionary as a history, and entries thus include thorough histories of the word.

Under *colour,* for example, you can trace "colour" as a noun through six columns and eighteen meanings. Those meanings the editors have grouped under four categories: "As a property or quality"; "As a thing material"; "Figurative senses"; and word combinations like "colour-washed" and "colour-party." Under each of the eighteen meanings, you'll find even further, finer shadings of meaning.

The OED offers a detailed chronology for each word's history. Under the fifteenth definition of "colour" as a noun (under the third broad category, "Figurative senses"), you read (and don't let the abbreviations throw you off—they're half the fun):

> 'Clang-tint.' (See CLANG sb. 3) timbre. Also, more generally, variety of expression in a musical composition (cf. next). **1597** MORLEY *Introd. Mus.* 166 To admit great absurdities in his musicke, altering both time, tune, cullour, ayre and what soeur else. **1866** ENGEL *Nat. Music.* v. 179 Almost every instrument has its peculiar colour of sound. **1876** *Bernstein's Five Senses* 247 Still they give to the fundamental tone a peculiar character: its quality or colour. **1887** *Daily Tel.* 14 Oct. 3 He has a keen sense of orchestral effect, a capital eye for colour. **1890** *Glasgow Her.* 19 May 9/2 New theories as to the causes of the varieties of tone colour or 'timbre' of different musical instruments.

**Assignment**: Choose one of four words—**air, earth, fire,** and **water**—and, consulting the unabridged OED (the multivolumed edition), read the history of your word.

Then, in an essay, summarize that history. In the first part, include all the meanings, citing dates and sources. In the second part, discuss the common denominator that links all the meanings.

**One note**: In your essay, write out all abbreviations, both terms and titles, present in the entries. At the start of the OED, you'll find a "List of Abbreviations," and at end, a "List of Books Quoted." Thus 1597 MORLEY *Introd. Mus.*, rescued from the cramping of an abbreviation, becomes Thomas Morley, *A Plaine and Easie Introduction to Practicall Musicke* (1597).

## Project 13: Writing a Research Paper: Popular Culture

(Since the assignment requires that you summarize sources, you'll probably want to tackle Projects 8-11 [especially 11]).

In this project, you won't be able to rely solely on the Internet. You'll need to conduct full-blown, trips-to-the-library, works-cited, scholarly research: In other words, for this project, you'll write an academic paper. No serious academic paper can come solely off the Internet.

First off, what *is* an academic paper? Although you'll find many kinds, generally an academic "paper" (the term scholars use more often than "essay," which historically suggests less formal writing) needs research as its foundation (unlike the essay, which can spin off from an idea you haven't researched).

Research can have many forms, from conducting a lab experiment to poring over library archives to interviewing experts or people in the street. **Research** means learning all you can to solve a problem; it's the tool to find answers.

The "formal" aspects of the academic paper are its foundation in research, its tendency to **prove** rather than **show** (see pages 2-7 on proving and showing), and its conventional organization.

Academic papers, whatever the discipline (or research area, such as biology or art history), normally break into these parts:

1. Here's the problem (presented in the Setup)
2. Here's what the research says about it (Development)
3. Here's my interpretation of the research (Wrap-up)

Because disciplines approach these conventions differently, you must look at a number of papers in your field. Begin by asking a librarian for a list (or bibliography) of journals (a periodical devoted to scholarship in one discipline). Then pull journals from library racks, pile up a bunch, and read through them, taking notes on:

1. Typical titles (a good title will sum up the research problem)
2. Average length
3. Number of endnotes
4. Number of sources in the bibliography (sometimes called "Works Cited")

When you find an article that's appealing and the length you want to write, print or photocopy it: This article will be your model, your Bible of how to do things.

Using the chart on page 13, analyze the article carefully. You'll want the research paper you write to look like the model essay. Mark up the copy with different colored inks, asterisks, and marginalia. During this project, it will become your best friend. You want to read it so many times **that it feels as though you wrote it**.

Since we're working with popular culture, you already have a topic to explore. If you're in a situation, however, for which you have no topic, follow the brainstorming strategies, pages xx-xxiv.

Once you have a topic, the trick is to find an approach to it that will let you accomplish one clear goal:

**To take an original slant toward your topic: You don't want to write a paper another scholar has already written.**

Let's imagine two situations in which you might do research. In both situations, you have the same problem: a computer software glitch that you can't figure out. In the first situation, you call a software help line, talk to friends who use the same software, and dig around through manuals and reference books for the answer. At last, tucked away in the appendix of a manual, you find what you've been looking for. Research has solved the problem. If you wrote a memo to a colleague about what you'd found, the memo would **show** your discovery (rather than **prove** something new).

But in the second situation, after consulting the same sources, you realize that **you're** going to have to solve this problem—if there's to be a solution. The sources have provided helpful clues, but the final piecing together of the information—along with original thinking that you bring to the problem—is entirely yours: You're the detective who comes up with a solution. Your memo to a colleague would thus try to **prove** what you'd found; since it's a new idea about the software, the burden would fall on you to provide proof of its validity.

Scholarly research often takes place within the first situation. While researching, you might discover, buried in the medical lore of the Brazilian rain forest, an indigenous cure for a disease. Your task as a scholar would be to **show** this cure to the world, via a published paper.

However, the second situation probably accounts for the greater share of scholarly research. Here, you're the detective who cracks a case that has baffled the cops on the staff. You take a new look at old evidence (research put in to find a killer). Not satisfied, you conduct your own investigation to find new evidence; then, joining the old with the new, you solve the case and come up with the killer's ID. The report you write for case files will **prove** why you've nabbed the right guy.

Our project will take place within the second situation. You'll come up **with your own solution to a problem.**

Before you can solve a problem, you must know just about everything that's been written about it. Since you're writing a short paper, **you must narrow your topic**—but don't narrow it so far that **you can't find information about it** or **that you don't have enough to write about.**

Narrowing the topic thus makes your research infinitely easier.

Let's imagine, too, that you want to write on the late actor River Phoenix. You read all that you can find (not much, though since his 1993 death an increasing number of publications have begun to appear). You brainstorm what you can write about . . .

You realize that one reason you admire Phoenix is his extraordinary ability to burrow inside a character—like his portrayal of Mike in *My Own Private Idaho*. You've never seen another performance like this.

But then one night on cable you see an old western called *Red River* with John Wayne and an actor who reminds you of River Phoenix. There's something about how he handles his eyes, his quiet delivery, the intense calm that he projects . . . How extraordinary to find River Phoenix's mannerisms and demeanor in a 1948 movie with Montgomery *Who?*

Intrigued, you research Montgomery Clift (1920-1966) and discover that scholars have said he was the father of movie method acting: a realistic, natural style of acting that extends from Clift to Marlon Brando to James Dean to Robert DeNiro to River Phoenix to James Franco.

But in your research of both Clift and Phoenix, nowhere do you discover a link mentioned. **You** decide to make this link. This link will be original research: your original argument that Montgomery Clift influenced the acting style of River Phoenix.

Thus, rather than write about "River Phoenix," you narrow your topic to "The Influence of Montgomery Clift on the Acting Style of River Phoenix." Your research includes analyses of Clift's acting art (scholars have published many), whatever you can find in print on River Phoenix, close study of their movies, maybe an interview with a knowledgeable actor or director, and you look on the Internet for information about Clift and Phoenix (you find a lot—even a "River Phoenix Shrine").

You're going to **prove** that an obvious link exists between the two actors. So your thesis goes something like:

**Montgomery Clift is the major influence on the acting style of River Phoenix because—**

Note that "because." By definition, a thesis needs a "because." It requires the writer to prove the claim, and in this case the proof will not come from what's already known but from what you've puzzled out, your original thinking **based on research**.

The "because" demands proofs (see page 2). Some of these come from what's already known; others may come from what you discover. In both cases, they add up to "proofs" that support your claim.

Rewrite your thesis until you can say it in a sentence. Make sure to include "because."

**Several Rules of Thumb about Sources:**

**Rule of Thumb 1:** Use many sources—journals, popular magazines, newspapers, pamphlets, books, interviews, published archives, government documents, oral (tape-recorded) histories, TV and radio programs, the Internet, etc.

**Rule of Thumb 2:** Never rely on just **one** kind of source. Don't take all your material from only books or only popular magazines or only interviews. Use a mixture.

**Rule of Thumb 3:** For the most part, avoid books if you're examining a current topic. Books are outdated by the time they hit print; periodicals carry the most recent material.

**Rule of Thumb 4:** Don't be lazy and use only Internet sources. Many websites are shallow, full of errors, and written by idiots. *Wikipedia* is *not* necessarily a reliable source . . .

**Rule of Thumb 5:** The moment you finish with the source, write down **where** you found it; use a complete description so that you don't have to go back later.

**Rule of Thumb 6:** In the notes that you copy, **ALWAYS** use quotation marks for anything you take directly from the source—even just a word or two if they're key words.

**Rule of Thumb 7:** Avoid long quotations in your essay. Long = more than four or five sentences.

**Rule of Thumb 8:** Don't use more than two or three quotations per double-spaced page.

**Rule of Thumb 9:** Paraphrase (rewrite in your own words) as much of the source as you can and as many sources as you can.

**Rule of Thumb 10:** To be on the safe side, endnote (footnote) every source that you use in the paper, even if you paraphrase.

**Rule of Thumb 11:** Every endnote that appears in the paper must have a corresponding citation in the bibliography.

**A Note about Plagiarism:**

> 1. You must put quotations marks around any words that come directly from the source (even just a word or two if they're key words).
> 2. You must endnote all sources, even if you paraphrase.

**A Note about Citation Style:**

Use the style of your model. The two commonest styles are the MLA (Modern Language Association), used mainly for nonscience disciplines, and the APA (American Psychological Association), used mainly for science disciplines. You can find both styles explained in any college writing handbook, such as the *Harbrace College Handbook* (libraries catalogue these under the subject heading "Writing Handbooks").

**A Final Note: How Many Pages Should I Write?**

To do any research topic justice, the bottom limit is probably five pages. On average (with some variation according to the discipline—papers in the sciences tend to be shorter), a published research paper averages 15-20 pages.

## Project 14: Writing a Position Paper: The Environment

**First**: Read the directions for Project 13.

**Then**: Write a paper that **takes a position** on some aspect of one of the following topics. The point of the essay is to **persuade** your audience to take action—you may want to imagine that you're writing to the president, urging him to propose legislation based on your research.

Research your paper thoroughly. This project uses the same strategies as Project 13; the Setup, however, will argue a position, and the Wrap-up restate it (try to find new words for the restatement).

Under each general topic, there are subtopics: e.g., solid waste includes garbage, nuclear materials, used oil, etc. Be sure to narrow your topic to a subtopic under a general topic: "Air pollution" is far too broad for a short essay.

| | |
|---|---|
| Air pollution | Solid waste |
| Energy | Transportation |
| Food | Vanishing animal species |
| Genetically engineered plants | Vanishing plant species |
| Global warming | Water pollution |
| Noise | Wilderness |
| Population | Workplace pollution |

# Project 15: Writing a Second Position Paper: Social Issues

This project asks you to write about a social issues topic. Because it calls for opinions based on fact, you'll need to research your issue (read the directions for Projects 13 and 14).

**Warning:** Because these topics are so familiar, you must work especially hard to avoid writing clichés and secondhand thought.

**Assignment:** Pick a topic, research it, and write an essay that does the following:

1. Sets up the topic
2. Briefly discuss various views of the topic
3. Develops a detailed discussion of Side A
4. Develops a detailed discussion of Side B
5. Wraps up the topic with an analysis that argues which side (or their likely compromise) will prevail; use reason rather than emotion to support your choice

| | |
|---|---|
| AIDS | LBGT rights |
| Animal welfare | Medical ethics |
| Anorexia/bulimia | National health care/insurance |
| Battered women/children/old people | Needle distribution to drug addicts |
| Capital punishment | Nuclear arms control |
| Censorship | Prayer in public schools |
| Condom distribution in public schools | Racism |
| Cults | Rape |
| Death and dying | Sex education in public schools |
| Drugs | Surrogate motherhood |
| The elderly | Teenaged pregnancy |
| Fetal alcohol syndrome | Terrorism and torture |
| Gangs and violence | Welfare reform |
| Gun control | Women's safety |
| Health care | World hunger |
| Incest | Youth crime |

# Project 16: Writing a Personal Essay

Traditionally, the essay has been short (usually no more than twenty or so pages—though sometimes it will run book length). An essay is a **personal** expression about an idea. Essays can take many forms, from an editorial to a character profile to a sermon to the essay you read in *Scientific American*. They traditionally develop in one of eleven ways (by **chronology, cause to effect, effect to cause, inductive reasoning, deductive reasoning, familiar order to unfamiliar, climactic order, anticlimactic order, spatial order, the whole to the parts**, and **the parts to the whole**).

An essay traditionally has one (or more) of seven aims:

- to **identify** a topic "(One cause of cancer is smoking cigarettes")
- to **define** a topic ("Cancer is a disease sometimes caused by smoking cigarettes")
- to **compare** or **contrast** a topic ("People who smoke cigarettes get cancer more often than those who don't")
- to **classify** a topic ("Cigarette smoke is an example of environmental pollution")
- to **analyze** a topic ("Smoking cigarettes can damage many parts of the body")
- to **illustrate** a topic ("Let's look at the medical history of a cigarette smoker")
- to **show cause and effect** in a topic ("Smoking cigarettes today often leads to cancer tomorrow")

Essays can use library sources and endnotes to prove their case, just as they can rely on the writer's own experience. A church sermon, for example, uses both. A preacher typically kicks off a sermon with a Bible reference appropriate to the church year, uses one (or more) of the seven aims to explore the topic ("The need to respect our elders"), and relies heavily on his or her experience for personal stories to illustrate and prove the case.

Whatever the aim or type of development, an essay grows out of the writer's **voice**: which is to say, an essay is rooted in our unique take on the world. Our voice is our soul, our essence, our interests, our passions. This is how *I* see the world; *I* see it differently from *you*. This is *my* voice. (Of course, like an actor, you may want to develop more than one voice.)

All writing obviously carries the writer's voice, but essays, especially personal essays, have a special affection for it. And just as the voice loves to digress in a conversation, so does the personal essay love to wind around a topic. (Again, think of a sermon and how long it takes a preacher to come to the point.)

A personal essay, then, is an essay that originates in the voice and its passions, brings a personal and particular observation to the topic, relies on the writer's own experience, and tends to follow a looser shape; it may or may not use library research.

"A looser shape" doesn't mean that you do away with the Setup (and Big Picture), Development, and Wrap-up. But it does mean that you may want to journey from the topic for a bit. Or that you don't neatly tick down through a list of points. Or that you're not especially obvious in making the point. (In many good essays, the point sneaks up on you.) Hence, you may not want to place a pointed topic sentence at the front end of every paragraph.

Given that looser shape in the personal essay, a good strategy for maintaining control is to make sure that you start and stop with the same idea—like a piece of music that comes back to the same melody it started with. If you let the personal essay digress too freely and forget to return to the opening topic, you'll probably end up with a grab bag of unrelated ideas. But circling around to the start pulls the essay together and lets you get away with just about anything in between.

Obviously, you need to look at models. Fiction writers produce some of the best personal essays available. See James Baldwin's *The Fire Next Time*, Joan Didion's *Slouching Towards Bethlehem*, Annie Dillard's *Pilgrim at Tinker Creek*, Ivan Doig's *This House of Sky*, Louise Erdrich's *The Blue Jay's Dance*, Thomas McGuane's *An Outside Chance,* Norman Mailer's *Advertisements for Myself*, Peter Matthiessen's *The Snow Leopard*, William Maxwell's *Ancestors*, V. S. Naipaul's *An Area of Darkness*, Richard Rodriguez's *Hunger of Memory*, John Updike's *Self-Consciousness*, and Eudora Welty's *One Writer's Beginnings*. Look, too, at Robert Pirsig's *Zen and the Art of Motorcycle Maintenance* and any book by Pauline Kael, Tom Wolfe, Edward Hoagland, John McPhee, and Joseph Mitchell. Each of these writers carries a powerful voice, rooted in passion, and some, like Mailer, try on more than one voice.

And many of these writers owe a debt to the great essayist Henry David Thoreau (see pages 50-52), whose *Walden* sets the standard for the personal essay—the essay rooted in a passionate voice.

Please read the following passage from *Walden* ("The Pond in Winter"):

As I sounded through the ice I could determine the shape of the bottom with greater accuracy than is possible in surveying harbors which do not freeze over, and I was surprised at its general regularity. In the deepest part there are several acres more level than almost any field which is exposed to the sun, wind, and plow. In one instance, on a line arbitrarily chosen, the depth did not vary more than one foot in thirty rods; and generally, near the middle, I could calculate the variation for each one hundred feet in any direction beforehand within three or four inches. Some are accustomed to speak of deep and dangerous holes even in quiet sandy ponds like this, but the effect of water under these circumstances is to level all inequalities. The regularity of the bottom and its conformity to the shores and the range of the neighboring hills were so perfect that a distant promontory betrayed itself in the soundings quite across the pond, and its direction could be determined by observing the opposite shore. Cape becomes bar, and plain shoal, and valley and gorge deep water and channel.

When I had mapped the pond by the scale of ten rods to an inch, and put down the soundings, more than a hundred in all, I observed this remarkable coincidence. Having noticed that the number indicating the greatest depth was apparently in the centre of the map, I laid a rule on the map lengthwise, and then breadthwise, and found, to my surprise, that the line of greatest length intersected the line of greatest breadth *exactly* at the point of greatest depth, notwithstanding that the middle is so nearly level, the outline of the pond far from regular, and the extreme length and breadth were got by measuring into the coves; and I said to myself, Who knows but this hint would conduct to the deepest part of the ocean as well as of a pond or puddle? Is not this rule also for the height of mountains, regarded as the opposite of valleys? We know that a hill is not highest at its narrowest part.

\*\*\*

If we knew all the laws of Nature, we should need only one fact, or the description of one actual phenomenon, to infer all the particular results at that point. Now we know only a few laws, and our result is vitiated, not, of course, by any confusion or irregularity in the calculation. Our notions of law and harmony are commonly confined to those instances which we detect; but the harmony which results from a great number of seemingly conflicting, but really concurring, laws, which we have not detected is still more wonderful. The particular laws are as our points of view, as, to the traveler, a mountain outline varies with every step, and it has an infinite number of profiles, though absolutely but one form. Even when cleft or bored through it is not comprehended in its entireness.

What I have observed of the pond is no less true in ethics. It is the law of average. Such a rule of the two diameters not only guides us toward the sun in the system and the heart in man, but draws lines through the length and breadth of the aggregate of a man's particular daily behaviors and waves of life into his coves and inlets, and where they intersect will be the height or depth of his character.

This project has three steps:

**Step One:** Take a trip to the library or bookstore. Browse through collections of essays (perhaps by the authors recommended) and choose several to use for models. Then, using your Journal of Ideas, jot down characteristics you notice of the essays and their authors. If there's any one personal characteristic that stamps the voice of the writer you're reading, what is it?

**Step Two**: Reread the passage from *Walden*. In your Journal of Ideas, respond to the following:

1. What theme connects the first two paragraphs and the last two?
2. What does Thoreau mean (last paragraph) when he says, "What I have observed of the pond is no less true in ethics?"
3. What is the "rule of the two diameters" (last paragraph)? How does the "rule" explain this passage?

**Step Three:** Position yourself near a pond, lake, or river; or in the woods; or on a mountain or the desert—somewhere beyond concrete and high rises (even it's just a park). Using Thoreau as a model, compose an essay that, in its first part, uses your lake or mountain or desert as a means to set up the philosophy you'll deliver in the second part.

That is, isolate some fascinating aspect of your own lake—some truth revealed—and from that point of fascination (the first part of your essay, like the Thoreau, will describe a scene), argue your own philosophical revelation: My lake looks like this, and it makes me think of the following . . . and the philosophical truth about the world that I find in my lake is . . . (In other words, you're moving from the micro to the macro level.)

The essay should be at least as long as the passage from *Walden*.

## Project 17: Writing a Second Personal Essay

Write an essay about a person, place, thing, or idea that (choose one):

1. Fills you with hope
2. Fills you with love
3. Moves you to despair
4. Moves you to anger
5. Makes you laugh
6. Makes you weep

Be sure to explain **why** your subject brings on such a profound emotion; use many examples from your life to vivify the essay.

## Project 18: Writing an Argumentative Essay: Alice vs. Humpty

In a scene from Lewis Carroll's *Through the Looking-Glass*, Humpty Dumpty comments upon a mathematical problem that Alice has just solved for him:

"As I was saying, that *seems* to be done right—though I haven't time to look it over thoroughly just now—and that shows that there are three hundred and sixty-four days when you might get un-birthday presents—"

"Certainly," said Alice.

"And only *one* for birthday presents, you know. There's glory for you!"

"I don't know what you mean by 'glory,'" Alice said.

Humpty Dumpty smiled contemptuously. "Of course you don't—till I tell you. I meant 'there's a nice knockdown argument for you!'"

"But 'glory' doesn't mean 'a nice knockdown argument,'" Alice objected.

"When I use a word," Humpty Dumpty said in rather a scornful tone, "it means just what I choose it to mean—neither more nor less."

"The question is," said Alice, "whether you *can* make words mean so many different things."

"The question is," said Humpty Dumpty, "which is to be master—that's all."

In a two-page essay, discuss Humpty Dumpty's and Alice's positions about language:

1. What do they believe? Comment on the validity or logic of each.
2. What consequences for communication logically lead from Humpty's position?
3. Alice's?
4. Are their positions irreconcilable, or do you see a compromise?

## Project 19: Writing a How-To Essay

Write an essay that tells the reader how to do something—repack the ball bearings in the hub of a three-speed bike, make blueberry waffles, lay ceramic tile, install a ceiling fan, tan a piece of hide, mount an advertising campaign, build a rare book collection, tune a piano, save money on a vacation, hook up a modem . . . you name it.

Treat the Big Picture with special care. Without a clear Big Picture, your reader will have no chance. "How-to" essays require instant clarity from step one. You must also make certain not to leave gaps in logic as you advance from one step to the next.

Before you write, try out your how-to process on a friend. Lay out the Big Picture, then move step by step through the Development. Are you being clear? Have you defined all terms? Spot any holes in the process?

This time work from an outline—even if you hate outlines and never outline. It's for the sake of your reader.

In fact, in this essay, you must never lose sight of the reader:

1. **What does the reader need to know?**
2. **How can I help the reader to understand?**
3. **If I were the reader, what would I want to read?**

## Project 20: Writing a Book Review

Remember giving a book report back in seventh grade?

The junior high book report usually offers a long summary of the plot ("and then, at the end, everything works out, and Marcy finds the will her granddad hid in the old barn") and the briefest possible recommendation ("So I guess I like it"). By contrast, the book review offers a brief summary of a book (a one- or two-sentence synopsis of the plot or Big Picture) and a much longer recommendation. In fact, "recommendation" doesn't describe the job expected of the reviewer, which is a fully fleshed-out judgment of the book's aims.

Book reviewers usually use two criteria for judgment:

1. **How well does the book compare with books it resembles?**
2. **How well does the book succeed on its own terms?**

That is, when we read a book, we compare it with other books of the same genre—or **kind** of work that it resembles. If it's a novel, how well has the author handled the characteristics of the novel: plot, character, language, tone? And within the genre of the mystery novel, for example, how well has the author handled the murder, the suspects, the motives, and the solution?

But we also try to be fair to the book and judge it on its own terms. The book may resemble other comic novels about adolescents, but in terms of its own structure—the unique terms it creates for itself—how well does it succeed?

For example, if the book is a nonfiction study of the Puerto Rican sugar industry, how well does it compare with similar studies? But more important, how well does it stand on its own—as a piece of unique work?

If you're reviewing a mystery novel, you should look up sample reviews of mystery novels. How do reviewers review? You should also read several mystery novels so that you have a basis for comparison. (If you've never read a mystery, your complaint about the book in hand—"They don't tell who did it till the end!"—may miss the point of the genre.) You want to consider the generic requirements of the mystery review as well as the generic requirements of the mystery novel.

Write a review of a book. Be fair to the writer. Don't review the book that you would have written; rather, review the book that the writer has written.

And don't forget to quote samples of the writer's prose.

## Project 21: Writing a Movie Review

Read the directions for Project 20. In your review, consider script, acting, direction, special effects, sound, and music. Before you write the review, find out what you can about the director's role: The director will be key to the success of the movie.

Remember not to criticize a movie because you don't like a character (although it's fair to criticize an actor's interpretation of a character). That is, if a character offends you for being a foul-mouthed sexist racist homophobic slimeball, the inclusion of such a character doesn't automatically make the movie bad.

Nor is it fair to say, for example, that a movie is bad because you "don't like horror films." Hollywood makes good horror films and bad horror films: You should review a horror film according to other horror films and according to how well it succeeds on its own terms.

In other words, you must distinguish **between your own prejudices and the movie on its own terms**. In fact, as an exercise, it's healthy to review a genre that you don't like; you may come to the writing with a fresher eye.

And remember that your assignment isn't to recapitulate the movie's plot; limit your summary to a sentence or two—just enough to let the reader know the premise and genre.

The great movie critic Pauline Kael wrote some of the finest reviews of the last century. To find admirable models, read any of her collections (available at most libraries). You may want to rent a movie she reviewed; then to write your response. Try not to read her review before writing your own.

## Project 22: Writing Literary Analysis Using Comparison and Contrast

### Sonnet 18
### William Shakespeare

Shall I compare thee to a summer's day?
Thou art more lovely and more temperate:
Rough winds do shake the darling buds of May,
And summer's lease hath all too short a date;
Sometime too hot the eye of heaven shines,
And often is his gold complexion dimmed;
And every fair from fair sometime declines,
By chance or nature's changing course untrimmed:
But thy eternal summer shall not fade,
Nor lose possession of that fair thou ow'st,
Nor shall death brag thou wand'rest in his shade,
When in eternal lines to time thou grow'st.
   So long as men can breathe or eyes can see,
   So long lives this, and this gives life to thee.

### Sonnet 19
### William Shakespeare

Devouring time, blunt thou the lion's paws,
And make the earth devour her own sweet brood;
Pluck the keen teeth from the fierce tiger's jaws,
And burn the long-lived phoenix in her blood;
Make glad and sorry seasons as thou fleet'st
And do whate'er thou wilt, swift-footed time,
To the wide world and all her fading sweets;
But I forbid thee one most heinous crime,
O carve not with thy hours my love's fair brow,

> Nor draw no lines there with thine ántique pen.
> Him in thy course untainted do allow,
> For beauty's pattern to succeeding men.
>    Yet do thy worst, old time; despite thy wrong,
>    My love shall in my verse ever live young.

*

Although Shakespeare wrote these sonnets four hundred years ago, historians still call their language "modern English," and you'll find that it will open up with less work than old or middle English, the language of *Beowulf* (the eighth century) or Chaucer (the fourteenth).

Don't be intimidated by the sound of Shakespeare; he's not impossibly difficult—just different from what we're used to. Learning Shakespeare's language is worth the effort. He's smart and funny, and nobody knows more about the heart and mind.

**First**: Look up a definition of "sonnet" in a literary handbook (which the library catalogues under "English literature—terms and phrases"). In particular, what defines a "Shakespearean sonnet"?

**Then**: Here's how you can learn Shakespeare's language:

1. **Look up every puzzling or curious word. (In fact, look up every word!)**
2. **Paraphrase every line. But don't change the meaning! If you don't understand a word or phrase, write out the original words rather than a garbled translation.**

**Next** write up two lists:

1. **Similarities in the sonnets?**
2. **Differences?**

Now you're ready to write. Compose a one- or two-page essay that **compares** and **contrasts** Sonnets 18 and 19. Each sonnet deals with the same theme, but each differs in how it handles that theme.

In the Setup, mention the numbers of both sonnets, the author (once you state his whole name, thereafter call him "Shakespeare"), and your thesis. The thesis should briefly state the common theme and the major differences.

In the Development, point out the similarities; then the differences. Quote words, phrases, or lines to support your claims.

Since the essay is so short, you don't need to write a formal Wrap-up. A sentence or two should do the duty.

Your title should be detailed and refer to your thesis; don't call your essay "Sonnet 18 and Sonnet 19" or "Shakespeare" or "Analysis," etc.

**Note 1**: Literary analysis, like all analysis, depends on evidence to make its case. You want to avoid making claims that you can't support in the sonnets. If you're a doctor who tells a patient that she has gall bladder problems, the patient wants evidence of that diagnosis; likewise, unless you can provide textual evidence, the reader won't take your word that a certain line means such-and-such.

**Note: 2**: Be sure to stay in present tense when you discuss the sonnets. (You can use past when you refer to historical fact—like "Shakespeare was born in 1564"—but for matters that aren't factual, like your interpretation of the sonnets, you must then move into present.)

## Project 23: Writing about the Ideal Job (with a Résumé and Cover Letter)

What job would you most like to have?

Write an essay that describes that ideal job.

To complete this assignment, you'll have to research a job. (See Project 13 on writing research papers.) You'll want to interview people who work at this job, to read trade publications and journal articles, and to consult the Internet. You must learn all that you can about your ideal job.

In the essay, respond to the following questions, organizing them within our traditional Setup, Development, and Wrap-up:

1. Why does this job appeal to you? Emotionally? Intellectually?
2. How will you stay on the cutting-edge? How will you keep up with developments?
3. What are the hiring requirements? Do you need work experience? Degrees? Anything else?
4. Salary range? High-end possibility?
5. Will technology ever displace your job? Do you see other threats to job security? (In other words, should you think twice if you want to shoe horses or repair typewriters?)
6. Do you see any possibility for burnout? What? What can you do to counter burnout?
7. Over the course of your career, what do you want to accomplish? What goals have you set for yourself?
8. How does your job matter to the world?

Now imagine that you're applying for this job. The personnel office asks for a cover letter and résumé.

A cover letter typically has three paragraphs. The Setup paragraph announces what position you're applying for and how you learned about it; the Development paragraph expands on the résumé, giving a reason or two why you're the ideal candidate for the job; the Wrap-up thanks the recipient and asks for an appointment, at her convenience.

Since résumés can take various forms, you should find a model for your area. If you want to be a firefighter, what kind of résumé do firefighters submit? What kind do high school teachers submit? Occupational therapists?

Take great care to proofread both and attach them to the job essay.

# Glossary

**Absolute**—A word or phrase not specifically linked to a sentence. **TRUE, the dog is barking. CONSIDERING HOW LOUDLY THIS DOG IS BARKING, I'm surprised somebody hasn't called the cops.**

**Active**—Normal sentence order (SUBJECT plus VERB plus OBJECT): **I** [subject] **HEARD** [verb] **the barking DOG** [object].

**Adjective**—Describes a noun or pronoun: **The BROWN dog.**

**Adverb**—Describes a verb—but also an adjective, a phrase, or another adverb: **The dog barks LOUDLY.**

**Adverb clause**—A fragment used as an adverb: **The dog barks BECAUSE IT WANTS TO.**

**Antecedent**—The noun (person, place, or thing) a pronoun stands for: **The DOG** [antecedent] **barks because it** [pronoun] **wants to.**

**Appositive**—A word that renames a noun: **The dog, A COLLIE, is barking.**

**Big Picture**—The main point in a work or within a section or paragraph.

**Clause**—Any group of words with a subject or verb (but can be a sentence or fragment): **THE DOG BARKS.** (sentence) **ALTHOUGH THE DOG BARKS.** (fragment)

**Command (Imperative)**—Giving someone or something an order. To the barking dog: **SHUT UP, Fido!**

**Conjunction**—Connects words in a sentence (FANBOYS: for, and, nor, but, or, yet, so): **The brown dog AND the yellow dog bark.**

**Development**—Body or middle of a work or section; where you open up and elaborate the Main Sub-points supporting the Big Picture.

**Diction**—Choice of words, grammatical or not, plain or fancy.

**Direct object**—*See* Object.

**Expletive**—Filler words that start a fragment or sentence: **It is, it was, there is, there are,** etc. **THERE IS a barking dog outside my window.**

**Essential**—A fragment needed to identify a noun. In a sentence like the following, the essential fragment thus wouldn't receive commas: **The dog THAT IS BARKING irritates me. WHICH dog is barking?** (Compare to **nonessential**, below.)

**Fragment**—A group of words that needs more words to complete its meaning: **ALTHOUGH THE DOG BARKS**. What? Finish up. **ALTHOUGH THE DOG BARKS, I don't mind.**

**Gerund**—A word that comes from a verb, ends in -ING, and functions as a noun: **BARKING is noisy.** (subject) **I don't like BARKING.** (direct object) **By BARKING, the dog will irritate the neighbors.** (object of the preposition)

**Idiom**–A phrase in a language that you can't translate word for word to another language: **DOG-AND-PONY SHOW.**

**Indicative**—*See* Mood.

**Indirect object**—*See* Object.

**Infinitive**—Any verb plus "to": **The dog likes TO BARK.**

**Interjection**—Breaks up the sentence; an exclamation/cuss word that has no grammatical connection to sentence: **DAMN! The dog barked.**

**Jargon**—Technical slang. Can be good (slang that belongs to a field) or bad (slang that prefers pretentious words to plain): **The DOG BARKED.** (good) **AUDIBLE RESONANCES were APPRECIABLY EFFECTUATED by the CANINE'S LARYNGEAL APPARATUS.** (bad)

**Linking verb**—A verb that hooks up a word to the subject: **The dog SOUNDS loud.** Examples include **seem, become, appear, taste, smell, look, sound,** and forms of **to be: am, is, are, was, were.**

**Main Sub-points**—The primary proofs or examples you offer to support the Big Picture.

**Modifier**—A word or group of words describing another word or group of words: **The BROWN dog barks.** (adjective as modifier) **The dog barks LOUDLY.** (adverb as modifier) **BARKING AT THE MAILMAN, the dog tried to attack him.** (participial phrase as modifier)

**Mood**—The way you phrase what you say: as a statement (**indicative: The dog barks loudly**); as a command (**imperative: Shut up, Fido!**); and as a wish or statement to the contrary (**subjunctive: I wish the dog were quiet**).

**Nonessential**—A fragment not needed to identify a noun and thus receives commas: **My dog, WHICH IS BARKING, irritates me.**

**Noun**—As we all learned in school, a person place, or thing; can be used as the sentence subject (**The DOG barks**), direct object (**I saw the DOG**), predicate noun (**Fido is a DOG**), and object of the preposition (**I took a picture of the DOG**).

**Object**—A noun or pronoun that follows the verb or preposition: **The dog gave ME** [indirect object] **a NIP** [direct object] **on the LEG** [object of the preposition].

**Participle, Present or Past**—A word that comes from a verb, regularly ending in **-ING** (present), **-D** or **-ED** (past) or irregularly with various past endings. Participles can be part of the verb or used as an adjective: **The dog was BARKING.** (verb) **The BARKING dog bit me.** (adjective)

**Particle**—A preposition added to a verb to form a common verb phrase: **jump OFF, start IN, calm DOWN**, etc. **Has the dog calmed DOWN?**

**Passive**—A sentence whose real subject follows the verb as an object: **The barking dog was heard by ME.** (= I heard the dog.) Sometimes the real subject is implied: **The barking dog was heard [by me].**

**Phrase**—A fragment lacking a subject or verb or both: **AT THE DOG.** (prepositional phrase)

**Possessive**—A word or the apostrophe that shows ownership: **MY dog. The DOG's barking.**

**Predicate**—The part of the sentence that isn't the subject; in other words, the part focused on the verb: **The dog BARKED ALL THROUGH THE NIGHT.**

**Predicate adjective**—Adjective that follows a verb of being or linking verb: **The dog is GOOD at barking. The dog feels GOOD barking.**

**Predicate noun**—Noun that follows a verb of being or linking verb: **The dog is a BARKER. The dog became a BARKER.**

**Preposition**—Found in phrases; connects words in a sentence, often showing location or direction: **The dog barked IN the yard DOWN the street.**

**Pronoun**—Takes the place of the noun: **dog** = **he**. ~~The dog~~ **He barks.**

**Run-on sentence**—A sentence punctuated with nothing or a comma when it should have a period or semicolon or conjunction plus comma. A run-on has nothing to do with how many words you stick into a sentence; rather, it's defined by having the wrong punctuation. **The dog was barking, the dog bit me.** (run-on) **The dog was barking; the dog bit me.** (correct punctuation)

**Sentence**—A group of words with enough information to make sense on its own (unlike a fragment): **THE DOG BARKS.** (sentence) vs. **ALTHOUGH THE DOG BARKS.** (fragment). A **simple sentence** has just a subject and verb: **THE DOG BARKS.** A **compound sentence** combines two simple sentences with a conjunction: **THE DOG BARKS, SO I CLOSE THE WINDOW.** A **complex sentence** combines a fragment and a simple sentence: **ALTHOUGH THE DOG BARKS, I DON'T MIND.**

**Setup**—Introduction of a work or section; where you set up the Big Picture and Main Sub-points that support the Big Picture.

**Subject**—The sentence part the verb talks about: **THE DOG barked all through the night.**

**Subjunctive**—A verb construction that shows a condition contrary to the real one (often a wish) or that makes a recommendation: **I wish that barking dog WERE dead. He suggested that the barking dog BE PUT out of its misery.**

**Tense**—The verb form that shows time (present, past, or future): **The dog barkS; the dog IS barking. The dog barkED; the dog HAD barkED. The dog WILL bark**, etc.

**Topic sentence**—The main sentence in a paragraph; it sets up (or sums up) the rest of the paragraph: **A barking dog has many annoying qualities.** (From here the paragraph discusses those qualities.)

**Transition**—A word, phrase, or sentence (or sentences) connecting two related words or ideas: **The dog was barking; AS A RESULT, the neighbors complained.**

**Verb**—Shows action (**The dog BARKS**) or doesn't show action (a state of being as in **The dog IS a barker**).

**Verb of being**—A "nonaction" verb, showing a state of being rather than action (**am, is, are, was, were, could be, should be, should have been**, etc.): **The dog IS a barker.**

**Voice**—The verb form that tells whether a subject controls the sentence (**active voice**) or is controlled by it (**passive voice**). **THE DOG sees the cat.** (active) **The cat is seen by THE DOG.** (passive). In the second, though "cat" is the subject, dog is the *real* subject, buried now in a prepositional phrase at the sentence end—hence in a passive position.

**Wrap-up**—Conclusion of a work or section; where you wrap up the last remarks about the Big Picture and the Main Sub-points.

# Suggested Readings

Bernstein, Theodore M. *The Careful Writer: A Modern Guide to English Usage.* New York: Free Press, 1995. An A-through-Z listing of word problems; enjoyable compilation.

Bush, Donald W. and Charles P. Campbell. *How to Edit Technical Documents.* Phoenix: Oryx, 1995. Solid practical advice by seasoned editors; comes with workbook.

Cook, Claire Kehrwald. *Line by Line: How to Improve Your Own Writing.* Boston: Houghton Mifflin, 1985. Terrific book for editors; particularly valuable for its "Glossary of Usage," which tackles, in depth, topics like **that** and **which**; and other word confusions.

Edgerton, Larry. *The Editing Book: Crafting Graceful Prose.* Dubuque: KendallHunt, 2008. A look at organization (writing for an audience and emphasizing key ideas) and sentence-editing (problems with passive, jargon, wordiness, etc.), with 276 exercises and their answers.

Graves, Robert and Alan Hodge. *The Reader over Your Shoulder.* 2nd ed. New York: Random House, (1943) 1979. A pioneering look at clear thought and language.

Lanham, Richard A. *Revising Prose.* 5th ed. New York: Longman, 2006. A no-nonsense, succinct approach to editing; Lanham's "paramedic" method cuts right to the sentence bone.

Lutz, William. *The New Doublespeak: Why No One Knows What Anyone's Saying Anymore.* New York: Perennial, 1997. Hilarious but sobering look at dishonest language.

Orwell, George. "Politics and the English Language" (1946). *Shooting an Elephant and Other Essays.* New York: Penguin, 2003. The major essay on dishonest language.

Sabin, William A. *The Gregg Reference Manual.* 10th ed. New York: Career Education, 2004. It's hard to find a better collection of the rules.

Strunk, William, Jr., and E. B. White. *The Elements of Style.* 4th ed., foreword Roger Angell. Boston: Allyn & Bacon, 1999. Graceful and wise; classic survey of writing problems.

University of Chicago Press. *The Chicago Manual of Style.* 15th ed. Chicago: University of Chicago Press, 2003. The bible of manuals. Along with a dictionary, the one book serious writers and editors usually own.

Williams, Joseph M. Style: *Lessons in Clarity & Grace.* 8th ed. New York: Longman, 2005. Helpful; many excellent exercises.

# INDEX

## A

absolute phrase
    defined, 277
    to vary sentence beginning, 46
active voice, 52-56, 65, 77, 277
    bureaucrat and responsibility, 56
    defined, 57, 277
    in parole board memo, 48, 50, 53
    inconsistent structure, 65
    subject-verb-object order, 77
    vs. passive, 52-56, 65, 77
address and comma, 167
adjective
    bad jargon and, 70-71
    capitalization with, 179-180
    comma with, 161-162
    comparison, 143-144
    defined, 118, 277
    hyphen with compounds, 184
    linking verb with, 141
    predicate, defined, 279
adverb
    defined, 118, 277
    hyphen with, 183
    -ly ending with, 140
    to vary sentence beginning, 46
    where do I put it, 143
adverb clause
    defined, 277
    to vary sentence beginning, 46
*affect/effect*, 87, 192
*after*, comma after, 165
agreement
    pronoun, 128-130, 198
    subject-verb, 130-133
*all-* with hyphen, 183
alliteration, assonance, and echo effects, 81
*alot* vs. *a lot*, 88
*although*, comma after, 165, 196
*am* and colon, 197
*and*
    comma after, 165, 197
    comma before, 160, 165, 177
    "rule" not to start sentence with, xv
apostrophe
    contraction, 172, 174-175
    exercises, 231-232,
    possession, 175
appositive
    defined, 277
    to vary sentence beginning, 47
*are* and colon, 197
argumentative essay, 270
*as*, comma after, 165, 196
assonance, alliteration, and echo effects, 82
audience, xiii-xxiv, 18-20
    determining, 199
    fragments and, 41
    general, 21
    specific, 21

## B

*because*, comma after, 165, 196
    "rule" not to start sentence with, xv
*before*, comma after, 165, 196
beginnings, sentence
    in Thoreau, 50-52

techniques to vary, 45-46
Big Picture, 1-2
    content, 2-8
    defined, 277
    finding, exercise, 188, 199
    finding, exercise revision, 202
    paragraph lacking, 33
    transition to another, 26-27
    with titles, 25
body, see Development
book review, writing a, 271
brackets, 184
brackets and sic, 185
brainstorming, xix-xxiv
    group exercise, 254
*but*
    comma after, 165
    comma before, 152, 177
    "rule" not to start sentence with, xv

## C

capitalization, 179-180
    adjective, 179
    compass directions, 180
    colon with, 179
    proper noun, 179
clause, defined, 118, 277
colon, 170-171, 178
    after preposition, 171, 178
    after verb of being, 171, 178
    *am* with, 171, 178, 197
    *are* with, 171, 178, 197
    capitalization after, 179
    elaboration with, 178
    exercise, 229-230
    explanation, 178
    *is* with, 171, 178
    quotation, introducing with, 178
    quotation marks, 196
    preposition with, 178
    scriptural reference, 178
    series, starting with, 178
    starting formal letter, 178
    time reference, 178
    *to be* verbs (of being), 171, 178, 197
    *was* with, 171, 178, 197
    *were* with, 171, 178, 197
combining simple sentences, 45
    in Thoreau, 50-52
comma
    address, 167, 178
    adjective, 161-162
    *after*, after 165
    *although*, after, 165, 196
    *and*, after, 165
    *and*, before, 152, 165
    *as*, after, 165
    *because*, after, 165, 177
    *before*, after, 165
    *but*, after, 165
    *but*, before, 151, 165
    compound verb with, 161, 177
    conjunction, after, 165
    conjunction, before, 152, 177
    date with, 161
    deleted words with, 162
    essential fragment with, 150-151
    *even though*, after, 165
    FANBOYS, see conjunction
    *for*, after, 152, 165
    *for*, before, 152, 165
    fragment, introductory, after, 150, 167, 177
    fragment, in middle of sentence, with, 148, 168-169, 177
    fragment, at end of sentence, 169-170
    before, 177
    *hence*, after, 166-167
    *if*, after, 165
    interrupters, 160, 165
    introductory fragment, 150, 167, 177

introductory word, 177
*next*, after, 159, 166
nonessential fragment, 151, 177
*nor*, after, 165, 177
*nor*, before, 159, 177
*now*, after, 166
*or*, after, 159, 165
*or*, before, 152, 165, 177
quotation marks with, 159, 174
run-on, 153, 177
sentences, connecting with, 153, 166, 177
series, separating with, 160
series, optional with, 165
*since*, after, 165
*so*, after, 165, 177
*so*, before, 152, 165, 177
subject and verb, separated, 163
*such as*, after, 197
*then*, after, 166
*though*, after, 165
*thus*, after, 166
title, before, 166-167
verb, before, when not to put, 159-164
verb from object, separating, 159-164
*while*, after, 165
common denominators as transitions, 38-39
comparison, adjective, 121
comparison, developing ideas by, xxii-xxiii
comparison and contrast essay, 273
compass directions and capitalization, 180
compound verb and comma, 161, 177
compound nouns (word in common), hyphen with, 183
compound modifiers and hyphen, 183
conclusion or Wrap-up, 2-12, 21-24
how to write, 21-24
purposes of, 22-24
when to write, 21-24
Wrap-up, 2-12, 21-27
confusions in word usage (list), 87-98
conjunction
comma after, 165, 177
comma before, 152, 177
conjunction, defined, 118, 277
to connect sentences, 152, 177
connecting words, bad jargon and, 85
content, organizing the, 1-13
contractions
apostrophe with, 159, 175
"rule" not to use, xvi
contrast, developing ideas by, xxiii-xxiv
conventions and communication, xvi
cover letter, writing a, 275-276
cramming nouns together, 74-75

# D

*-d* on *supposed* and *used*, 193
dangling modifiers, see modifiers
dash, 167-169
date and comma, 160
deleted words, comma with, 162
deletion, apostrophe to show, 159
Development, 2-11
defined, 277
of content, 7-11
Dickens, Charles, punctuation examined in *Dombey and Son*, 146-147
dictation, exercise, 233-236
answers, 237-240
diction
defined, 277
mistakenly choosing complex over plain, 78-79
to vary sentence, 49-52
direct quotations and quotation marks, 176

direct object
    defined, 277, 279
    to vary sentence beginning, 46

# E

*each-their* agreement, 129, 198
echo effects
    alliteration and assonance, 82
    syllables, 82
    words, 81-82
editing
    exercises, 207-250
    forty-four reminders, 191-198
    nineteen suggestions for, 204-205
    test, 221
effective sentences, exercise, 215-216
eight punctuation patterns, 150-155
eight parts of speech, 118
elaboration, colon to start, 171
*-elect* and hyphen, 183
ellipsis and period, 182
emphasis and dash, 167-169
errors, *sic*, and brackets, 185
essay, 266-270
    argumentative, 270
    how-to, 271
    personal, 266-270
    vs. research paper, 259
essential fragments
    defined, 278
    exercise, 227-228
    punctuation with, 150-151, 154-155, 177
    *that* vs. *which*, 127
*even though*, comma after, 165, 177, 196
*ex-* and hyphen, 183
exclamation point, 181
    overusing, 181
    question mark with, 181
exercises for editing, 207-250
explanations, colon to start, 178

# F

fallacies, thirteen logical, identifying, 254-256
family relationships and hyphen, 182
FANBOYS, see conjunction
finding the Big Picture, exercise, 209
*for*
    comma after, 165, 177
    comma before, 152, 165, 177
formal letter, colon to start, 178
forty-four editing reminders, quiz, 241-248
fractions and hyphen, 182
fragment, 41-42, 150-152, 157-158, 177
    audience and, 42
    defined, 41, 278
    at end of sentence, comma with, 150-152, 177
    at end of sentence, dash with, 167-169
    essential defined, 278
    essential, exercise, 227
    essential, punctuation with, 150-152, 177
    introductory, comma with, 150, 165, 177
    introductory, dash with, 167
    in middle of sentence, comma with, 151, 177
    in middle of sentence, dash with, 168-169
    nonessential defined, 279
    nonessential exercise, 227
    nonessential, punctuation with, 150-152, 154-158, 177
    *that* and, 127
    traditional writing and, 41-42
    *which* and, 127
    when not to connect to sentence with comma, 150, 177

when to connect to sentence with comma, 177
free association, developing ideas by, xxiii

## G

genre and paragraph, 31-32
gerund, defined, 278
gerund and possessive, 144
glossary, 277-280
*good* or *well*, 142
grammar problems, nineteen famous, 120-144

## H

*hence*, comma after, 166,
hollow phrases, 66
how-to essay, writing a, 271
hyphen, 182-184
    compound modifiers and, 183
    compound nouns (words in common) and, 184
    family relationships and, 182
    fractions and, 182
    letter and word with, 184
    *-ly* adverb and, 183
    *non* and, 184
    predicate adjective and, 184
    to avoid misconstruing verbs, 184
    *to be* verbs and, 183
    with prefix and capitalized root word, 183
    verbs of being, see *to be* verbs

## I

I, "rule" not to use, xiv
ideas
    developing and focusing, xxii-xxiii, 7-11
    finding, xix-xxii, 253-254
    focusing in a sentence, xxiv
    journal of, compiling a, 253

*if*, comma after, 165
indirect question and question mark, 180
indirect object, defined, 278
infinitive,
    defined, 278
    to vary sentence beginning, 47
    use with to determine who or whom, 125
institutional language, 70-83
    in parole board memo, 48-49, 53-54, 71, 76
    defined, 70
interjection, defined, 118, 278
interrupters, sentence
    comma with, 160-161, 196
    dash with, 167-168
introducing, explaining, or elaborating, colon with, 170
introduction, see Setup
introductory fragment, comma with, 150, 167-169
introductory word, comma with, 177
irregular verbs, 133-135
is and colon, 171, 178
*it is*, 65
*it's/its*, 94, 192
italics and titles, 25, 176

## J

jargon, 70, 278
    bad, 70-83
    bad and word endings, 83
    bad, characteristics of, 73-83
    bad, defined, 70, 278
    bad, vocabulary of, 83-85
    good, 70-72
    good, defined, 70-71, 278
job titles to avoid sexism, 66
journal of ideas, compiling a, 253

## L

language, institutional, 70-74
    defined, 70
length, sentence
    in Thoreau, 50-52
    to vary, 47-48
letter, to develop and focus ideas, xxiv
letter and word with hyphen, 184
letters and plural apostrophe, 176
*lie* or *lay*, 136-138
    chart, 137
linking verb
    adjective with, 141
    defined, 278
list, colon with, 170
literary analysis (comparison and contrast), writing, 273
*-ly* ending
    adverb, 140
    hyphen with, 183
logical fallacies, thirteen, identifying, 254-256

## M

Main Sub-points
    broken into sub-points (chart), 8
    defined, 278
    to support Big Picture, 4-13
memos and conclusions, 23-24
misplaced modifiers, see modifiers
models
    best way to learn to write, 14, 259, 266
    paragraphs and, 31
    questions to ask of models, 31
modifiers
    dangling, 56-58, 177
    defined, 278
    describing the wrong word, 58
    exercise, 213-214
    misplaced, 58-59

movie review, writing a, 272

## N

*next*, comma after, 166, 177
*non* and hyphen, 184
*none*, singular or plural, 129
nonessential fragments
    defined, 279
    exercise, 227
    punctuation with, 150-152, 154-155, 157-158, 177
    *that* vs. *which*, 127
*nor*
    comma after, 165, 177
    comma before, 152, 177
noun
    apostrophe with, 175-176
    bad jargon and, 74
    defined, 118, 279
    plural and apostrophe, 176
    predicate, defined, 279
    sexism and, 66
    verb turned into, 73-74
nouns, crammed together, 74-75
*now*, comma after, 166
*number*
    with *a*, 132
    with *the*, 132
numbers used as words and plural apostrophe, 176

## O

object, defined, 279
object and verb, when not to separate with comma, 164, 177
object pronoun
    after preposition, 124
    after verb, 123-124
*or*
    comma after, 165, 177
    comma before, 152, 165, 177
organizing the content, 2-11

outlines
    danger of traditional, 15-17
    informal grouping, 15-19

# P

pages
    how many to write and convention, 11-13
    how many to write and models, 13
    rule-of-thumb proportions, 13
paragraph
    Big Picture and, 28
    classic form of, 27
    defined, 27
    examples to support, 28
    fixing bad, 32-35
    genre, 31-32
    how long should it be, 31-32
    lacking Big Picture, 34
    loose, 30
    models and good paragraphs, 31
    number per page, 30
    one topic per, 30
    overdeveloped, 33-34
    revising exercises, 211-212, 249
    theme and variations, 30
    topic sentence and, 29-30
    underdeveloped, 33
parallel structure, 60-61, 192
parentheses, 184
parole board memo
    echo effects, 81-82
    institutional prose, 48-49, 53-55, 70-71, 76
    passive, 53-56
    stacked prepositional phrases, 75
participle
    past defined, 279
    past to vary sentence beginning, 48
    present defined, 279
    present to vary sentence beginning, 48
parts of speech, the eight, 118
passive voice, 52-56, 65, 77
    bureaucrat and responsibility, 56
    defined, 53, 279
    in parole board memo, 53-55
    inconsistent structure, 65
    subject-verb-object order, 77
    vs. active, 52-56, 65, 77
period, 182
    quotation marks and, 174-175, 196
    to show material left out (ellipsis), 182
personal essay, 266-170
    aims, 266
    development, 266-267
    "loose" shape, 267
    voice, 266-267
phrases, wordy and redundant, long list of, 99-110
plural noun and apostrophe, 175
pompous phrases, 78-79
position paper, 264
possessive, defined, 279
possession, apostrophe to show, 175
possessive pronoun
    gerund with, 144
    no apostrophe with, 175
predicate
    adjective, defined, 279
    adjective and hyphen, 184
    defined, 279
    noun, defined, 279
prefix and capitalized root word, hyphen with, 183
preposition
    colon with, 170, 178
    defined, 118, 279
    object pronoun after, 124
    "rule" not to end sentence with, xv

prepositional phrase
    in parole board memo, 76
    strings of (stacking), 66, 75-76
    to vary sentence beginning, 46
profile of the writer, writing the, 253
pronoun
    after preposition, 124
    agreement, 128-129, 198
    always plural, 129
    defined, 118, 279
    either singular or plural, 129
    eliminating to avoid sexism, 66
    object after verb, 123-124
    possessive, see possessive pronoun
    subject, 120-121
    subject after verb of being, 122-123
    subject in comparison, 121
    to avoid sexism, 66
    vague reference, 59
proofreading
    nineteen strategies for, 189-190
    two stages of, 188
proper noun and capitalization, 179
proving vs. showing Big Picture, 2-10
punctuation
    ear and eye to punctuate, 146-149
    least I should know, 145-146
    examined in Dickens, 146-147
punctuation patterns
    eight, 145, 156
    quiz, 222

# Q

question mark, 180
    with indirect question, 180
    with quotation marks, 181
quotation, colon to start, 178
quotation marks
    colon and, 196
    comma and, 163, 174, 196
    double, 176
    exclamation mark and, 181
    period and, 174, 196
    question mark and, 181
    semicolon and, 196
    single, 176
    title and, 25, 176
quotations (quoted passages)
    brackets and, 185
    comma to introduce, 163, 171
    direct, 176
    in research paper, 259
    overusing, 174
    within quotations, 176

# R

reader-writer relationship, xiii-xvi
readings, suggested, 281
*real* or *really*, 142
redundancy exercises, 219-220
redundant phrases, long list of, 99-110
reference, vague pronoun, 59
related sentences and semicolon, 178
repeated key words as transitions, 38
repetition, needless, 66
research, developing ideas by, xxiv, 259-261
research paper, 259-263
    essay vs. research paper, 259
    models, 259
    narrowing topic, 261
    original research and, 261
    pages, how many, 264
    quotation marks and sources, 264
    sources, 263
résumé, writing a, 275-276
revision, 187-203
    exercises, 210-211, 249
    lessons to be learned from, 203
    stages of (chart), 188
"rules" of English, healthy distrust of, xv

run-on
  defined, 279
  exercise, 225-226
  to avoid, 153
  to fix, 153, 194

## S

-s ending, 193
scriptural reference, colon to start, 178
*self-* and hyphen, 183
semicolon, 153, 167, 178-179
  quotation marks and, 196
  related sentences and, 178
  series and, 167
  transition and, 179
sentence
  defined, 280
  interrupters, comma with, 160-161, 196
  monotony to ear, 45
  parallel structure, 60-61, 192
  punctuation connecting two, 152-153
  related, with semicolon, 178
  run-on, 153
  run-on exercise, 225-226
  separated, parts of, 52-53
  simple and less simple, 46-47
  simple, combining, 45-51
  subject, defined, 280
  subject identified and use of comma, 154, 177
  subject not identified and use of comma, 154, 177
  variety, creating, 45-46
  varying beginning of, 46-47
  varying diction of, 49-52
  varying length of, 47-49
  what goes wrong with, 56-57
series
  colon to start, 178

  comma with, 160, 177
  optional comma with, 160, 177
  semicolon with 167
Setup, 4-12
  Setup, defined, 4, 280
sexist language, 66
*shall be* and colon, 178
showing vs. proving Big Picture, 2-13, 260
*sic* and brackets, 185
simple sentence, defined, 280
*since*, comma after, 165
*sit* or *set*, chart, 138
*so*
  comma after, 152, 165, 194
  comma before, 152, 165, 177
  leaving out necessary word with, 62
splitting subject and verb, 57
stacking (strings of) prepositional phrases, 66
starting to write, where, 14-15
strong verbs, list of, 111-112
subject-verb
  agreement, 130-133
  separating with comma, 163
  splitting with words, 57
subject of sentence, defined, 280
subject pronoun, 120-123
  after verbs of being, 122-123
  in comparisons, 121
subject-verb-object order, 77
subjunctive, 139-140, 280
  defined, 280
sub-points
  levels, chart of, 9
  Main, defined, 4, 278
  number of, 10
*such as*
  with colon, 197
  with comma, 197
suggested readings, 281

summaries, writing, 257-258
    more than one source, 258
    one source, 257-258
*supposed*, 193
*sure* or *surely*, 142
syllables that echo each other, 81
symbols and plural apostrophe, 176

# T

tenses, verbs, mismatched, 63-65
test, editing, 221-223
test, eight punctuation patterns, 222
test, forty-four reminders, 241-248
*than/then*, 97, 192
*that, which,* or *who*, 127
*that* and essential fragments, 127
*the/a/an,* using to avoid sexism, 66
*then*, comma after, 166, 177
*there is/are/were*, 65
*there/their/they're*, 97, 193
*There is/there are* and plurals, 198
Thoreau, Henry David
    essay on passage from *Walden*, 267-269
    passage from *Walden* examined for sentence diction, length, beginnings; sentence combining, 46-47
*though*, comma after, 165, 196
*thus*, comma after, 166
time reference, colon to start, 178
title
    Big Picture and, 27
    comma before, 167, 195
    italics (underlining), 25, 176-177, 195
    stealing title from other works, 25
    title and quotation marks, 25, 159, 174, 176
    what title to use, 25, 260
*to/too*, 97, 192
*to be* verbs and hyphen, 183
transition
    chart, 37
    comma and, 153, 177
    common denominator as, 40
    connecting two sentences, 35-40, 153, 179
    defined, 280
    punctuation with, 153
    repeating key words as, 38
    semicolon and, 179
    three kinds of, 35-37
    to vary sentence beginning, 46-47
    words and phrases as, 35-37

# U

underlining and titles, 25, 174-176
usage and word confusions, 87-89
*used*, 193

# V

vague pronoun reference, 59
verb
    bad jargon and, 72-73
    comma, when not to put before, 151, 177
    defined, 118, 280
    forms of, mismatched, 63-64
    hyphen to avoid misconstruing, 184
    irregular irregular, 133
    irregular regular, 133-134
    linking, defined, 278
    linking with adjective, 141
    object and, comma separating, 163, 177
    object pronoun after, 123-124
    principal parts of, 134-135
    strong, list of, 111-112
    tenses, mismatched, 63-64
    *to be* verbs (of being) and colon, 171, 178
    *to be* verbs (of being) and hyphen, 183

*to be* (of being), subject pronoun after, 122
   turning into noun, 73-74
   weak, use of, 77
vocabulary lists, 83-85
   all-purpose fancy words, 112-115
   bad jargon, 70
   individual (problem) words, 86-87
   strong verbs, 111-112
   word confusions (affect/effect, etc.), 87-98
   wordy phrases, 99-110
voice, defined, 266
   in the personal essay, 266

## W

*was* and colon, 171, 178
weak verbs, 77
*were* and colon, 171, 178
Windbag, Senator, speech examined for complex diction, 78-79
*which, that,* or *who,* 127
*which* and nonessential fragments, 127
*while,* comma after, 165, 177
*who, that,* or *which,* 127
*who* or *whom,* 124-127
*will be* and colon, 171, 178
word
   confusions (*affect/effect,* etc.), long list of, 83-85
   endings of jargon, 83
   pairs (rhythmic), 79-81
   triplets (rhythmic), 79-81
wordiness, 65
words
   fancy, all-purpose, list of, 112-115
   more-than-one syllable and sentence variety, 49-50
   necessary, leaving out, 62
   one-syllable and sentence variety, 49-50
   phrases and, as transitions, 35-37
   to watch out for, 86-87
   words that echo other words, 81-82
   wordy phrases, exercise, 219-220
   wordy phrases, long list of, 99-110
   wordy sentences, exercise, 217
Wrap-up or conclusion, 2-11, 21-24
   defined, 2, 280
   how to write, 21-24
   purposes of, 22-24
   when to write, 21-24
writing projects (exercises), 251-276
   argumentative essay, 270
   book review, 271
   brainstorming in a group, 254
   finding ideas inside yourself, 253
   finding ideas outside yourself, 254
   how-to essay, 271
   identifying logical fallacies, 254-256
   job essay (with résumé and cover letter), 275-276
   journal of ideas, 253
   literary analysis (comparison and contrast), 273-274
   movie review, 272
   personal essay, 266-269
   position paper, 264
   profile of the writer, 253
   research paper, 259-265
   summarizing more than one source, 258
   summarizing one source, 257-258

## Y

*yet*
   comma after, 165, 177
   comma before, 152, 159, 177